family life *and* **sex education:**

curriculum and instruction

family life *and* sex education: *curriculum and instruction*

Esther D. Schulz, *Ph.D.*

Associate Director for Educational Services, SIECUS

Sally R. Williams, *R.N.*

Director, Family Life and Sex Education Program,
Anaheim Union High School District
Anaheim, California

HARCOURT, BRACE & WORLD, INC.

New York Chicago San Francisco Atlanta

Library of Congress Catalog Number: 68-58082

Printed in the United States of America

foreword

Dear Dr. Mary S. Calderone:

Please help me. I have a serious problem. I am 15 years old--going into the 10th grade and have never been told the facts of life. My mother and father refuse to talk about sex. I've asked my mother hundred of time if she'd sit down and explain to me how I was born, why I have my menstrual period and stuff like that. She won't answer--always make up excuses or say I'll learn as I get older. Just because her mother didn't tell her she thinks she shouldn't tell me. She had older sisters--I don't. I'm awfully scared that I'll get pregnant and worse of all I don't know how. I have tryed to learn by myself--but its very hard in today's society. I tryed reading books or magazine articles but they're filled with grown-up vocabulary--impossible to understand. I spend half the time looking words up in the dictionary and getting all mixed up. I do have some ideas on sex but I want to get them straight. What am I supposed to do? Would you please tell me the honest truth about sex? You are a doctor and I know you can do it. Please, this is very important to me. I know there are thousands of kids like me--trying to find out where they came from, etc. My turn has finally come up. I'll never forget you for this. I hope you won't let me down. Thanks alot.

G--L--

This letter, received after this book was written, is one of many similar ones received by the Sex Information and Education Council of the U.S. (SIECUS) from young people of both sexes. It points up the first of the two main reasons for sex education: Children need to be given simple, honest information, at appropriate times in their lives, regarding the human body and its functioning in reproduction.

The second main reason for sex education, and the touchstone of the sex education movement now sweeping major segments of society, is suggested by the title of the first chapter in this book, "Education for Human Sexuality." Quite literally, we now realize that human sexuality—that is, the quality of being sexual—must be educated *for.* True, the infant is born with the chromosomal and anatomical configurations that permit us to assign him to one of the two sexual collectivities, male or female. But the assignment alone will not guarantee his evolution from child to adult as a fully developed and functioning member of his collectivity, for in his day-to-day and almost breath-by-breath experience as infant, toddler, child, pre-adolescent, and adolescent, a multiplicity of things happen —or fail to happen—to him, any one of which may swing the tide against him and distort his orderly evolution into a sexually mature person. Many children share the dangerous, warping experience of the young girl who wrote to SIECUS: their parents keep them in abysmal ignorance about their own bodies' functioning. Other children suffer an opposite, no less dangerous warping when they experience sex precociously, either directly or by observation, of life or films. In society today many new factors impinge on the child's sexual evolution from his earliest years. Many parents are unaware of these factors or are tempted to ignore them, but the school is obligated to take them into account.

The school has been given by society a clear-cut role to play, to be a primary and trustworthy source of truth and factual knowledge for every child. Every right-thinking parent should welcome the honest efforts of educators to present the true facts about human sexual behavior at those moments in the child's evolution when such facts are most necessary to him for his protection and orderly development. Never, under any circumstance, can the school be considered as trying to replace the parents—its aim is rather to supplement and complement their efforts so that all of us may share the same knowledge and live in mutual respect of it.

The program in Family Life and Sex Education on which this book is based was developed in the Anaheim Union High School District by Superintendent Paul Cook and by Mrs. Williams well before SIECUS was established. The book itself was completed before Dr. Schulz became SIECUS' Associate Director for Educational Services, and before Mrs. Williams was invited to membership on the SIECUS Board of Directors for the standard three-year term. Therefore SIECUS, while joining in the general recognition of the book's excellence, nevertheless can claim no credit for it. The two authors deserve great credit for putting into usable form some of the basic principles and materials developed so successfully at Anaheim. Both recognize that the book will best serve its function simply as a departure point for other communities as they begin the search for patterns most appropriate to their specific needs. This is a point that SIECUS has emphasized over and over again: Responsibility for programs in education for sexuality rests within each individual community. No program can be shifted unchanged from one locality to another; community leaders must bestir themselves to seek the best possible resources in arriving at their decisions on form and content.

Throughout the United States responsible bodies of trained men and women in the various professions—teaching, medicine, nursing, education, the ministry—are recognizing the serious need of young people for the kind of solid approach exemplified in this book. Certainly the churches have underlined their position on sex education in the recent statement published jointly by the United States Catholic Conference, the Synagogue Council of America, and the National Council of Churches. This book is a fine example of the happily increasing number of efforts now being made to set the stage for honesty and intelligence as regards teaching about human sexuality. Hopefully parents will read it as well as educators. When they do they will realize what our religious leaders have underlined, that the development of sound moral values about sexual behavior, as with any behavior, can come only from the honesty and integrity with which adults present facts to the young. Sound sex education for our children will be possible when educators and parents learn how to *tell it like it is* about sex.

Mary S. Calderone, M.D.
Executive Director, SIECUS

preface

This book has been written to serve as a guide for the development of family life and sex education programs in public schools. The authors wish to stress that this book is not a detailed outline to be followed in its entirety as such. The grade level outlines, developed for a hypothetical school, make specific recommendations for concepts, content, and learning experiences. These recommendations are based upon knowledge of the growth and development of children, experience in developing family life and sex education programs, and close observation of typical recipients of this curriculum. Our hope is that the book will serve as a *starting point* from which creative teachers, school nurses, and administrators throughout the country will develop and implement their own specially tailored family life and sex education programs.

Colleges and universities, in their departments of curriculum, health education, elementary education, social studies, home economics, physical education, and others, are preparing teachers to teach and administer the family life and sex education program. This book will provide teachers in training with extensive background materials and help them envision in concrete detail what are the opportunities and challenges of teaching the course day by day. Experienced teachers attending special family life and sex education workshops or institutes who work through the entire sequence of the book will be able to envision the specific requirements of a total school effort in their own districts.

We have attempted to omit generalities. We also hope that this book will assuage the fears of some school administrators concerning "How far do you intend to go?" It is our feeling that we have spelled out in specific terms how far we intend to go, particularly in the sex education sections.

One strong plea is made to teachers reading this book: Please do not underestimate the ability of students to handle this content material. We also hope that you will not segregate the sexes or suggest that the course be an elective. As we listen to students in classes, we are continually surprised by the fearful misconceptions with which students have been trying to live. Each class is different, but the opportunity to share problems and concerns under the skillful guidance of well-prepared teachers will be a milestone in the lives of many students.

The general content chapters, 1 through 3, and the section on Teacher Aids and Techniques, were the responsibility of Dr. Schulz. Those chapters containing specific course suggestions and evaluation, 4 through 12 and 14, were contributed by Mrs. Williams.

The course outlines for grades 7 through 12 are adapted from the Family Life and Sex Education of Anaheim Union High School District, Anaheim, California. Under the dynamic leadership of Mr. Paul Cook, Superintendent, the Board of Trustees directed that a staff develop a course of study. Particular credit should be given to teachers who volunteered to serve as a steering committee under the chairmanship of Mrs. Sally R. Williams that produced the course outlines for pilot classes: Mrs. Beverly McCall, physical education; Mr. Barry Williams, language arts; and Ronald D. Cohen, science. Many hours were spent reviewing films and books, searching for materials, talking, arguing, writing, and rewriting.

Lastly, our thanks go to our families for tolerance and understanding during the long hours of writing and research. Particular appreciation is extended to our daughters and their friends for serving as youthful resources.

Esther D. Schulz, Ph.D. — Sally R. Williams, R.N.

contents

family life *and*
sex education:
curriculum and instruction

part I

planning a family life and sex education program

chapter **1**

education for human sexuality*

Historically, most schools in this country have carried on the day-to-day business of educating the young as though sex did not exist. With few exceptions, the formal educational approach to sex, if indeed there was any approach, consisted in presenting a rainy-day film in an all-girl or all-boy physical education class or a hasty, embarrassed lecture on the dangers of venereal disease. Within the last two years, however, schools seem to have discovered sex. From New York to California and from Alaska to the Virgin Islands, sex education programs are beginning to appear. Teachers, administrators, and parents inevitably have the subject on the agenda at meetings, and newspapers, national magazines, and television have joined in enthusiastically with features on "The Birds, The Bees, and The 3 R's."

The three main components of sex education programs—philosophy, curriculum, and teacher training—are all caught up in the explosion of interest that has transformed a subject once spoken of only in whispers in schools into a subject as talked about and respectable as the new math.

Although some schools and individual teachers have for years been giving their students a little information about sex, the extent and intensity of interest is new. And while those of us who have been working in this field for years are pleased that a long-neglected area has finally come to the surface of public attention, we see some danger signs. For example, the "bandwagon" approach to sex education that is building up in many communities is similar to the atmosphere that marked the launching of Opera-

* Chapter 1: Published in *The Humanist,* May/June, 1968.

tion Headstart—the early childhood enrichment program that was hailed as the educational salvation of the disadvantaged child. Oversold and under-planned in many communities, the program left behind it a residue of disillusionment that did much to discredit an excellent principle. As they rush to begin sex education programs without proper preparation or teacher training, some schools and communities seem bent on repeating the Head-start experience.

To avoid this pitfall and lay a firm basis for a family life and sex education program, schools and communities must first work out their own, mutually satisfactory answers to the three basic questions of sex education: Why teach about sex? What is to be taught? Who is to do the teaching?

The first question—Why teach about sex?—is the most important one in many respects, because the answer to it will provide the philosophy and set the tone and direction of the course. Dr. Lester A. Kirkendall, a noted authority and a pioneer in sex education, says, "The purpose of sex education is not primarily to control and suppress sex expression, as in the past, but to indicate the immense possibilities for human fulfillment that human sexuality offers."[1] Unfortunately, this positive approach is far from characteristic. The real impetus behind much of the clamor for sex education programs is the desire on the part of parents and educators to reduce the number of out-of-wedlock pregnancies, to curb venereal disease, and to counter what many adults see as a frightening revolution in the sexual mores of teenagers. (Whether there is actually a significant change in behavior as opposed to *talk* about behavior is a moot question.)

While these suppressive aims are often unspoken, numerous contacts with schools and parent groups throughout the country indicate that they are often the real goals behind the drive for a sex education program. It is not surprising, therefore, that many programs contain a "hidden agenda" designed to get students to conform to what parents and teachers see as the moral status quo, an idealized image of adult morality that often has very little to do with reality.

Courses that begin with this "stay-out-of-trouble" mentality and go on to establish specific and limited guidelines for student thinking defeat the very purpose of sex education. First, they do not work. Experienced teachers know that young people simply drop a mental curtain when the moralizing and sermonizing begin. Second, this approach hardly prepares young people to deal with a complex and uncertain world where standards of all kinds are in a state of upheaval. And finally, whose code is to be taught in the schools of this pluralistic society? The minute a school tries to establish a code about masturbation, for example, or premarital sex, petting

[1] Lester A. Kirkendall, *Sex Education,* SIECUS Study Guide No. 1 (SIECUS Publication Office, 1855 Broadway, New York, N.Y.), 1965, p. 14.

and necking, dating, and other such subjects, it is placing itself in a precarious position. If the school system takes one position and youngsters go home to parents who have opposing standards, the children are confused and the system is likely to be discredited.

In contrast to this "tell-them-what-is-right" approach, the ideal family life and sex education program gives students a chance to assess a wide span of behavior, to see how it applies to the society in which they live, and to determine whether they are ready to abide by the sanctions society offers. It prepares students to decide on a set of values that they choose for themselves, values on which they base their behavior and make their judgments.

The reverse of the moralistic approach is the attempt to avoid entirely the sensitive area of values and judgments and to simply "give them the facts"—to center the sex education program on biology, anatomy, and the mechanics of reproduction to the exclusion of all else. A limited approach of this sort is a disservice to young people. Sex should be presented to students as something more than a biological function and the results of that function. It should be taught from a broad-based approach and include the behavioral aspects of sex studied in psychology and sociology, as well as the purely biological aspects. The primary aim of sex education is to help each individual to understand himself as a sexual being in the total sense and to use that knowledge in a responsible manner.

Given this framework, with its positive orientation and broad scope, the answer to the second question about sex education—What is to be taught?—follows naturally. The approach to planning a sex education curriculum should be no different from the approach to English or math. Young people are not expected to learn English in one course or from sporadic presentations. Neither should sex education be handled this way. The sex education curriculum should be a sequential learning experience planned in levels that can be assimilated by the students in various age groups. As in other courses, the presentation and material will change as the child's understanding grows and develops. There is fairly general agreement that children should have a sound understanding of the biology of reproduction and the physical changes of puberty by the time they reach junior high school so that as adolescents they can focus instead on the values and attitudes and relationships that are so crucial during these years.

In addition to being sequentially planned, sex education, if it is to be an academically respectable part of the curriculum, must make use of the insights into the entire learning process that we have gained over the last few years. In all other areas we have moved away from the old concepts of rote learning, drill, and memorization of facts. We now start in the earliest grades with a research approach to learning. In math we want students not merely to memorize the multiplication tables but to understand numerical concepts. In history, instead of asking for a textbook list of five causes of the Civil War, we give students documents and newspapers from the period and urge them to reach their own conclusions. Only when we come to sex education do we lose faith in this approach and revert to telling students what to think. If sex education is to take its rightful place in the curriculum, it must be as soundly planned as the math courses and just as free from cant and indoctrination.

It would be a mistake to give the impression that planning a good course and putting it into practice is an easy matter. Even schools that start out with the best intentions can bog down in the execution. A recent evaluation of one program that had been functioning for several years showed that although its objectives had a heavy behavioral science emphasis, little of this emphasis had filtered down to the classroom. The students were receiving mostly information on reproduction and the negative aspects of the sex act. Parents seemed delighted with the program, but student reaction was decidedly less enthusiastic. The students wanted more opportunity to discuss their real concerns, such as responsibility for sexual interaction, the double standard, and other ethical–moral problems.

The sex education course, then, must include discussion of sensitive issues and guidance for students who are searching for answers. This conclusion about content leads to the third basic question about sex education—Who is to do the teaching? In the minds of many educators and parents, this question is the crucial one. There is almost universal agreement that the teacher is the key element in a good program. No matter how carefully planned the course, how sound the philosophy, how strong the community backing, the ill-prepared or fearful or embarrassed teacher can defeat the entire effort.

To teach a sex education course properly, a teacher must have not only extensive knowledge of a variety of subjects—biology, psychology, sociology—but, more important, an attitude of openness and understanding, a self-knowledge and awareness of hidden prejudices, and a willingness to be honest with students. Although these qualities are certainly not present in every teacher, there are people in every system who have the basic attitudes and who can be trained in subject matter and methodology. In many successful programs teachers of various subjects, including a librarian and a chemistry teacher, were chosen on the basis of their interest and willingness to participate and then given intensive and extensive preparation.

The preparation of teachers is currently perhaps the major problem in the development of good sex education programs. With communities pressuring school administrators to do something *now,* much teacher education amounts only to stop-gap measures. Workshops varying in length from one or two days to six weeks are cropping up across the nation. An integral part of a teacher's preparation involves his own attitudes: he must become aware of his own biases and learn to feel comfortable in handling all topics. The attempt has been made to help teachers acquire awareness or readiness of this kind through the use of sensitivity training in various forms. This process, unfortunately, when attempted by unskilled leaders, has occasionally had dire consequences: it has resulted in a depth or group psychotherapy format that is properly a tool to be used only with the guidance of persons with formal psychiatric preparation. Another training technique used has been to involve young people in group discussions with teachers, in the hopes that this would "sensitize" the teachers to student reactions and to their own attitudes. This technique, like the T-group process, can have serious drawbacks. While the practice of having secondary level students state their major interests as a basis for planning course content is clearly valuable, a similar use of adolescents in short-term sensitivity groups with no follow-up for those who have "bared their souls" seems highly questionable. Finally, a third type of teacher preparation now in use is complete concentration on methods and materials; this reverts to earlier and now discredited patterns of Normal School preparation.

We can only hope that, when the flurry of activity and atmosphere of panic in which many schools and communities are approaching sex education has leveled off, there will be an opportunity for some sane and sober thinking. When this period comes there will be time to look with some depth at what we are trying to do in preparing our youth to meet the challenge of life as *individuals.* If the school is to prepare students for a productive and satisfying life in today's stressful and challenging world, a curriculum must be established that will contribute to family stability and to a healthy, positive attitude toward the sexual aspects of man's nature. When this is accomplished, hopefully the individual's sexual nature will contribute to his self-development and happiness and at the same time conserve and advance the welfare of society.

The major hope, then, is that we will not have tried to turn out a group of conformists into a society that demands individual choice. Ignorance, misinformation, fear, and negative attitudes about being a male or female member of society can and must be dealt with in sex education. Helping young people to find well thought-out and comfortable patterns for expressing their sexuality is the ultimate goal of sex education. If we succeed we will see the results not only in individual lives but in a healthier and sounder society.

chapter 2

community acceptance

As communities across the nation begin to stir and waken to the need for a realistic approach to sex education, a basic problem arises: How does one go about initiating such a program in the school curriculum? Does the impetus come from the school? from the parents? from the community in general? from a combination of all three?

There is no set answer. Communities and their school systems differ in size, sophistication, and readiness to accept new courses of study. There are regional differences and differences in the degree and kind of cooperation between a community and its school board. In a largely urban area, with its sprawling population and stratified school system, there is not likely to be strong or particularized community involvement in school policy. The impetus for initiating a family life and sex education program in an urban center would thus most often come from the school board, working with community leaders. In rural and suburban areas, where parents of school-age children are likely to be the community leaders, the involvement would have a more "grass roots" character.

But no matter where the impetus comes from, the school and community need to work together closely to implement a sex education program. If the leadership comes from the school, parents and interested civic groups must be invited to participate in getting the program started. Their views should be solicited, their doubts and concerns sympathetically listened to, their suggestions carefully considered—for their support is absolutely essential if the program is to be a success.

Where the mandate for a sex education program comes from the community, those who are spearheading the drive may sometimes, in their enthusiasm, attempt to impose upon school administrators and personnel a prescribed sequence of courses. This not only tends to alienate the very people whose responsibility it will be to administer the program; in most cases the attempt will fail. If a sex education program is to be successfully introduced in the school curriculum, those responsible for planning the school curriculum must be the ones to evolve the basic outline or overview of the proposed new program. Parents and other concerned groups may, and indeed should, suggest overall areas to be included and perhaps recommend the general manner in which they would like to see the program presented to students. But it is up to the school authorities to determine how active a role the community will play in planning the specific contents of the program and the way it is to be implemented.

One of the most widely and successfully employed means of launching a family life and sex education program is the formation by the school board of a citizens advisory committee, made up of a cross section of civic leaders in the community. This committee serves as a consulting body during the formation of the program and then as a spearhead for gaining community support and acceptance.

An excellent means of fostering community acceptance is to initiate a year's pilot run of the developed curriculum. This may be done one class per grade level in one or more schools within the district. Almost without exception students and parents are enthusiastic about this sort of sequentially planned program, and their enthusiasm about the pilot project can ease the task of the advisory committee and school board in publicizing a comprehensive program.

Another basic purpose of the citizens advisory committee is to reflect and report upon the attitudes of citizens living within the school district regarding family life and sex education as part of the school curriculum. The advisory committee members then discuss these attitudes with the school board and school personnel charged with carrying out the program.

In one community[1] that was very successful in winning support for its family life and sex education program, the citizens advisory committee, in conjunction with the school board, employed a commercial market research firm to determine the attitudes toward sex education of parents whose children would be part of such a program. A subcommittee of the advisory committee was selected to cooperate closely with the research firm. Working with this committee the firm developed an interview survey questionnaire to be asked of a cross-sectional representation of the residents of the local school district. The residents were told that the citizens com-

[1] Anaheim Union High School District, Anaheim, Calif.

mittee would make recommendations to the school board based on the responses to the questionnaire and that the school board would in turn decide the course of action to be taken in determining whether a family life and sex education course would be developed for the school district.

Since an earlier attempt to introduce some sort of sex education in the school curriculum had failed, the survey was directed to a particularly sensitive group. The parents were asked whether sex education should be taught only with the parents' permission, whether it should be taught in separate classes for boys and girls or in joint classes, and whether it should be offered as a required or an elective course. They were also asked at what grade sex education should begin and whether it should continue through high school. Another question elicited opinions about the inclusion of specified topics in the program at different grade levels; then the respondents were asked to suggest others that they felt should be included.

Though as might be expected a variety of opinion was expressed about these and many other questions covered in the survey, the respondents were almost unanimous (92% answered the question positively) in believing that there is a need to help children understand that there are appropriate sources from which they can learn about family living and the role sex plays in everyday life. Even those who had doubts about including such courses in the school curriculum because of religious beliefs or other reasons still believed that children should have access to proper sources of information. Virtually no one thought that children would not seek and obtain sex information from some source, and almost all seemed aware that if sex education were not taught in a formal manner somewhere, children would get misleading "gutter"-type information instead.

The survey, of course, was only a beginning step, but it provided a foundation on which the school board and its advisory committee could build a well-planned, comprehensive family life and sex education program. The program that resulted has been a respected part of the school curriculum in the district for four years and enjoys community support.

The school board in this particular community took the lead in launching a program of sex education in its schools. In other communities the initiative had come from ordinary citizens—parents, clergymen, PTA groups, women's clubs, and fraternal and professional organizations. Following are a few examples of how concerned citizens have kindled community and school board support for such a program.

A mother in a western town, shaken by a magazine article describing the sexual unrest and rebellion of teenagers, invited a group of neighbors and friends to her home to discuss the problem as it related to their community. The other women shared her concern, and soon they had enlisted the interest of doctors and clergymen in sex education and were sponsoring guest speakers to address community assemblies. Word spread, and other parents joined the group. A series of weekly parent education meetings was held, in which small discussion groups heard guest speakers and reviewed films, books, and other sex education resources. Audio-visual aids were found to be very helpful in sensitizing and informing community members about the need for family life and sex education in the schools. Two filmstrips were found useful. One, entitled "Sex Education U.S.A.,"[2] gave an overview of parent reactions and some scenes from classrooms. The other, "Sex: A Moral Dilemma for Teenagers,"[3] helped the viewers to see the need for sex education from the viewpoint of the students. A film, "Parent to Child About Sex,"[4] served to enlighten the parents about the differences between positive and negative sex education. The response to these meetings was so enthusiastic that the participants began to have difficulty finding large enough quarters for their future gatherings. At the end of six weeks the group, now a considerable force in the community, recommended that the Board of Education mandate a program of sex education extending from kindergarten to grade twelve.

In another small town the school health section of a local medical society sponsored an address by a sex education specialist at a community meeting. Community response was encouraging, so committees composed of medical and lay leaders were formed to investigate and report on sex education programs being offered in other communities. Result: a recommendation to the Board of Education that it adopt a comprehensive sex education program in the schools. A curriculum-writing committee of teachers was appointed and charged with developing a K through 12 program of Family Life and Sex Education.

In a large city the County Mental Health Association mounted an intensive three-day campaign to introduce sex education in the city's schools. A sex education specialist was engaged as a consultant, funds were solicited from interested parents, and a widespread radio, television, and newspaper publicity campaign was organized. The specialist held a whirlwind series of discussion meetings with the Neighborhood Youth Corps and teenage YMCA–YWCA groups and with medical leaders, the clergy, and their wives, and gave radio and television interviews. The campaign culminated in a one-day forum that began with a keynote speech by the sex education consultant. Local professional people and lay leaders then presided over a series of concurrent special-interest group sessions at which a broad spectrum of sex education topics was discussed. High school classes

[2] *Sex Education U.S.A.*, Guidance Associates, color, Part 1, 20 min; Part 2, 19 min.

[3] *Sex: A Moral Dilemma for Teenagers,* Guidance Associates, color, Part 1, 14 min; Part 2, 20 min.

[4] *Parent to Child About Sex,* Henk Newenhouse, color, 31 min.

were taken by bus to attend these sessions. In the evening session the sex education specialist spoke to parents and educators on the specifics of developing and implementing a sex education program in the schools. As a result of this intensive campaign, the County Education Department formed a broad-based advisory organization of parents, clergymen, teachers, and teenagers. The members were assigned according to their special interests to committees and subcommittees set up to explore the ways and means of developing both a school curriculum guide and adult education courses.

In some communities where Boards of Education and school administrators have not yet implemented a program of sex education in the curriculum, professional and lay leaders have established nonprofit organizations to serve primarily as catalysts. Serving as information centers, these organizations offer materials on sex education and suggest speakers willing to address local organizations. They also offer resources for the development of a curriculum guide. Such organizations do much to help establish constructive dialogue between the community and its school board.

The impetus for initiating a course of study in family life and sex education may spring from a variety of sources. It matters little whether the school board or the community took the first steps, or whether it was a combined effort. What does matter is that the two groups work together with mutual regard for each other's point of view and with a certain amount of give-and-take. The parents of the community must be assured that their voice will be heard in the overall planning of the program; the school must be allowed to exercise its rightful authority to spell out and implement the specifics of the program; each must realize that success cannot be achieved without the full cooperation of the other. Together, parents and school can help prepare young people to view the world and their role in it with healthy sexual attitudes and a meaningful awareness of the joys and responsibilities of family living.

chapter 3

preparing school personnel

When a school system adopts a family life and sex education program, the effect may be likened to dropping a pebble in a pool. The ripples spread outward to other courses in the curriculum, and teachers in virtually every discipline feel the effects. For this reason it is essential that all members of the faculty have some knowledge of the program if they are to be comfortable in dealing with their students. They need to understand the program's rationale, be in accord with its hoped-for results, and have a degree of familiarity with the content as it will be presented to the students.

In some courses, such as sociology and literature, there will be an inevitable "spillover" of student opinion and information from the sex education course, and teachers working in these fields need quite intimate knowledge of what is being taught in the latter course. In other classes the course relationship is more tenuous—but even so, there usually will be some intellectual crossover from the sex education coursework, and a teacher needs to be informed enough to be able to make a meaningful contribution should a discussion arise in his class.

The teachers who are directly responsible for teaching a designated course in family life and sex education need considerably more than a general knowledge of the subject. They need to be thoroughly grounded in classroom methodology. They need to understand and know how to use effectively the teaching aids and resources available to them. A vocabulary they can handle with ease and confidence is essential. Above all, they need to have the firmest understanding and conviction of the value content in family life and sex education and their own ability to handle this content in an objective, unbiased manner.

The importance of content cannot be emphasized too strongly. Sophisticated teaching techniques and methodology, necessary as they are to successful presentation of a sex education course, are merely the icing on the cake. The cake itself—the heart of the matter—is content. One simply cannot teach in this custom-ridden and sensitive area without a firm and thorough grasp of the subject. If a pupil has beliefs that are incorrect because of misinformation, lack of information, or unsatisfactory experiences, he may pose a threat to the teacher who is not prepared to answer hard questions and handle detailed discussion by the class members. This then threatens the whole image of the teacher and his sense of worth.

The teacher of family life and sex education must be aware of his own feelings and attitudes about the subject. Of particular interest to the teacher is where and how the study of sex fits into the whole learning process. He must understand himself and his attitudes, for this is a prerequisite to understanding and teaching children. Indeed, a great deal of self-evaluation is necessary. The teacher must assess his strengths and weaknesses; he must examine his biases lest they invade his presentation of the material and effect the student's learning; finally, he must ponder the image of himself that he projects to his students. Children copy adults for whom they feel respect or love. When adults set an example of integrity and thoughtfulness, of friendship and cordiality between the sexes or in family groups, young people are apt to internalize these behaviors and demonstrate a similar pattern. A simple act of courtesy on the part of a respected male teacher—opening the door for a woman or helping her with parcels —observed by a boy who is hostile toward girls in his class or toward his sisters at home may do much to help him re-evaluate his attitude.

When a teacher knows himself and his subject he will find that he can speak of sexual matters with confidence and authority, using "those words" without embarrassment. The children will respond to his ease and confidence, and the proper atmosphere for teacher–pupil discussion is thus established. Equally important, the child who learns to use a socially acceptable vocabulary naturally and spontaneously has taken an important step in his sex education.

Many young people, even in the lower grades, have an astonishing knowledge of gutter language. The wise teacher recognizes this and does not express shock when he hears a youngster use an objectionable or socially questionable word or expression. At times the teacher may even inject some of these words into the discussion himself to relate them to their correct scientific counterparts if this is necessary to help a child understand what a particular bodily part or act is. But it can be a mistake for us but somehow he just doesn't seem to be lucky. He doesn't really plan his marriages that well, I think, but he's a wonderful guy to us. I just want to try to plan better. But there are times when divorces are necessary."

The professional training of a teacher places heavy emphasis on a critical examination of the experiences of other people but does little to help the teacher turn that critical eye on himself. For this reason awareness or sensitivity training is a valuable tool. Yet there are hazards inherent in any technique that probes inner feelings and doubts, as we mentioned in Chapter 1. The person in sensitivity training, like a patient undergoing psychotherapy, must be brought along at the right pace or he may experience emotional trauma. It is imperative that trained leaders preside at all group discussions to forestall this unhappy event. Probing with the group may also give rise to hostility between persons with opposing viewpoints. The experienced leader will be alert to any such signs and will lead the discussion into constructive channels before harm can be done.

In some sensitivity training sessions, high school students have been invited to attend the group discussions, the purpose being an exchange of views between teachers and pupils in preparation for classroom teaching. While no one would question the value of student thinking in this area (students are, after all, the whole reason for a sex education course), and while adult–adolescent dialogue is a healthy and desirable thing, consideration must be given to when the dialogue takes place. If students ask questions that the teacher is unable to answer, or feels embarrassed or inadequate to handle, the teacher–student relationship is weakened. Seeing a teacher in a state of unreadiness can shake the student's confidence in the teacher's ability to conduct a sex education course, for the student envisions his own teacher as inadequate. The teacher's confidence is also likely to be shaken by the experience.

Until teachers have had the strongest possible grounding in content and a thorough indoctrination in classroom methodology and techniques, it is best not to expose them to student question-and-answer sessions. At earlier stages of teacher training, student views can be more constructively presented at general sessions rather than in small group discussions. An all-student debate on the subject of sex education is an excellent means of ascertaining how students feel. Young people usually "open up" in discussions with their peers, and teachers will find that they can learn much of value from this method.

A surprising number of people tend to think that sex education means primarily instruction for the adolescent student. This is a fallacy. We are all, from the moment of birth, sexual beings, and, as with other aspects of human health, there is hardly an age too young to begin education on sex

to make too liberal a use of this teaching device. "Dirty words" are, after all, "dirty words"—and children can be as much offended by their overuse as adults. It is equally mistaken for a teacher to use gutter language for its shock value or in a misguided attempt to establish a "hail fellow" rapport with older students; to do so will confuse the young person's attitudes and values and may also seriously diminish his respect for his teacher.

To help teachers understand, accept, and want to work in an area that will cover sensitive subject matter, a variety of resources can be used. The well-informed administrator, school psychologist, guidance counselor, and professional school nurse are all people who might contribute their skills and experience. Case studies of student–teacher interaction are extremely useful. Through identification with the people and situations in a case study, teachers can begin the critical self-evaluation so necessary in this field of teaching. Other resources are films, selected readings, pamphlets, and charts to be used in the course sequence.[1]

The responsible school administrator has a great stake in the successful implementation of a family life and sex education program, once it has been decided to add family life and sex education to the school curriculum. There are many ways he can help the teachers in his school to prepare for full constructive participation in putting the program into effect:

1. He may arrange visits and other experiences for teachers to increase their understanding of the socio-economic conditions in the community where they teach. School personnel can teach more effectively if they are aware of the environmental factors that impinge upon their students. Every community has its special needs; a sequence of courses in sex education that has worked successfully in a suburban community, with its traditionally sheltered youth, may not reach slum children, or children from rural areas, who have their own special knowledge and problems.

2. He may help teachers to make parent–teacher conferences meaningful and productive. When parents have questions relating to the family life and sex education program, it is often the class or homeroom teacher to whom they turn, rather than the teacher whose job it is to teach in the program. When teachers are adequately prepared to answer these questions —and this means when ample time has been set to prepare for the questions—there is a much better chance for mutual understanding.

3. He may schedule periods of in-service education for teachers to help increase their self-knowledge and understanding. Seminars can be held in these periods on course content, or a sex education specialist may be enlisted to demonstrate teaching techniques that have been found appropriate for the whole area of family life and sex education. There should also be

[1] Many such resources are listed and described throughout this book.

frequent meetings of the teaching staff to explore ways in which other curriculum areas may contribute to the success of the sex education program. An exchange of views with the literature, drama, and physical education instructors, for example, can result in new ideas for enriching the sex education curriculum.

4. He may provide opportunities for teachers to talk out their problems with people in a position to help them. The school psychologist, the school nurse, and the guidance counselor, with their experience in interpreting behavior, can be of much help with certain kinds of problems. Teachers also need to exchange among themselves information on teaching techniques and experiences. This can be done through small group discussions, through workshops, or through planned conferences. Teachers like to share successes as well as mistakes, for much of their work is necessarily independent, and they need assurance from other teachers tackling the same problem that they are on essentially the right track. This is particularly true in family life and sex education classes where content and methods are still being explored. Hearing the unusual questions asked by students in one class helps other teachers prepare for questions of the same sort.

5. He may encourage teachers to take college courses in growth and development or family life and sex education. Some scholarships are offered in these fields, particularly in the summer workshops. When teachers can be sent to workshops in teams of two or more, the shared experience can result in concepts and specific programs to fit a wider range of grades.

In these ways the school administrator can greatly help teacher preparation. It is in the longer-term woıkshops and institutes that teachers really come to grips with the subject, however. These workshops provide teachers with intensive training in methods of instruction and curriculum building. Resources of all sorts are reviewed in depth, and teachers are taught to use the most effective teaching aids and techniques.

In some workshops, unfortunately, there is a tendency to stress classroom methodology and teaching techniques more than course content. This is putting the cart before the horse. Teachers need complete mastery and understanding of the content in their area of study; without it they may never be able to teach a course with any degree of success.

Many workshops and institutes employ sensitivity training, or other self-awareness techniques, to help teachers prepare for classroom instruction in family life and sex education. This usually takes the form of the small group discussion, where group members speak freely of their private doubts and biases regarding sex education. Sensitivity training or awareness sessions seek to help the individual to recognize his own biases and to react with tolerance and understanding when he encounters different biases in others. It also teaches that in sex education, as in other fields of study, there

may be more than one answer to a given problem. For example, som teachers may have personal reservations about the propriety of a se education course as part of the curriculum or may disagree with certai parts of the coursework. Their teaching role is likened to that of an instructor in social studies or government who permits a latitude of beliefs viewpoints, and concepts to be discussed, whether or not they agree witl his own. A teacher of sex education courses can also confidently allow a free discussion of content areas and viewpoints opposed to his own beliefs without in any way compromising those beliefs. What follows is one illustration of a teacher's response to student questioning before and after attending a workshop where sensitivity training was part of the preparation course.[2]

> At the beginning of a classroom discussion on divorce, Jim, a high school student, asked his teacher for his views on the subject. Mr. R. replied, "I'm totally opposed to divorce. My religious faith does not permit it. But my wife comes from a different religious background and could accept divorce. We thought the whole matter through in great detail before our marriage and decided that the religious issue was only part of the picture. We discussed every possibility we could envision that might result in divorce and how we could prevent this from happening."
>
> Jim did not respond after he heard the teacher's reply. Later, Mr. R. learned from the school guidance counselor that the boy had had four stepmothers. His father was thoughtful and affectionate where Jim was concerned and took his son on fishing trips, to ball games, and the like. Jim could not reconcile the polar opinions of the two men for whom he felt respect and liking.
>
> After attending a summer institute that included awareness of biases the following summer, Mr. R. taught in another school. A student, John, asked him for his opinion of divorce. Mr. R. replied that he would answer the student after the subject had been covered in class. Following a detailed study of all the religious, legal, social, and emotional ramifications of divorce, John again asked the teacher for an answer. Mr. R. gave John substantially the same reply he had given earlier to the other boy. He then asked John what he thought.
>
> John's response was, "Well, I think sometimes divorce is the best thing, but I want my marriage to be a success. My father's been married three times. My last stepmother was ruining my thirteen-year-old sister. She would make a big fuss over her when my father was home but would treat her terribly when he was away on business trips. She was jealous of the attention my father gave my little sister. If my father hadn't divorced her I don't know what would have happened to my sister. My father tries to do what's right

[2] This case was reported personally to the authors by the teacher involved.

and its ramifications within the family. Current theories of cognitive development suggest that teachers in the lower grades are in a strategic position to help young children develop positive attitudes about interpersonal family relationships, role requirements, and sex in the whole life process. The objectives of the family life and sex education program can usefully be taken into account, for example, by a teacher who is using an organic approach to reading. Very young children often give words such as "mommy," "daddy," "kiss," "love," and "touch" as words they would like to work with. These words can be used as beginning reading–spelling–storytelling words. They can serve equally well to introduce the concepts of sex.

Too often teachers, like mothers, give evasive answers or redirect the discussion when certain words are used. Teachers in the early grades must be ready to let children not only mention words that have implications in family roles and sex, but also to explain why the words are of interest to them.

Teachers at every grade level, from kindergarten through high school, must remember that children come to school from a variety of backgrounds and with a wide variation in their understanding of social behavior and social obligations. Helping children to establish proper attitudes about their role in life is the primary purpose of a family life and sex education course. When the school has done its job well, there will be less need to spend society's money at a later date to correct confusion and poorly developed moral codes or ability to make judgments. Although one does not like to stress the dollars-and-cents value of any phase of education, it is sometimes necessary. Training teachers for a new family life and sex education program costs money, but the money will be well spent. The plain fact is that juvenile delinquency is destructive and wasteful, and a great deal of effort, time, and money must now be spent combating it. Hopefully, much of this expenditure will become unnecessary once competently run sex education courses have been widely adopted. Sex education can be regarded, among other ways, as a measure in preventive physical, psychological, and social health. An old adage applies to the economics of teacher training for the family life and sex education program: an ounce of prevention in the form of the money spent is worth a pound of cure for students improperly taught.

Summary of the Types of Teacher Preparation

A. In-service at the local level (offered by individual schools or school districts).

1. *Concentrated workshops* lasting from one day to two weeks. The longer workshops generally include only those teachers who will have specific teaching assignments in sex education or those who are charged with developing and writing a curriculum guide for the course. The one- or two-day workshops are conducted for the entire faculty, and their purpose is to familiarize the teachers with the general content of the family life and sex education program. Usually a sex education specialist describes the aims and content of the program and explains how they appear in a typical course. The specialist's talk is followed by small group discussions meant to give everyone a better general view of the program; the groups are formed without regard for the teaching disciplines or grade of the participants.

In the second stage of the workshop the faculty is addressed by a second speaker (often the school curriculum director or chairman of the planning committee), who discusses specific problems of introducing a sex education program in the curriculum. A panel of high school students may give their views on what should be taught and how. Following this the teachers again meet for small group discussion, this time grouped according to their individual disciplines and grade levels. Materials and resources in current use are reviewed, and suggestions are made about how they might be improved or expanded for use in the particular school or school district.

2. *Seminars,* held weekly or monthly, in which outside experts (biologists, psychologists, marriage and family counselors, gynecologists) speak on a broad range of topics within the authority of their individual fields. Usually all faculty members attend these seminars.

3. Regularly scheduled *after-school sessions* for the entire faculty using community resources, for example, local physicians, ministers, psychologists, and other professional people. Audio-visual aids are shown and discussed. Sometimes an outside sex education specialist may be brought in to address the group.

4. *Meetings* of teachers with community leaders who serve as an advisory committee to the family life and sex education program. These sessions usually take place during school hours or in the evenings, with only those teaching personnel present who are charged with drawing up guidelines for the course.

B. At institutions of higher learning (colleges, universities, special institutes).

1. *Seminar workshops* varying in length from one to six weeks, and usually offering both graduate and undergraduate credit. The workshops are open to teachers, public health personnel, social and community service workers, religious educators, and the like. Specialists in a number of fields

address the group on the general content of a family life and sex education program; the responsibilities of home, school, church, and community in this area; biological aspects of sex; moral and ethical aspects; premarital sexual relations; homosexual and other deviant behavior; laws affecting sex relations or behavior; the changing role of women in society; and other topics related to family life and sex education.

Besides hearing these informational lectures, the seminar participants are individually prepared to teach or to lead discussions on human sexuality. Usually such preparation takes the form of sensitivity training or other self-awareness techniques.

2. *Teacher workshops,* geared exclusively to the needs and interests of school personnel. Methods of teaching and curriculum building are the primary concerns. These workshops usually carry graduate credit and last two to eight weeks. Intensive study is given to specifics of putting together a course of study, and the format relies heavily on small group discussions.

3. *Institutes* lasting from one day to two weeks, with half-day or evening sessions. In these, guest speakers or guest panelists, often medical practitioners or members of the clergy, address the teachers. The range of topics is much the same as that included in workshop discussions, and the speeches are often followed by question-and-answer periods.

4. Regular *summer sessions courses,* which meet one hour daily and are taught by one faculty member assigned to the course. The coursework consists primarily of the study of methods and materials for use in a family life and sex education course.

5. Courses offered during the academic year, usually off campus and by the *division of continuing education.* In some instances these are conducted solely for a single school system but are given for credit and thus require regular attendance. As in the summer sessions courses, the emphasis is usually on methods and materials.

Professional Book List

A "p" following the date indicates paperback.

Annals Amer. Academy of Political and Social Science, "Sex and the Contemporary American Scene," vol. 376; Pennsylvania, 1968.

Bailey, Sherwin, *Sexual Ethics.* New York: Macmillan, 1963*p.*

Bieber, I., et al., *Homosexuality.* New York: Vintage, 1965*p.*

Blitsten, Dorothy, *The World of the Family.* New York: Random House, 1963.

Blood, Robert O., *Marriage.* New York: Macmillan, 1962.

Blood, Robert O., and Donald M. Wolfe, *Husbands and Wives.* New York: Macmillan, 1960. Also available in paperback.

Bossard, James H. S., and Eleanor S. Boll, *One Marriage, Two Faiths.* New York: Ronald, 1957.

——, *Why Marriages Go Wrong.* New York: Ronald, 1958.

Bowman, Henry A., *Marriage for Moderns,* 5th ed. New York: McGraw-Hill, 1965. Text edition and teacher's manual also available.

Broderick, Carlfred, and Jessie Bernard, eds., *The Individual, Sex, and Society,* a SIECUS handbook for teachers and counselors. Baltimore, Md.: Johns Hopkins, 1969.

Caldwell, Edson, and Clarence Mahler, *Group Counseling in the Secondary Schools.* Chicago: Science Research Associates, 1961*p*.

Caplovitz, David, *The Poor Pay More: Consumer Practices of Low-Income Families.* New York: Macmillan, 1963.

Cassara, Beverly B., ed., *American Women: The Changing Image.* Boston: Beacon, 1962.

Cavan, Ruth S., *American Family,* 3rd ed. New York: Thomas Y. Crowell, 1963.

Cavan, Ruth S., ed., *Marriage and Family in the Modern World,* 2nd ed. New York: Thomas Y. Crowell, 1965*p*.

Child Study Association of America, *Sex Education and the New Morality.* New York: Columbia Univ. Press, 1967*p*.

Christensen, Harold T., ed., *Handbook of Marriage and the Family.* Skokie, Ill.: Rand McNally, 1964.

Coleman, James S., *The Adolescent Society.* New York: Macmillan, 1961.

Collier, J., *The Hypocritical American.* New York: Macfadden, 1964*p*.

Committee on Adolescence, Group for the Advancement of Psychiatry, *Normal Adolescence.* New York: Scribner, 1968.

Crawley, Lawrence Q., et al., *Reproduction, Sex, and Preparation for Marriage.* Englewood Cliffs, N.J.: Prentice-Hall, 1964. Also available in paperback.

Driver, Helen I., et al., *Counseling and Learning Through Small Group Discussions.* Madison, Wis.: Monona-Driver.

Duvall, Evelyn M., and Reuben L. Hill, *Being Married.* New York: Association Press, 1960.

Duvall, Evelyn M., *In-Laws Pro and Con.* New York: Association Press, 1954.

Duvall, Evelyn M., and Sylvanus M. Duvall, eds., *Sex Ways—In Fact and Faith.* New York: Association Press, 1961.

Ellis, Albert, *The American Sexual Tragedy.* Boston: Stuart, 1962.

Erikson, Erik H., ed., *The Challenge of Youth.* Garden City, N.Y.: Doubleday (Anchor), 1963*p*.

Filas, Francis L., *Sex Education in the Family.* Englewood Cliffs, N.J.: Prentice-Hall, 1966.

Fishbein, Morris, and Ernest W. Burgess, eds., *Successful Marriage,* rev. ed. Garden City, N.Y.: Doubleday, 1955.

Fitzsimmons, Cleo, *Consumer Buying for Better Living.* New York: Wiley, 1961.

Fletcher, Joseph F., *Situation Ethics: The New Morality.* Philadelphia: Westminster, 1966. Also available in paperback.

Ford, Clellan S., and Frank A. Beach, *Patterns of Sexual Behavior.* New York: Ace, 1961*p*.

Friedenberg, Edgar Z., *The Vanishing Adolescent.* New York: Dell, 1962*p*.

Fromm, Erich, *The Art of Loving.* New York: Harper & Row, 1956. Also published as a Bantam Book, 1963*p*.

Fromme, Allan, *The Ability To Love.* New York: Farrar, Straus & Giroux, 1965. Also published by Pocket Books, 1966*p*.

Ginzberg, Eli, ed., *The Nation's Children.* New York: Columbia Univ. Press, 1960. Available in three volumes or in the one-volume edition.

Glueck, Sheldon, and Eleanor Glueck, *Family Environment and Delinquency.* Boston: Houghton Mifflin, 1962.

Hechinger, Grace, and Fred M. Hechinger, *Teen-age Tyranny.* New York: Morrow, 1963.

Hettlinger, Richard F., *Living with Sex: The Student's Dilemma.* New York: Seabury, 1966.

Hoffman, Lois, and F. Ivan Nye, *The Employed Mother in America.* Skokie, Ill.: Rand McNally, 1963.

James, E. D., *Marriage Customs Through the Ages.* New York: Macmillan (Collier), 1965*p*.

Jenkins, William A., et al., *These Are Your Children,* 3rd ed. Glenview, Ill.: Scott, Foresman, 1966.

Jourard, Sidney M., *The Transparent Self.* Princeton, N.J.: Van Nostrand, 1964*p*.

J. Social Issues, "The Sexual Renaissance in America," vol. XXII, no. 2, April 1966, 611 South Maple Rd., Ann Arbor, Mich.

Kirkendall, Lester A., *Premarital Intercourse and Interpersonal Relations.* New York: Julian, 1961.

Kirkpatrick, Clifford, *The Family, As Process and Institution,* 2nd ed. New York: Ronald, 1963.

Kling, Samuel G., *The Complete Guide to Divorce.* New York: Geis, 1963.

Landis, Judson T., and Mary G. Landis, *Building a Successful Marriage,* 4th ed. Englewood Cliffs, N.J.: Prentice-Hall, 1963.

Lantz, Herman R., and E. C. Snyder, *Marriage.* New York: Wiley, 1962.

McCary, James L., *Human Sexuality.* Princeton, N.J.: Van Nostrand, 1967.

McKinley, Donald G., *Social Class and Family Life.* New York: Macmillan, 1964.

Martinson, Floyd M., *Marriage and the American Ideal.* New York: Dodd, Mead, 1960.

Maslow, A. H., *Motivation and Personality.* New York: Harper & Row, 1954.

Mead, Margaret, *Male and Female: A Study of the Sexes in a Changing World.* New York: Morrow, 1949.

Missildine, W. Hugh, *Your Inner Child of the Past.* New York: Simon and Schuster, 1963.

Moskin, J. Robert, *Morality in America.* New York: Random House, 1966.

Peck, R. F., and R. J. Havighurst, *The Psychology of Character Development.* New York: Wiley, 1960. Also available in paperback as a Wiley Science Edition.

Pike, James A., *Teen-agers and Sex.* Englewood Cliffs, N.J.: Prentice-Hall, 1965.

Reiss, Ira L., *Premarital Sexual Standards.* New York: Macmillan, 1960. Also available in paperback.

Rodman, Hyman, ed., *Marriage, Family and Society.* New York: Random House, 1965*p*.

Ruitenbeek, Hendrik M., ed., *The Problem of Homosexuality in Modern Society.* New York: Dutton, 1963. Also available in paperback.

Russell, Bertrand, *Marriage and Morals.* New York: Liveright, 1929.

Scheinfeld, Amram, *Your Heredity and Environment.* Philadelphia: Lippincott, 1965.

Schofield, Michael, *The Sexual Behavior of Young People.* Boston: Little, Brown, 1965.

Schur, Edwin M., ed., *The Family and the Sexual Revolution.* Bloomington, Ind., Indiana Univ. Press, 1964. Also available in paperback as a student edition.

Shultz, Gladys D., *How Many More Victims: Society and the Sex Criminal.* Philadelphia: Lippincott, 1965. Also published by Ballantine, 1966*p*.

Simpson, George, *People in Families: Sociology, Psychoanalysis, and the American Family.* Cleveland, Ohio: World (Meridian), 1966*p*.

Sorokin, Pitirim A., *The American Sex Revolution.* Boston: Sargent, 1956.

Sussman, Marvin, *Sourcebook in Marriage and the Family,* 2nd ed. Boston: Houghton Mifflin, 1963*p*.

Wentworth, Harold, and Stuart Berg Flexner, *Dictionary of American Slang.* New York: Thomas Y. Crowell, 1967. Also published by Pocket Books, 1968*p*.

Womble, Dale L., *Foundations for Marriage and Family Relations.* New York: Macmillan, 1966.

Wyden, Barbara, and Peter Wyden, *Growing Up Straight.* New York: Stein & Day, 1968.

Wynn, John C., ed., *Sex, Family and Society in Theological Focus.* New York: Association Press, 1966.

chapter **4**

questions children ask

Introduction

The teacher preparing to teach a family life and sex education course must be aware of the types of questions that the students may ask and be ready to deal with them in a relaxed and objective manner. This chapter presents a sampling of questions placed in the question box[1] by students in a Western public school system. The questions are generally reproduced as they were written, complete with misspelled words and occasional uses of gutter terminology. Some teachers may be shocked by several of the questions, or by the chapter as a whole, but the shock is of reality and the teacher must prepare himself to deal with it. Better than anything else, the questions demonstrate for the prospective teacher the seriousness and wide variety of student interests in sexual and family matters, and also the extent of their misconceptions and lack of knowledge.

Student questions sometimes shock because of the language in which they are posed. Classroom discussions of human sexuality normally employ a dignified scientific vocabulary, but occasionally the vernacular is required. The teacher must remember an important educational admonition: "Start where the student is." Students ordinarily use vernacular words in class because they know no other language; if they are to ask any questions at all, they must be permitted to use the vernacular. Furthermore, a teacher

[1] For a description of this device, see Chapter 13, page 271.

achieves little by initiating a discussion of masturbation, for example, if three-fourths of the students are unfamiliar with the term and know the practice only by some other name or names.

Once a question has been posed in the vernacular, the teacher supplies the needed scientific words in a rephrasing of the question, or in his answer. This must be done tactfully; the aim is not to suggest that the questioner is uncouth, but rather to carry the discussion to a level that will permit all members of the class to consider the topic with unembarrassed honesty and to understand what is being said. It is important to remember that the students' command of vernacular is no more uniform than their knowledge of scientific terminology; the teacher cannot assume that every student knows a particular word, or that all the students understand a word in the same way. The students' understanding of vernacular varies initially with their regional and social backgrounds, and they are apparently prevented by considerations of peer-group status from asking each other for definitions so that common meanings might become widely shared.

Ambiguities and handicaps of language like these can be dissolved in the classroom if the teacher will carefully lead the discussion from the private, individualistic level implicit in many questions to a suitably public and scientific level of expression. The students will learn a language that they may use in discussing problems with their parents as well as with each other. Naturally, for this result to be achieved, the teacher needs tact, nerve, and practice—success is no more automatic in the family life and sex education course than in any other course in the school curriculum. The enterprise of gradually improving the students' vocabulary cannot be separated from work with their attitudes and beliefs; thus, it is not a peripheral, embarrassing annoyance but a challenging task that is very central to the course. Hopefully, the questions that follow will help teachers prepare themselves for their difficult but rewarding role as discussion leaders.

Typical Questions Asked: The Primary Grades

What is being born?
Where was I before I was born?
Why can't I have a baby?
Why does a baby chick come from an egg?
Did I come from an egg?
Why doesn't my mommie get a baby?
Why can't I marry Daddy?
Where is the seed?

The Intermediate Grades

Why are some people bigger than others?
Why do some people have red hair?
Why do some babies die?
Why do I look like my uncle instead of my father?
Why do some people have twins?
How do babies start?
How does the sperm get into the egg?
Can two sperm enter the egg cell?
What happens if there is no egg cell?
How long does it take for a baby to get ready to be born?
What happens if the sperm misses the ovum?
How can you tell if the baby will be a boy or girl?
Why do people have birth marks?
Can a baby that is born too soon live?
How does the baby eat inside the mother?
Can the baby move inside the mother?
What causes freaks to be born?
How can two babies come out at the same time?
Can two babies fit in the mother?
Is one pocket for boys and one for girls?
Do boys menstruate?
What is mating?
When are we old enough to mate?
Why is it wrong to mate before marriage?
Do you have to mate each time in order for a baby to be formed?
When the husband and wife mate, does menstruation occur?
Do you have to go to the bathroom to bleed?
Is it all right to go swimming during your period?
Can you have a baby when you are 13 years old?
Does it hurt to have a baby?
Why do mothers nurse their babies?
When do boys start to change?
Why do some girls have larger breasts than others?
Can a boy have a baby?
What happens to the other organs when the mother carries a baby?
How does a boy know when he is growing up?
Why do some babies have hair and teeth when born?
Why does a baby have a soft spot on its head?
Why does a woman get fat when she is going to have a baby?

Why are you born upside down?
If a baby gets stuck can the doctor help?
Does cutting the cord hurt the baby?
Why does the doctor spank the baby?
What is a breach baby?
Why do some mothers die when babies are born?
Why don't some women have babies?
Do you menstruate the rest of your life once you start?
What is meant when they say you're born with a veil over your face?
Why do some mothers have an operation to born the baby?
Will working too hard make a baby come too soon?

Seventh, Eighth, and Ninth Grades

About Dating

Is it bad or good to go steady?
Do you have to have a sense of humor to be popular? Do you think you have to follow the fad to be popular?
What do you do if you're chicken to ask a girl to go on a date?
What do boys look for in a girl?
If a boy asked you in his house should you go?
Is it all right to go to these school dances?
What does a girl look for in a boy when she goes dating?
Why do boys take girls to drive-ins and not to theatres?
At what age do you think it appropriate for dating?
When should you be home at night?
Why shouldn't a girl call boys if she is bored?
Do you think going steady is a normal thing at the ages of 13 and 18?
I'm 14 and the boy I like is 12 he's a real sharp guy. I am invited to a party for teen agers about 15 & up do you think I should ask him to go with me or do you think he would feel funny being around an old crowd?
Where is the best place to go on the first date?

About Petting

What is petting?
In a date, is it customary to kiss the girl after the date? If so, under what conditions should you do it?

How do you French kiss a girl?
Do boys get a thrill out of playing with girls?
What is meant by necking?
Why do parents think it is so terrible for kids our age to make-out? (heavy kissing)
What does a fellow get out of giving hickies?
Is it ok to kiss for fun?
Why do boys give girls the finger? Should I give it back? (I am not trying to be funny).
Do the boys blow in your ear to get you turned on, so he can get something off you?
What should a girl do or say if her boy friend wants to have sexual intercourse with her but she doesn't, but she still wants to keep him as a boy friend?
Do boys get aroused easily at this stage?

Terminology

What does molested mean?
What is an off-spring?
What does rotate mean?
What does flat as a board mean?
What is nude?
What is a cherry that is inside the girl?
What is a jock?
What causes a boner?
What is a queer?
What is sex cell?
What is the womb?
What is navel?
What are the testes?
What does circumsize mean?
What is a "fairy"? What does "screw" mean?
What is a Kotex?
What is a gene? What is abdomen?
What is a playboy?
What is sex?
What does rape mean?
What does making out mean?
Is "bitch'n" a dirty word?
What's an erection?
What is a peter?

What is coitus?
What does bastard mean?

About Anatomy

Why are most boys at ages 9–14 so wanting to know about the other sex? Why do they want to know and find out in the wrong way?
When does one start to mature and to stop?
Do some people still grow when they are 20?
Why can't men have babies?
Why don't girls produce their own sperms?
Why do junior high boys and girls have pimples on their face?
Why don't girls have a penis?
Why do some people not grow any taller than about three feet?
Why do women have bigger breasts than men?
I would like to know what growing pains mean?
Why does a sex appeal start at adolescence?
About what age does a boy become a man?
Do girls change voice?
How is a women's life changed in adolescent years?
How does the pituitary gland influence the growth function?
Does the pituitary gland send the message every month?
How do the sweat glands know when to work? What are hormones?
Can you go through life without blackheads?
Why do you get hair in the lower tract?
Why do women have two ovaries?
How big are ovaries? Big or small? What are pituitary and testes?
If the skin is still on the penis can you still have a family?
Why do the testes sometimes stay inside of a boy?
Why can't some men become fathers?
Do fat boys develop slower than thin boys?

About Growth and Development

Do boys have periods like girls?
Why does a boy's penis get hard and stiff when he gets sexually emotional?
How are the spermatozoa produced?
What are the testes?
Is there any limit to a boy's sperm?
What makes people voices different?
What does circumsize mean?

Will we discuss about why you have black hair, if your parents have blonde?
What are the mammary glands for? What do they do?
Is it milk in the girls breast? Is the vagina between the girls legs?
Why don't boys have cramps? It's not fair for the girls to have all the pain.
What happens if the pituitary gland sends some message that are not supposed to be sent?
Why are cromesonses so important to the looks and personalities of a child?
Do girls always grow faster than boys?
What does the semen look like?
Does a girl ever have a wet dream?
How does ovary make egg?
Do men have something like memopause?
Why do people have a "sex urge"?
What makes a girl attracted to a boy?
Why do some people have big feet and some small feet?
What makes you perspire?
What are the woman's breasts filled with when they're not pregnant?
What is inside of the female breast?
Why do people have hair? (In the productive area)
Why are the girls' breasts filled and boys aren't?
Why do girls hips wiggle?
What is the part called on the outside of the body on a girl?
Where does the blood come from to make the penis erect?
Is a boy's penis suppose to be bent?
What do girls do to stop the blood coming out?
Do boys have almost the same problems as girls do?
Why do girls have vaginas and boys don't? Why do both girls and boys have ovaries?
Does the tube which the sperm passes through grow at adolescences or while you're a baby?

About Menstruation

When do you start?
When does the period end; does it keep on forever?
What color is menstruation?
What is a period?
If you have cramps is it a sign of the starting menstruation?
Why do some girls start menstruation later or earlier than others?
Is it unusual to start your period at 9 years of age?

Is there any special kotex to wear?
Does a boy have cramps while growing to a man?
How many days are there between menstrual periods?
Do cows and horses have menstruation?
When girls start to menstrate do they need kotex?
If girls do not menstruate is there something wrong and do they have to menstruate?
What makes a girl have menstruation?
What if you do actually have cramps during your period? Is it a reflection on your eating habits and emotional stability?
Do you menstruate even if you are going to have a baby?
During your menstruation the little egg which goes through once a month, do they come out every month? At what age does the menstruation end?
Is it possible to get pregnant during your period?
Why would a cold make a girl irregular?
If a girl never has a period is it because of an accident?
Can you horseback ride while you have your period?
What if you get bad headaches and cramps every time you have your period and your doctor says its normal?
Why are girls using tampax?
Can menstruation be stopped when it first starts and you don't like it?
Some people say that you can't go swimming when you are on your period.
What makes women so nervous and cranky during their period?
Where does blood come from before entering the uterus?
Does a boy flow?

About Personality

How many different personalities can one person have?
What do you do when a person hates you?
What all does your personality include?
Why do you have to be popular?
How can you become more sociable?
Why does a person feel left out when he's around a group of friends that don't even know he's there?

About Reproduction

If you are over 80 can a girl have a baby?
How does the baby grow inside the woman? If a woman has twins, does she usually die? Do women die if they have too many babies?

Where is the cord connected?
Do the hormones stop because the baby is finished or the baby is finished because of the hormones?
Does the male ever run out of sperm cells?
When does a baby's eyes open?
When a woman is so old that she cannot have a baby is this because she used up all of her eggs?
How is the ovum drawn into the tube?
How does the baby come down from the vagina?
What causes Siamese Twins?
What happens to the tail of the sperm? Where does it go?
Have any boys had babies? If so why?
How big is a sperm?
How can a doctor tell you are going to have a baby?
Does it hurt when the doctor cuts the cord connecting you and your baby?
What makes the baby be born retarded besides heredity?
Why are some babies born dead?
Does German measles cause a deformed baby while the mother is pregnant?
If the mother does not eat the right food can it kill the baby during pregnancy?
If a girl is pregnant can she still have her periods?
Does a woman have to have sexual relations with a man in order to have a baby?
Why doesn't any doctor or person know before we are born what sex we are?
How many children can a mother have?
What is the tube in which the little egg goes into to make an infant?
Do you have to mate every time you have a baby?
How does a miscarriage start in a lady's stomach?
Will you explain how the umbilical cord actually feeds the baby? Explain the placenta? Does the egg come out of only one ovary?
What happens to a baby who's mother wore a girdle when pregnant?
If you're pregnant and have a miscarriage where does it go?
Is it all right for a pregnant woman to ride a bicycle or motor bike?
How long does it take the sperm to get in the egg?
When a baby is ready to be born how long does it take to have it?
What if a whole bunch of sperm cells were going down the tube and all of them bypassed the egg and all those sperms entered the ovary?
How come babies come out of the mother before they are supposed to, like at 8 months?
Can a woman become pregnant before menstruation?

How did the family first start? For instance who gave birth to the first people?
Is the mother awake when she has her child? Could the mother feel the baby turn its head down in the position ready for birth?
How does the milk come out of the breasts?
In the beginning how were people combined in skin color?
How old is the youngest girl to give birth?
Does it take 9 months all the time for the girl to have a baby or more?
After the egg passes through the uterus, what color is the nourishment? Is it red?
How long can sperm stay in the women?

About Babies

If one parent has a certain disease and other one doesn't would the child be likely to have this disease too?
What makes a baby have a hole in its heart? Is the eyes of an animal open at birth?

About Masturbation

Is is bad for boys to masturbate?
What is masturbation?
If you play with yourself, and are not able to stop, what will it do and can it be stopped? I have been doing this for a long time. I need help.
Do all boys masturbate and at what age?

About Seminal Emission

If a boy does menstruate with his sperm, Why? How? When?
Can you wake up when you are going to have a wet dream or are having a wet dream?
How long between boy's period? How long does it last too?
Do the boys automatically have wet dreams during the time they make a woman pregnant?
One book says a wet-dream is accompanied by a special dream. What is this special dream?
Does ejaculation take place often, or does it take place only during sexual intercourse?
If you have wet dreams, are you mature?

Are wet dreams like menstruation?
When boys have wet dreams do they use such things like napkins of some sort? If it happens during the day what do they do?
Why is nocturnal emission necessary?

About Homosexuality

What should you do if a man gets friendly?
Are there such things as homosexual women?
Is there such a thing as half boy half girl?
Who do sometimes men marry men and women marry women?
What is the difference between homosexual, lisbians, queers, morf?

About Sexual Intercourse

When you want a child what do you say to your wife?
When you are going to have a baby and you mate before the baby is born what happens?
Can the boys possibly go to the bathroom during the time they make a woman pregnant? What position are men and women in when the man makes the woman pregnant?
Are the testes empty after sexual intercourse?
If you get married to have a baby would you have to be raped? What would happen if you weren't married and were raped?
Does sexual intercourse hurt?
What happens when the male has sexual intercourse with his wife once every month?
What does sexual intercourse mean?
Why do people want to have sexual intercourse when they don't want children?
What would happen if a boy 12 years old had sperm and mated with a girl 12 who had eggs?
Why do men and women kiss and mate in bed?
Is it wrong to have sexual intercourse in the morning?
How long does a penis have to stay in the vagina to let out the sperm?
When a couple is married is it natural to feel shy before having sexual intercourse (shy about expecting to have it the first time with one another)?
How, when, where does reproduction take place? How is the penis put into the vagina?

About Contraceptives

In what ways does a man *not* become a father?
Why do women have to take birth control pills? A lady said that she had a pink pill baby. What is that supposed to mean?
What is a rubber used for?
Do women take pills to keep from having babies?

About Premarital Coitus

Can a doctor tell if a girl has mated but is not going to have a baby?
How can some girls in high school have babies when they are not married yet?
Young people that are not married and have sex relationship. What happens to them when they are too young to get married and the girl is going to have a baby? And what happens to the baby?
Why do some girls have a baby when they are not married?
Is it bad for boys and girls to have sexual intercourse?
What causes sex intercourses between young people of young ages?
Why is it bad for kids our age to have sexual intercourse with a rubber?
Are you "No good" if you get pregnant before you are married?
Does the girl have to get pregnant every time she and a boy get together?
When a girl has a baby under age what happens?

About Family Problems

Why are your parents so mean to you? What do you do if you are sixteen and your parents treat you as a baby?
Why do parents disagree with the new styles?
Why are parents so stupid?
Why do my parents say I can't stay out late when my friends stay out to about 8:00 clock or sometimes even later, I never have any fun?
How come the baby of the family is pushed around most of the time?
What do you do when your brother hits you and if you hit back you get in trouble?
What should I do if I'm put on restriction for something I didn't do wrong?
What do you do when you have friends over and you father is just laying around and is cranky at them?
Why can't we have any secrets of our own?
What do you do when you get in a fight with your mom?
What if you've tried to be friends with your sister but you can't? What

should I do if I talk to my mother and my sister buts in with a sarcastic remark?
If you try to be nice to your sisters and brothers why don't they appreciate it?
Why do adults quarrel so much?
Why do parents try to baby you?
How old should a girl be before shopping with other girls?
Can you drink alcohol when your parents are home?
Why are people so worried about young people all of a sudden? When my father was a teen-ager nobody worried but his mother?
The kids across the street like to start fights with rocks. What can I do?
How can you stop fighting with brother and sister?
What causes a person to have arguments with his grandma? She always says I used to keep my bedroom neat and clean and it starts an argument.

Miscellaneous

What is real love?
Why doesn't it hurt a baby boy when he is getting circumcized?
Why do people get married?
Why do people have families?
If you get married do you have to support your wife and family. Why can't they support themselves?
Why do you ever need sex?
When you get old why do you have to die?
Is Playboy magazine illegal?
Should you tell your parents about this class?
How did the stone age people know about having babies?
When your nose bleeds does the blood come from the uterus?
Can girls get ruptured (in the public area) just like boys?
What is love?
How do you know when you are in love?
Why do boys hate girls when they are young?
Do Teenage marriages work out?
Should you get married before you get too old and settled in your way?
What are falseys?
Why does a lady wear a bra?
Why are girls called whores?
Why is sex so complicated?
Why do the boys pretend they don't know the girl's pregnant?
Why can't you smoke in school?

Tenth, Eleventh, and Twelfth Grades

Terminology

What is prostitution?
Is "making love" to a person the same as sexual intercourse?
What is petting? What is stroking and fondling? What is chastity?
Is erection the same meaning as dick?
What does the word seduced mean?
What is organsm?
What is a vergin?

About Dating

Do you think that "parking" is bad?
What do girls really want in a good date?
How should a boy who is very shy go about overcoming his problem and asking a girl for a date? Where should a boy take a girl if he doesn't have a car?
Should a boy "pick up" a girl at a show or if his friends with him do?
How do you get a girl to kiss you?
What is the boys role in dating?
How does going steady usually end? When do parents let their children date?
Do you think that a girl who really likes a boy should ask for a date?
Does a girl wait for a boy to actually say he likes her? This is very unnerving, because then you ask them to go out and you find them already going with someone else and they hadn't mentioned it. It's come natural to me this last year to be easy in the company of girls. The only trouble is that I feel I don't hit off exactly right with them, I'm more a friend than a boy.
How many boys should a girl go with?
Why do boys always have to make the first "move" when it comes to relations with the opposite sex?
How should a girl refuse a date?
How far should a girl go on a date? What about a kiss on the first date?
Do boys respect you if your ideas are right and his wrong and you admit to him he's right? How to start a conversation with a boy on the first date? Should you have dated by 15?
If two people had been going steady for quite a while and decided they would break up and date other people, do you think it would be a good way of knowing if they really liked each other?

Does it mean that a girl is cheap if she sneaks out?
How can you tell a guy that you don't want him to drink while you are on a date?
When you're going steady who gets tired of the other person first, the boy or girl? When going steady who gets tired of physical relationships first, the boy or the girl? What are boys most impressed by in girls?
Why are we so self-conscious when we meet new boys?
Is it wrong to go with a guy for two years, and he is 18 and you are 15? Should a boy tell his steady if he has ever touched a girl before?
Is it possible to really love a boy or man at age 15? Should you worry if you don't have dates right away?
Would a boy rather date a slim girl with a lousy personality rather than a plump girl with a real nice personality?

About Petting

Why are boys so aggressive?
Why do girls let boys play around with them? If they know what might happen because they have the most to lose.
Why does society condemn teenagers for necking and such?
Do girls like to be petted as much as some boys like to do it?
If a boy and girl are going together for around 9 months do you think petting is out of place? Do you think that physical contact with the opposite sex has anything to do with showing how you feel about each other? What is considered wrong with a girl when she doesn't know where to draw the line? (sex wise)
How can people control their sex emotions?
Why do most girls pet if they don't expect to have sexual intercourse with the boy? Why do they do things like that to encourage the boy?
What are sex standards? You just can't say one hour's kissing and petting and then stop.
Are there any advantages to necking and petting?
Why do boys always test girls?
What should a girl do if a boy shows a desire to have sex relations (if she likes him but doesn't want to have these relations)?
Do you think if you have been going together for quite awhile and the boy doesn't try anything, does he have respect for you? If you are engaged to be married is it wrong to pet?
Are two people who have no desire wants for petting until marriage compatible or still in love?

About Engagement

What is engagement exactly?
What do you think of long range engagements, such as the boy you are engaged to is over-seas? Do you think that they could be faithful easily?
How long should engagements last?

About Sexual Intercourse

Are sex relations habit forming?
What is sexual intercourse?
Is there a certain time to have sexual intercourse? Does it hurt?
Who would suggest sexual intercourse between a married couple? How?
I read in a medical book that during sexual intercourse that the woman's conclusion takes longer than mens, also that during the time you should change the subject and talk about the walls or curtains in the room. What does this mean? (especially the conclusion). And how do you know when the end comes?
Is intercourse fun?
How does the sperm get from the mate to the body of the female?
After marriage when you have your first sexual relations, is it possible you can be wrong for each sexually?
At what time, if you wish to have a baby, are you suppose to have sexual intercourse?
Why does a man or woman become dissatisfied sexually?
If a girl can't have children can she still have sexual intercourse with her husband?
How many times do married people have sex?
Do married people get embarrassed after intercourse?
How long does intercourse take?
When you have intercourse is there always a result?
Must the male penis fit snugly into the girls vagina in order to make a successful relation when secreting the sperm?
What is the proper way to act at the time of intercourse?

About Premarital Coitus

When you make out, pet and really get turned on then have to stop, does this make the sex act when you are married a disappointment?
Is it good to have sexual intercourse before marriage if you are serious about someone?

Doesn't sexual intercourse get boring after being married about 10 years? If you were about 20 would it be all right to have sex intercourse before marriage even if you were getting married?

Is there any harm in having sexual relationship with a person of your family?

How much of an affect do surroundings have on the enjoyment of intercourse? How do premarital relations effect ones outlook on marriage?

Does the average person perform sexual intercourse before the age of 21 or before they are married?

Why do boys always want to sex relations with a girl and still want a virgin for a wife? Can a girl have intercourse and not get pregnant?

Do you believe that an unmarried girl's parents should take in the girl's baby?

If a young girl got involved with a boy and she gave her consent, but then she turned against him, would the court still defend the girl?

Why should a person wait until after he or she married for sexual intercourse?

Out of all the times a person has intercourse what is the percentage of risk of getting pregnant?

Intercourse, would you know it after you recovered from being drunk?

Is there something wrong with a boy who believe in sexual intercourse with birth control before marriage?

What does it mean when a girl doesn't satisfy a boy?

Why do girls seem to get all the blame when she get pregnant before marriage and the boy is just treated as an innocent bystander?

Do you think that if the boy or the girl have ever been in trouble, such as the girl having been pregnant or the boy the father, that they should tell their future mate about it either before or after marriage?

What is the main cause of premarital pregnancies?

If a girl becomes pregnant before marriage what possible action can be taken? (expenses, home, the baby)?

How should you tell your parents if you are pregnant?

About Marriage

How can the man tell if his wife has had sexual intercourse?

When it comes to deciding how many children to have, who should have priority? Who should bring up the question of how many children? Wife or husband?

Does marriage to most people mean having children or just having sexual intercourse?

What does a man expect of his wife sexually and otherwise?

Why are girls more interested in marriage than boys?
Does an early marriage usually divorce in a few years?
How do you get a successful marriage? How do you pick a good mate?
How long do you believe a girl and a boy should go together before they take serious steps (age 18–30)?
Do you think when a girl is married, would it be all right to stay in school, while married, or go to night school. Do you think it would harm the marriage?
Why are grown-ups afraid of teenage marriages not working out?
Should you marry for love or security? Is a good marriage always happy? Of what importance is money in marriage? Is religion a necessary part of marriage?
What should you tell your children when they start asking about "The Birds and the Bees". Should you tell them a fairy tale or explain it the right way?
If your wife had a baby and it was born with one arm, is it true that the mother has bad blood?
Is it good to elope?
Should a wife work after she has had her first child? Why or why not?
How can you tell if a man can't have children? Do you think children make a stronger marriage?

About Contraceptives

When you're married, are there certain precautions that you must take during an intercourse?
Is is true that you can't get pregnant a few days before and after your period? If not what is approximate number of days?
Is there any sure way to keep from getting pregnant?
What are birth control pills and how do they work?
Is there a time system that is used to prevent pregnancy and is used very much, and is reliable?
How does a boy get steril?
What's a rubber?
If you use a "rubber" can the girl ever get pregnant?

About Venereal Disease

What is syphilis?
If the boy has syphilis will he always give it to the girls?

Can either sex carry a venereal disease?
Can syphilis be exchanged in kissing?
Have they found a cure for syphilis?
What are the symptoms of syphilis?
When a parent has syphilis will the child have the same disease?

About Menstruation

When and why does menstruation stop in a woman?
Should a girl whose period is very irregular go to a doctor?
Is it all right for a 15 year old to use tampons?
How often does it happen that a girl of 8 or even younger starts having periods?
How do you get rid of cramps? Why do you get them?

About Masturbation

Why do boys stimulate themselves?
What happens if you sperm too much?
Is ejaculation the same as masturbation?
How long does masturbation last?
Is a fellow who masturbates a homosexual?

About Seminal Emission

What is a seminal vesicle?
Do boys know when they're having a wet dream?
What are wet dreams?
How often does a wet dream occur?
How do you know if hormones or sperms have been released during sleep?

About Love

Do girls respect a boy who jumps from one romance to another?
Can you tell if you are just physically attracted to a guy, or you think you really do like him?
What is love?
Do you think it is entirely impossible for a sophomore to really be in love and not just puppy love?

About Growth and Development

Is forming sperm the only job the testes do? Why do many people take after there ansesters?

Where do characteristics and atitudes come from?

I would like to know at what age the sperm cells cease producing sperm?

Why do boys have adam's apples and girls don't?

What if a boy's penus is too big for a girl? or can it be?

What is the last mature development a normal male goes thru? What is the epididymis?

What causes an erection in the boys?

What causes the pituitary gland to become active in sending the "go ahead" to the sex organs (what tells it)? Can two eggs from the two different ovaries (one from each) ripen and pass into the falopian tube at the same time?

What is the piece of skin called that bleeds the first time you have intercourse? And why doesn't it get in the way when you menstruate? What is its purpose?

Why does hair grow by the sex organs?

Why is it that some women have a covering to the womb and others don't?

Exactly what is the prostate gland and where is it located? Do boys feel anything when the semen is ejected?

About Reproduction

Why can't some women have children? Are twins from two different eggs? Does it matter which ovary the egg comes from?

What do they call the reproductive fluid?

Does the father have anything to do with a premature baby?

Is it at all possible or has it ever happened where a woman has had a baby without the help of a man?

Are pregnant ladies self-conscious?

What happens to the sperm that are not united with the egg? How do they leave the body? Do they have an effect on the female?

Is it possible to stop a pregnancy at any time after conception without an abortion?

Why are siamese twins born? What causes birth defects?

Where is the sex of the child determined?

Are almost all relations successful if the sperms are released into the vagina when an egg is in the tube? How do you know when an egg is in the tube?

The human embryo gets its food how?
What are the symptoms of pregnancy and when do they occur? Can you be pregnant and still have your periods?
Is it okay to have intercourse during menstruation?
Do you have to check with the doctor to see if you or your husband can have a baby before sexual intercourse?
Would the child be defective if you did get pregnant during your period?
How long does a woman have her period after she has her baby?
What causes premature babies? What causes morning sickness?
What is a miscarriage and why does it happen?
Is there a prevention against pregnancy?

About Homosexuality

What is homosexuality?
What causes queers?
What's the best thing to do if a homo traps you in a car when you are doing 60 M.P.H.?
How do queers operate?
What makes a person a homo? Is he born one or does he develop the attraction to his own sex?

About Family Problems

Why do some parents hide sex from their children.
Why do little brothers always bother the old child, and then when the oldest child yells at him, he says to the parents, he hit me, mom?
Why are members of the family (brother and sisters) more apt to fight amongst each other than outside friends?
What do you do when your parents tease you about dating?
Why do parents tend to be more lenient with boys even though they may be younger than the girl?
Why do the kids have so much freedom?
If you can't talk to your parents what are you to do? If they just don't understand, through past experience you have had with them?

Miscellaneous

Can boys be virgins?
Can a rape ever result in a pregnancy?

Is there such a thing as a legal abortion in the United States or in any other society?
How does a prostitute keep from getting pregnant?
Can your hymen (maiden head) be broken at other times beside during intercourse? Is there any way to know when it is broken?
Why is sex regarded as a dirty word today?

chapter **5**

suggested content for the primary grades

Introduction: The Elementary Grades

Educating children about sex and family life is not simply a matter of answering their questions about biology. The classroom teacher acts as an aide to the pupil's family and has been entrusted with the privilege of supplementing the teachings of the parents and enriching the pupil's social life. He must acknowledge the importance of the pupil's family experiences at all times in order to create a family-accepting climate in the classroom. He should seek to develop attitudes and exhibit conduct that will assist the pupil in adjusting to the world around him with respect to his sexual nature. To understand the nature of his pupils better, he should become well acquainted with the growth and development patterns of children their age.

The sequence of learning opportunities suggested in these chapters for grades K–6 is especially suitable for use in conjunction with an integrated curriculum organization. The content listed will serve to make the teacher conscious of the family life and sex education elements that he is already introducing and will help identify the areas that need to be supplemented.

Children ages five to eleven are experiencing a period of relatively slow growth. An annual growth of two or three inches and an annual weight gain of three to six pounds are expected, but there are wide variations in these patterns, each significant for the individual concerned.

From five to seven, the child's legs are lengthening rapidly, although the rate of growth for the body as a whole is slowing down. The chest has become larger in circumference than the head or the abdomen. While the heart is still growing rapidly, the pulse and respiration rates are decreasing.

The average six-year-old girl is skeletally about as mature as the typical seven-year-old boy. Postural defects become quite apparent during this period. The six-year-old molars appear between five and six years of age and the deciduous teeth are lost.

Muscular development is still uneven and incomplete during the years from five to seven. Control over large muscles is usually more advanced than control over the small ones, although the activities of each child are indicative of the stage of his muscular growth.

Eye–hand coordination is also developed during this period, and manipulative skill is evident in the handiwork of children of these ages. At eight years of age, the small muscles are sufficiently developed to permit work requiring manual dexterity, such as writing, sewing, weaving, and woodwork.

Masturbation may continue through this period into the later years of childhood if a harmful attitude has previously been taken in dealing with it.

These years represent a period in which children tend to establish some independence from adults. Children often give evidence of this quest for independence by refusing to do what they are asked, or by accusing the adult of being too bossy, too strict, or "just not fair." They may take special delight in using unacceptable language, coming to the table with hands unwashed, or preferring to wear their most tattered sweaters. Yet the necessity for adult approval continues. The child desires the freedom to grow away from adults but must feel that they really care for and will "stand by" him.

Children up to eight or ten years seem to show contradictory social traits. They fight their best friends and brothers and sisters more than they fight other children, probably because they spend more time with these children. Yet the most aggressive are often the most sympathetic when anyone is hurt or in trouble. Research has found that children who showed outstandingly sympathetic behavior sometimes also displayed exceedingly unsympathetic or even cruel behavior.

Boys seem to have more enduring friendships than girls, and toward the end of this period there is the beginning of "gang" interests. Fear, anger, jealousy, joy, affection, and many other emotional patterns characterize the children's lives. Many of the fears that beset children after the age of five concern imaginary and improbable dangers. Children from six to ten, for example, show a fear of such things as blood, ghosts, death, a

part II

suggested content for the elementary grades

fainting person, dead animals, lightning, robbers, dark, solitude, and even the doctor; girls tend to show more fear than boys.

At six, both boys and girls readily play with companions of either sex, although boys fight girls and have no special courtesy toward them. Neither boys nor girls are self-conscious about their bodies, and neither are embarrassed by physical affection from adults or from the opposite sex. Up to the age of seven, boys and girls play together as equals, with no distinctions. This may continue beyond the age of seven, particularly if the girls are physically active in games and dramatic play.

Children of these ages have usually learned the difference between boys and girls and between men and women, and they are interested in the development of babies. Sexual modesty usually appears about the age of seven or eight years.

Overview of Growth and Development: Grades K–3

The primary grades are a natural time for the pupils to begin the study of the structure and functions of families. During this period the pupil is usually given more home responsibilities and can learn to understand his contribution to family life and the significance of family living. The pupil should be helped to gain new concepts of family relationships and the purpose of family life.

Before they get to kindergarten, little boys have already been admonished to be "little men" and not cry when they are hurt; little girls have been encouraged to act like "little ladies." When the youngsters enter school the differences between the sexes is made even clearer. The children need to develop an understanding of their psychological and physical differences.

Natural situations arise in primary classrooms that enable the teacher to help children learn about their bodies, about emotions, about reproduction, and about differences between boys and girls. Answering pupils' questions simply and truthfully without embarrassment will help children to develop constructive attitudes. Attitudes toward human sexuality develop during the child's early life and tend to remain with him throughout life. The emotional climate the teacher creates in the classroom will have a direct effect on the effectiveness of the family life and sex education program.

The following curriculum outlines are designed to be used by a regular classroom teacher in a hypothetical school. The *instructional objectives* at the head of the outlines are meant to guide the teacher in planning activities and in evaluating the effectiveness of the teaching–learning process. The *content* listed in the outlines represents the academic information that the teacher may suitably present. The *suggested learning opportunities* are classroom activities that can help implement the students' understanding of the content. Hopefully these suggestions will give the creative teacher ideas for additional learning situations that can be arranged in her classroom to meet the particular needs of her students.

A variety of books have been suggested for classroom use; these should normally be followed by discussion and other activities designed to reinforce learning that are usually carried on in the primary classroom. The books mentioned will frequently already form part of the school or classroom library.

For the typical primary class the teacher will wish to correlate or incorporate the content listed in the curriculum outline with the social studies and science curriculum. Many of the new social studies and science textbooks contain reading material on families and family patterns that is quite appropriate for use in connection with these outlines.

The curriculum outlines are not intended as a "bible" for family life and sex education courses but rather to stimulate the thinking of the classroom teacher. Each teacher has a classroom filled with pupils with a variety of interests, abilities, needs, and family backgrounds. Each school is located in a community that has special problems, educational goals, and interests in its schools. Each school has special educational procedures that control the educational format of the classroom—team teaching, flexible scheduling, ungraded classrooms, mixed grade classrooms, single sex classrooms, overcrowding. All these factors must be considered when drawing up a curriculum outline to be used in a specific classroom in a specific school district.

The curriculum outlines that follow should be studied carefully and adapted as necessary. The instructional objectives, content, activities, and materials should be considered concerning their appropriateness and practicality for each teacher's specific group of pupils and school district. The only methodological principle about which the authors are rigid is mixed sex classes. Boys and girls should be separated only when the separateness will enhance the pupils' learning. The underlying goal of family life and sex education is an understanding of male–female relationships. Learning in this area is impeded when one half of the relationship is missing during discussion.

A large fund of knowledge exists about family life and sex education. The teacher must become familiar with this knowledge and not just try to teach what he has always thought is true. The following bibliography was selected to enable the teacher to gain the greatest amount of information in the shortest period of time. Many other excellent books are available that will enhance the teacher's knowledge.

Teachers' References

Arnstein, Helene S., *Your Growing Child and Sex*. Indianapolis: Bobbs-Merrill, 1967.

——, *What To Tell Your Child About Birth, Death, Illness, Divorce and Other Crises*. New York: Pocket Books, 1962.

Association for Supervision and Curriculum Development, *Perceiving, Behaving, Becoming: A New Focus for Education*. Washington, D.C.: National Education Association, 1962.

Broderick, Carlfred B., "Sexual Behavior Among Pre-Adolescents," *J. Social Issues* ("The Sexual Renaissance in America"), vol. XXII, no. 2, April 1966, Ira L. Reiss, ed., Acme Printing and Reproduction, 611 South Maple Rd., Ann Arbor, Mich.

Child Study Association of America, *What To Tell Your Children About Sex*. New York: Pocket Books, 1959.

Crawley, Lawrence Q., et al., *Reproduction, Sex, and Preparation for Marriage*. Englewood Cliffs, N.J.: Prentice-Hall, 1964.

Crosby, Muriel, ed., *Reading Ladders for Human Relations*. Washington, D.C.: American Council on Education, 1963.

Duvall, Evelyn M., *Family Development*. Philadelphia: Lippincott, 1957.

Duvall, Evelyn M., and Sylvanus M. Duvall, *Sex Ways—In Fact and Faith: Bases for Christian Family Policy*. New York: Association Press, 1961.

Eckert, Ralph G., *Sex Attitudes in the Home*. New York: Popular Library, 1963.

Erickson, Erik H., *Childhood and Society*. New York: Norton, 1964.

Fromm, Erich, *The Art of Loving*. New York: Harper & Row, 1956.

Hoffman, Hans, *Sex Incorporated: A Positive View of the Sexual Revolution*. Boston: Beacon, 1967.

Hoffman, Martin L., and Lois Hoffman, eds., *Review of Child Development Research*, vols. I and II. New York: Russell Sage Foundation, 1964, 1966.

Jenkins, Gladys G., et al., *These Are Your Children*, 3rd ed. Glenview, Ill.: Scott, Foresman, 1966.

Johnson, Warren R., *Masturbation*. SIECUS Study Guide No. 3, 1966, SIECUS Publication Office, 1855 Broadway, New York, N.Y.

Kirkendall, Lester A., *Sex Education*. SIECUS Study Guide No. 1, 1965, SIECUS Publication Office, 1855 Broadway, New York, N.Y.

Mead, Margaret, *Male and Female*. New York: Morrow, 1949.

Museum of Science and Industry, *The Miracle of Growth*. New York: Pyramid Books, 1960.

Narramore, Clyde M., *How To Tell Your Children About Sex*. Grand Rapids, Mich.: Zondervan, 1958.

Rodman, Hyman, ed., *Marriage, Family, and Society: A Reader*. New York: Random House, 1965.

Rubin, Isadore, *Homosexuality*. SIECUS Study Guide No. 2, 1965, SIECUS Publication Office, 1855 Broadway, New York, N.Y.

Young, Leontine, *Life Among the Giants*. New York: McGraw-Hill, 1966.

Curriculum Outlines

Kindergarten

Instructional Objectives

The pupil:
1. Continues to develop a concept of his self-worth and sexual identity.
2. Begins to develop an understanding of love.
3. Recognizes that there are sex differences between boys and girls.
4. Begins to recognize the role of the family in his life.
5. Understands that a human baby develops inside the body of the mother.
6. Understands that curiosity about his body and how it works is normal.
7. Begins to develop a correct vocabulary for body parts and body functions.

Content	Suggested Learning Opportunities
Learning About the Family Families differ in size and makeup.	· Have the pupils paint or draw a picture of their family. · Ask pupils to tell the class about the size of their family, about their brothers, sisters, etc.
Learning About Love A. There are various kinds of love. B. People are alike in needing love.	· Have the class discuss what love is. What does the word mean to them? · Read and discuss the book *Love Is a Special Way of Feeling.*[1] · Have the pupils tell how they show their love.
Learning About Babies A. Babies need a lot of care from their families. B. Babies grow inside the mother in a special place called the uterus.	· Read and discuss stories like *Animal Mothers and Babies. A Baby for Betsy. Judy's Baby. The Story of a Baby. The New Baby.* · View and discuss the film *Human Beginnings.* · Have the class share what they know about babies in their families.

Learning About Individual Differences

A. All people are different in some ways and alike in others.

- Discuss how boys and girls are alike and different physically, using correct terminology for body parts.
- Have pupils tell about their favorite activity at home and at school.

B. Everyone has something to contribute.

- Discuss some classroom activities such as cleanup to demonstrate how the class works together.

[1] Books and films mentioned as *Learning Opportunities* are cited fully in the *Resources* sections that immediately follow.

Resources

Books

Anglund, Joan Walsh, *Love Is a Special Way of Feeling*. New York: Harcourt, Brace & World, 1960.
Ets, Marie Hall, *The Story of a Baby*. New York: Viking, 1939.
Foran, Robert, *Animal Mothers and Babies*. New York: Warne, 1960.
Guy, Anne, *A Baby for Betsy*. Nashville, Tenn.: Abingdon Press, 1957.
Johnston, Dorothy, *All About Babies*. Grand Rapids, Mich.: Zondervan, 1962.
Scott, Sally, *Judy's Baby*. New York: Harcourt, Brace & World, 1949.
Shane, Ruth, and Harold G. Shane, *The New Baby*. New York: Simon and Schuster, 1948.

Films[2]

Human Beginnings, Association Films, color, 22 min. Depicts the beliefs of a group of primary children concerning the origin of human life by showing drawings they have made in kindergarten. Also pictures the reactions of a young boy and his parents to the coming of a new baby.

Study Prints

Anglund, Joan Walsh, *The Joan Walsh Anglund Sampler*. New York: Harcourt, Brace & World, 1967.

First Grade

Instructional Objectives

The pupil:

1. Continues to develop an understanding of love.
2. Recognizes and appreciates his role in the family.

[2] The distributor and not the producer is given for all films mentioned in this book.

3. Continues to develop a concept of his self-worth and sexual identity.
4. Develops a matter-of-fact attitude toward his body and body functions.
5. Continues to develop a correct vocabulary for body parts and body functions.
6. Understands that male and female are requisite for reproduction.
7. Understands and accepts reproduction as a natural process basic to all life.
8. Recognizes that attitudes of cheerfulness and unselfishness contribute to the family well-being.

Content	Suggested Learning Opportunities
Learning About Feelings A. Feelings can be either pleasant or unpleasant.	· Have the class talk about their feelings for their family and friends. · Read and discuss stories about children's feelings, such as *Boo, Who Used To Be Scared of the Dark. Timid Timothy. The Very Little Boy. The Very Little Girl.*
B. Love is an important feeling.	· Have the pupils draw pictures of love. · Read and discuss *What Color Is Love?* · Have the pupils tell how they felt when someone took away their turn on the playground equipment.
C. Failure is a way to learn.	· Have the pupils tell about situations in which they felt they failed. · Read and discuss stories like *While Susie Sleeps. Youngest One. Kate Can Skate. Jim Can Swim.* · Discuss what would happen if they and others never tried new things. · Collect and discuss pictures of children showing emotions, and/or have the pupils draw their own. · Read and discuss the book *Laugh and Cry.*
Learning About Family Relationships A. Family members help each other in many different ways.	· Show and discuss the film *Zoo Families.* · Have various pupils tell about their families.
B. Cooperation makes for a more	· Have pupils tell of the ways they

pleasant family life.

help at home or how they help mother, father, siblings, grandparents, etc.

- View and discuss the film *Beginning Responsibility: Taking Care of Things.*
- Have the pupils make a family scrapbook.

C. Both fathers and mothers take care of the children.

- Have pupils dramatize several roles of various family members.
- Have pupils make up songs about the work the members of the family do at home.
- Have pupils tell how their mothers and fathers provide and care for them.

D. Fathers do many kinds of work to support the family.

- Show and discuss the film *Fathers Go Away To Work.*
- Have the pupils discuss the work their fathers do.
- Have pupils draw pictures of their fathers at work.

E. Mothers do many kinds of work to contribute to the well-being of the family.

- Have the pupils describe several tasks that mothers do in the home.
- Read and discuss stories like *Family Helpers. The Way Mothers Are. Mommies at Work.*
- Have pupils draw pictures of their mothers at work at home and away from home.

F. Each family member has a place of worth in the family.

- Ask pupils to tell of experiences with family members on holidays, birthdays, and visits to relatives.
- Have pupils tell the class why they like their home.
- Have pupils tell how they help at home.

Learning About Human Reproduction

A. A new baby needs much care.

- Ask the class if anyone has a new baby in their home.
- Read and discuss stories like *We Want a Little Sister. I'm Going To Have a Baby. A Tiny Baby for You.*

B. Human babies need more care than animal babies.

- View and discuss the film *Kittens: Birth and Growth.*
- Discuss the study prints *Beginning*

the Human Story: A New Baby in the Family.
- Compare the way human babies develop before birth with the way animal babies do.
- Have the pupils tell how they can help with a new baby.

C. Both mothers and fathers are needed to create a new life.

- Show and discuss the slides *How Babies Are Made.*
- Read and discuss the book *The Wonderful Story of How You Were Born.*
- Have some pupils share some of their family stories about their birth.
- Discuss some of the problems that create one-parent families.

Learning About Individual Differences

- Have the pupils draw a self-portrait.
- Have the pupils discuss their concepts of sex roles. Help them identify the overlapping areas.

A. Boys and girls look different because boys are growing up to be men and fathers and girls to be women and mothers.

- Have the pupils discuss how they are different from each other with respect to eye color, size, and hair type.
- Read and discuss stories like *The Smallest Boy in the Class. Two Is a Team. Big Sister and Little Sister.*

B. Growing up is more than just getting older.

- Read and discuss stories like *Bridget's Growing Day. The Growing Story.*
- Discuss the importance of effective communication by using correct terminology: urine, bowel movement, penis, navel, uterus, etc.
- Discuss how each pupil is proud of his differences, and how all pupils work together in the classroom, school, family, and community.

Resources

Books

Anglund, Joan Walsh, *What Color Is Love?* New York: Harcourt, Brace & World, 1966.

Beim, Jerrold, *The Smallest Boy in the Class.* New York: Morrow, 1949.

——, *Laugh and Cry.* New York: Morrow, 1955.

Beim, Jerrold, and Lorraine Beim, *Two Is a Team.* New York: Harcourt, Brace & World, 1945.

Bromhall, Winifred, *Bridget's Growing Day.* New York: Knopf, 1957.
Gruenberg, Sidonie M., *The Wonderful Story of How You Were Born.* Garden City, N.Y.: Doubleday, 1952.
Hobson, Laura, *I'm Going To Have a Baby.* New York: John Day, 1967.
Hoffman, Elaine, *Family Helpers.* Chicago: Melmont, 1954.
Krasilovsky, Phyllis, *The Very Little Boy.* Garden City, N.Y.: Doubleday, 1962.
——, *The Very Little Girl.* Garden City, N.Y.: Doubleday, 1953.
Krauss, Ruth, *The Growing Story.* New York: Harper & Row, 1947.
Langstaff, Nancy, *A Tiny Baby for You.* New York: Harcourt, Brace & World, 1955.
Leaf, Munro, *Boo, Who Used To Be Scared of the Dark.* New York: Random House, 1948.
Mattmuller, Felix, *We Want a Little Sister.* Minneapolis, Minn.: Lerner, 1965.
Merriam, Eve, *Mommies at Work.* New York: Knopf, 1961.
Olds, Helen D., *Jim Can Swim.* New York: Knopf, 1963.
——, *Kate Can Skate.* New York: Knopf, 1960.
Schlein, Miriam, *The Way Mothers Are.* Chicago: Whitman, 1963.
Schneider, Nina, *While Susie Sleeps.* Glenview, Ill.: Scott, Foresman, 1948.
Williams, Gweneira M., *Timid Timothy.* Glenview, Ill.: Scott, Foresman, 1944.
Yashima, Taro, *Youngest One.* New York: Viking, 1962.
Zolotow, Charlotte, *Big Sister and Little Sister.* New York: Harper & Row, 1966.

Films

Beginning Responsibility: Taking Care of Things, Coronet Films, color, 11 min. Describes how to care for one's toys, clothing, and other things, putting articles back where they belong, and proper storing and handling of articles to prevent damage.

Fathers Go away to Work, Bailey Film Service, color, 11 min. Three fathers from one neighborhood are seen leaving home and at their respective jobs. One is a salesman who works in an office, one a commercial artist, and one a construction worker. The film illustrates the way many families are dependent on their jobs and services.

Kittens: Birth and Growth, Bailey Film Service, color, 11 min. An introduction to the birth, growth, and care of pets.

Zoo Families, Film Associates of California, color, 10 min. Tommy takes his mother to visit the zoo. The care the animal mothers take of their babies is shown.

Slides (35mm)

How Babies Are Made, General Learning Corporation, color. This series of 34 slides in three sections shows the story of reproduction in plants, animals, and humans. The teacher can employ one section at a time in order to meet the pupils' most immediate interests and needs. Each slide has beautiful paper sculpture illustrations and easily read descriptions.

Study Prints

Anglund, Joan Walsh, *The Joan Walsh Anglund Sampler.* New York: Harcourt, Brace & World, 1967.

Fricke, Irma, *Beginning the Human Story: A New Baby in the Family.* Glenview, Ill.: Scott, Foresman, 1967.

Second Grade

Instructional Objectives

The pupil:

1. Understands that there are many different patterns of family life.
2. Continues to develop an understanding of and respect for the rights of others, including the right to privacy.
3. Recognizes that growing up includes assuming more responsibility.
4. Continues to develop an appreciation of the importance of mutual love and consideration in the family.
5. Continues to develop an understanding of human reproduction.
6. Develops a regard for human reproduction as a privilege.
7. Continues to expand his concept of himself.

Content	Suggested Learning Opportunities
Learning About the Many Kinds of Families	• Have the pupils draw pictures of their families and tell about them.
A. The composition of the family may change from time to time.	• Discuss the various kinds of family groupings. Help the children to accept changes brought about by death, divorce, and separation.
B. Families have different ways of living in different countries.	• Ask the pupils to tell about some of their family customs that come from other countries.
C. Families have different ways of living in our country.	• Discuss the pictures in books like *Follow the Sunset. Family of Man.* • Read and discuss stories like *Papa Small. Home Is a Very Special Place. The Night When Mother Was Away. The Big World and the Little House.*

- Invite parents or other community people to talk to the class about their cultural background.
- Have pupils bring in pictures that illustrate such differences.
- Have pupils who have lived in other places tell how their homes were different.

D. A family's way of living is affected by the father's and mother's work.

- Have pupils tell of the different kinds of work their mothers and fathers do. Invite parents to visit the class and tell about their work.
- View and discuss the film *What Do Fathers Do?*
- Read and discuss stories like *Little Angela and Her Puppy. The Little Carousel.*

E. All family members care for and about each other.

- Have the pupils tell how their parents help them to grow up.
- Read and discuss books like *Where Are the Mothers? Growing Up with Daddy. Grandfather and I. Grandmother and I. The Littlest One in the Family.*
- View and discuss the film *Allen Is My Brother.*
- Have pupils discuss how they and other members of the family show their affection for one another.

Learning About People Outside the Home

- Read and discuss the book *A Friend Is Someone Who Likes You.*

A. Some qualities help us to make friends; other qualities make it difficult for us to play and work with others.

- Have the pupils tell what they like about a friend.
- Have the pupils tell what they do not like about friends.
- Discuss how to overcome these qualities.

B. Taking turns and cooperating help us to live more happily with people.

- Discuss ways of working and playing more harmoniously.
- Discuss ways of sharing equipment.
- Discuss ways of helping with classroom and home chores.
- Discuss taking turns in various situations. Dramatize ways that children may behave in a sharing situation.

C. Good manners and courtesy show kindness and consideration for others.	• Read and discuss the book *Kindness Is a Lot of Things.* • Have the pupils tell of a kindness they have done at home or school. • Dramatize simple courtesies and manners.
D. Respect for property is important for harmonious living.	• Dramatize family situations such as using something that belongs to another member of the family and not returning it. • Dramatize classroom situations to demonstrate respect for individual property. • View and discuss the film *Beginning Responsibility: Other People's Things.* • Read and discuss stories like *If Everybody Did. Let's Be Enemies.*
Learning About Growing Up A. Growing up gives one more privileges.	• Have the pupils describe the activities they may do this year that they were not allowed to do last year. • Have the pupils tell how they have changed in size and appearance. Compare current class pictures with last year's.
B. Growing up gives one new responsibilities.	• Have pupils tell about additional responsibilities they have this year both at home and at school. Also have them discuss the additional privileges granted.
C. Boys and girls have their own pattern of growth and development.	• Ask the pupils to talk with their parents about family patterns of growth and note the differences in class. • Have the class discuss the different kinds of physical changes experienced by growing boys and girls. • Compare the independence of the pupils to the helplessness and dependency of the human baby.
D. Human babies have both a mother and a father.	• View and discuss the film *Human and Animal Beginnings.* • Read and discuss the book *All About Babies.* • Continue the development of correct terminology during class discussion of the above material.

Learning About an Individual's Worth in Society

A. We learn from our successes and failures.

- Help each student to identify his talents.
- Have the pupils discuss their hobbies.
- Have a hobby show for the class, where each child who wishes may discuss his hobby with the others.
- Discuss the differences between boys' and girls' hobbies or activities.
- Read and discuss books like *Benjie. Swimming Hole. Jenny's First Party.*
- Discuss with the class what we can learn from failures.
- Have the pupils talk about the things they do well and things that are hard for them to do.

B. We are influenced by our environment.

- Show and discuss the film *Beginning Responsibility: Doing Things for Ourselves in School.*
- Have pupils tell of situations where people have helped them.
- Have pupils tell of situations where they have helped a friend or family member.
- Help the pupils to understand their limitations and to set realistic goals for themselves.

Resources

Books

Anglund, Joan Walsh, *A Friend Is Someone Who Likes You.* New York: Harcourt, Brace & World, 1958.

Averill, Esther, *Jenny's First Party.* New York: Harper & Row, 1948.

Beim, Jerrold, *Swimming Hole.* New York: Morrow, 1951.

Brown, Marcia, *The Little Carousel.* New York: Scribner, 1946.

Buckley, Helen E., *Grandmother and I.* New York: Lothrop, Lee & Shepard, 1961.

——, *Grandfather and I.* New York: Lothrop, Lee & Shepard, 1959.

Duncan, Lois, *The Littlest One in the Family.* New York: Dodd, Mead, 1960.

Eckblad, Edith, *Kindness Is a Lot of Things.* Norwalk, Conn.: Gibson, 1966.

Evans, Eva Knox, *Home Is a Very Special Place.* New York: Capitol, 1962.

Johnston. Dorothy, *All About Babies.* Grand Rapids, Mich.: Zondervan, 1962.

Krauss, Ruth, *The Big World and the Little House.* New York: Harper & Row, 1956.

Lenski, Lois, *Papa Small,* ITA ed. New York: Walck, 1966.
Lexau, Joan M., *Benjie.* New York: Dial, 1964.
Marino, Dorothy, *Little Angela and Her Puppy.* Philadelphia: Lippincott, 1954.
——, *Where Are the Mothers?* Philadelphia: Lippincott, 1959.
Schneider, Herman, and Nina Schneider, *Follow the Sunset.* Garden City, N.Y.: Doubleday, 1952.
Steichen, Edward, *Family of Man.* New York: Simon and Schuster, 1956.
Stover, Jo Ann, *If Everybody Did.* New York: David McKay, 1960.
Udry, Janice May, *Let's Be Enemies.* New York: Harper & Row, 1961.
Wilson, Christopher B., *Growing Up with Daddy.* New York: Lothrop, Lee & Shepard, 1957.
Zolotow, Charlotte, *The Night When Mother Was Away.* New York: Lothrop, Lee & Shepard, 1958.

Films

Allen Is My Brother, Churchill Films, color, 11 min. Designed to emphasize good family relationships. Karen, age seven, helps mother take care of Allen, age three, and learns that it can be fun.

Beginning Responsibility: Doing Things for Ourselves in School. Coronet Films, color, 11 min. Explains how a young boy learns to do things for himself by watching others, by profiting from his mistakes, by asking for help, and by practice. Emphasizes the importance of self-reliance.

Beginning Responsibility: Other People's Things, Coronet Films, color, 11 min. Explains how public and private property, as well as articles that are borrowed or found, should be cared for. Stresses the need for respecting the property of others.

Human and Animal Beginnings, Henk Newenhouse, color, 13 min. Presents in simple fashion the basic concepts of the family and reproduction.

What Do Fathers Do? Churchill Films, color, 11 min. On their way to Toby's father's construction job, Toby and his father meet other fathers going to their jobs. Toby learns how a father's earnings buy things the family needs.

Third Grade

Instructional Objectives

The pupil:

1. Continues to develop a greater understanding of his own identity.
2. Continues to learn constructive ways of using and resolving differences.
3. Continues to learn about the factors involved in a successfully functioning family.
4. Continues to learn how to handle feelings and act in a way that is acceptable to others.

5. Has respect for all parts of the body and uses correct terminology in referring to them.
6. Continues to develop a reverence toward and an understanding of the process of creating life.

Content	**Suggested Learning Opportunities**
Learning To Accept What Cannot Be Changed A. Body Structure	• Discuss the advantages and disadvantages of being a tall person; of being a short person. • Discuss hereditary traits.
B. Sex	• Have the class bring in pictures of boys and girls; discuss the differences. • Discuss how boys and girls are alike.
C. Intelligence	• Help the pupils to identify and discuss their academic strengths. • Discuss what qualities pupils admire in others.
D. Environment	• Have the pupils give ideas regarding how they can influence their environment. • Read and discuss stories like *The Fairy Doll. The Cowboy Surprise.*
Learning to Accept Consequences When Making Decisions	• Discuss the idea that love of and respect for others presupposes love of self. • Have the class tell what they would suggest if they had three wishes for all the boys and girls in the world. • Read some of the unfinished stories about possible choices, published in the *Journal of Education* each month. Have some of the pupils dramatize their choice and discuss. • Read and discuss stories like *Big Brother. The Lonely Doll Learns a Lesson. Tough Enough and Sassy.*
A. Some consequences cause conflicts.	• Ask the class to give their ideas about conflict, quarreling, and fighting. • Read and discuss stories like *The Carrot Seed. Belling The Tiger. Let's Be Enemies.*

Read and discuss *The Quarreling Book.*

B. Conflicts can be resolved.

- Have the pupils tell how they have resolved a conflict situation.
- Discuss how the following may help: (1) decision as a result of a conference, and (2) decision by a figure of authority.
- Demonstrate the use of a problem-solving technique.
- Have the pupils dramatize how to oppose others verbally while still respecting them.

Learning To Develop Acceptable Relationships

- Have the pupils tell about the different backgrounds represented in the classroom.
- Have the pupils discuss how the individual differences within the class contribute to class activities.
- Learn and sing the song "Getting To Know You," from *The King and I.*

A. With friends

- Have the pupils describe the qualities they admire in a friend.
- Read and discuss stories like *Fun For Chris. Peter's Long Walk. Exactly Alike.*
- Have the pupils list and discuss qualities in themselves that would make them a good friend.

B. With adults

- Discuss how adults can contribute to children's growth and development.
- Have pupils tell stories about their adult relationships.
- Read and discuss stories like *Bully Of Barkham Street. Mrs. Piggle-Wiggle's Magic.*

Learning That Families Can Be Fun

- Have the pupils tell about their favorite family outing.

A. Families work together.

- Have the pupils describe the chores they do at home. Discuss how everyone's helping out makes the family function smoothly.
- Have some of the pupils give situa-

tions and consequences when they did not do their chores.
- Discuss courtesies and privacy in the family.
- Read and discuss *Manners Can Be Fun.*

B. Family members share feelings, beliefs, and ideas with their families.

- Ask the class to share an idea with their family at dinner and be prepared to discuss the results of the discussion in class the following day.
- Discuss the idea that we do not always think and feel the same as our other family members.
- Read and discuss books like *It Looks Like This: A Point-of-View Book. Charlotte's Web.*

Learning How All Life Reproduces Its Own Kind

- Have the class grow different kinds of plants to show the different methods of reproduction.

A. Plants

- Read and discuss *How a Seed Grows.*
- View and discuss the film *Wonders of Plant Growth.*

B. Animals

- Read and discuss stories like *All About Eggs. Animal Families. Animals as Parents.*
- Show and discuss films like *The Day Life Begins. Development of the Chick Embryo. Mother Deer and Her Twins.*

C. Humans

- Read and discuss the book *A Baby Is Born.*
- Discuss what makes man different from lower animals.
- Have the class share stories about babies in their homes.
- Compare the way human babies develop before birth with the way animal babies do.
- Discuss the time it takes for a human baby to develop as compared to the time it takes for animal babies.
- Show and discuss the film *Fertilization and Birth.*
- Continue to help pupils develop a

correct vocabulary for body parts and functions.

- Have the class list the things that newborns need, for example, parents, home, and love.
- Discuss the father's contributions to the creation and care of a baby.

Resources

Books

Carroll, Ruth, and Latrobe Carroll, *Tough Enough and Sassy*. New York: Walck, 1958.
Godden, Rumer, *The Fairy Doll*. New York: Viking, 1956.
Jordan, Helene J., *How a Seed Grows*. New York: Thomas Y. Crowell, 1960.
Kingman, Lee, *Peter's Long Walk*. Garden City, N.Y.: Doubleday, 1953.
Krauss, Ruth, *The Carrot Seed*. New York: Harper & Row, 1945.
Leaf, Munro, *Manners Can Be Fun*. Philadelphia: Lippincott, 1958.
Levine, Milton I., and Jean H. Seligmann, *A Baby Is Born*. New York: Simon and Schuster, 1949.
MacDonald, Betty, *Mrs. Piggle-Wiggle's Magic*. Philadelphia: Lippincott, 1957.
Ness, Evaline, *Exactly Alike*. New York: Scribner, 1964.
Randall, Blossom E., *Fun for Chris*. Chicago: Whitman, 1956.
Selsam, Millicent E., *All About Eggs*. Glenview, Ill.: Scott, Foresman, 1952.
——, *Animals as Parents*. New York: Morrow, 1965.
Stolz, Mary, *Belling the Tiger*. New York: Harper & Row, 1961.
——, *The Bully of Barkham Street*. New York: Harper & Row, 1963.
Udry, Janice May, *Let's Be Enemies*. New York: Harper & Row, 1961.
Unfinished Stories for Use in the Classroom, No. 381-11766. Washington, D.C.: National Education Association.
Webber, Irma E., *It Looks Like This: A Point-of-View Book*. Glenview, Ill.: Scott, Foresman, 1958.
Weil, Ann, *Animal Families*. Chicago: Children's Press, 1956.
White, E. B., *Charlotte's Web*. New York: Harper & Row, 1952.
Wise, William, *The Cowboy Surprise*. New York: Putnam, 1961.
Wright, Dare, *The Lonely Doll Learns a Lesson*. New York: Random House, 1961.
Zolotow, Charlotte, *Big Brother*. New York: Harper & Row, 1960.
——, *The Quarreling Book*. New York: Harper & Row, 1963.

Films

The Day Life Begins, Carousel Films, b/w, 23 min. Traces the reproductive processes from the division of the one-celled amoeba to man. The scenes of births of turtles, sea horses, snakes, and puppies are excellent. Development of the human baby is explained by Dr. Milton Levine.

Development of the Chick Embryo, Coronet Films, color, 5 min. Studies the basic processes of one type of reproduction. Pictures live chick embryos and points out embryonic movement, blood circulation, heartbeat, and show the chick hatching out of the shell.

Fertilization and Birth, Henk Newenhouse, color, 10 min. An unusual new film that combines animation to describe the fertilization process and live photography of the births of a calf, a litter of puppies, and a human baby.

Mother Deer and Her Twins, Encyclopedia Britannica Films, color, 11 min. The story of twin fawns. Shows how the mother protects them at first but later teaches them to care for themselves.

Wonders of Plant Growth, Churchill Films, color, 11 min. A girl and her younger brother experiment with plants. They start plants from a bean and a squash seed, and from the root of a sweet potato plant. Growth is shown in time-lapse photography.

chapter 6

suggested content for the intermediate grades

Overview of Growth and Development: Grades 4–6

The major purpose of the family life and sex education program in these grades is to help the pupils improve their personal and social relationships through a better understanding of themselves and others. It is during these pre-adolescent years that pupils need specific and realistic information concerning family life and sex education that will prepare them for adolescence and help them through it.

Most intermediate pupils still have an impersonal and objective interest in the physical changes of adolescence. The pupils should know how they grow and develop, the major factors and influences that promote or retard physical, mental, emotional, and social growth, and how the different factors affect each other. They should also understand that physical and mental health are important in influencing behavior and developing the understandings, attitudes, and skills that cause the individual to work toward constant self-improvement in all his relationships.

In the past, many schools held assemblies and showed films on menstruation to the fifth- and sixth-grade girls. This program was usually conducted by the school nurse; in order to participate, each girl had to present a slip of paper with written parental consent. The assemblies were well done, but sex education was isolated as an extracurricular area, and the boys, who were not included in the presentation, had to rely on the interpretation they received from the girls. Sex education is only one aspect of the total family life and sex education program and must not be isolated if we wish to develop wholesome attitudes in pupils.

Between the ages of nine and eleven the children's growth in height and weight is normally slow and steady. The rapid growth of early childhood is over, and the changes of adolescence often begin to appear. Children tend to be long-legged and rangy because their legs grow more than their trunks. The period of relatively least growth in height is from nine to ten years for girls and from ten to eleven for boys.

The circulatory, digestive, and respiratory systems are mature in functions although growth still continues during these years. The lungs are almost fully developed, and the rate of respiration is eighteen to twenty per minute, which approaches the adult level. Blood pressure is increasing and is only a little lower than that of adults. The brain and spinal cord reach adult size by the age of ten, but the cellular development upon which mental development depends is not complete and continues for a number of years. By ten years the eyes have reached adult size and are completely developed in function.

At age eleven girls are a full year nearer to reproductive maturity than are boys. During that year some girls and fewer boys, through sudden and rapid growth, show signs of approaching adolescence.

Children ages nine to eleven enjoy being recognized as participants in making family plans, although they tend to reject many of the standards of home in favor of those of friends their own age, their "age mates." The standards set up for children by adults concerning private property, honesty, tidiness, and cleanliness often demand a higher level than the children are normally able to attain, and tension and conflict result. Age mates provide standards of oral speech, clothes, manners, and games, while parents and teachers still supply ideology, including race prejudices, religion, and morals.

At these ages teasing, rivalry, and fights between brothers and sisters are likely to occur. Sudden "crushes" and hero worship are to be expected, along with a strong concern over group recognition and approbation.

If a child's growth is normal, he is usually well established as a "clique" or club member by eight or ten. A password, a club house—in fact, anything that represents organization and secrecy—gives the child a great sense of importance and "belonging." The impulse to secrecy often causes parents to suspect unwholesomeness, but most of the secrets and activities characteristic of these ages are thoroughly wholesome.

Boys and girls in the intermediate grades do not play together as much as they did when they were younger. Their behavior and interests are becoming increasingly differentiated, and sex differences create difficulties between them. At about eight-and-a-half years children enter into a period of strong attachment for their own sex and also of sex antagonism. This lasts for a short period with girls, longer with boys. Toward the end of the period (eleven years for girls, twelve for boys) the child shows much self-consciousness when playing with children of the opposite sex.

Both sexes like to show their affection for their pals, but in different ways. Girls put arms around each other, boys substitute with punches. This is the age of "rassling," as the boys call it, and in spite of its outward appearance it is a very friendly activity. Poking, tripping, practical jokes for boys and incessant giggling for girls are characteristic of these ages.

Children have a heightened curiosity about the facts of reproduction as they approach the age of ten or eleven, and they will react to an explanation of human reproduction with understanding and objectivity.

Curriculum Outlines

Fourth Grade

Instructional Objectives

The pupil:

1. Continues to develop an understanding and appreciation for the roles of each member of the family as an individual and as a contributing member of the family unit.
2. Continues to build an image of self as a worthy contributing member of society.
3. Continues to develop an emotional acceptance of sex as a basic life function.
4. Continues to grow in self-understanding and personal responsibility.
5. Continues to learn to appreciate himself for what he is.
6. Becomes increasingly competent in developing and maintaining mutually satisfactory interpersonal relationships.

Content	Suggested Learning Opportunities
Learning About Our Capabilities A. Our strengths and weaknesses can	• Read and discuss stories about outstanding personalities in many fields.

be used positively in many different ways.

- View and discuss the film *Learning from Disappointments.*
- Read and discuss stories like *I Wonder Why. The Hidden You.*

B. Success means different things to different people, depending on their age and sex.

- Have the class discuss the meaning of success in the following areas: sports, appearance, neatness, popularity, and good grades.
- Have the class discuss what areas are important to their parents for success and why.
- Read and discuss stories about Lincoln, Helen Keller, and others who achieved success after initial failure.

C. Learn to face reality.

- Have pupils discuss how they can help each other in facing their strengths and weaknesses and how they can help each other to grow, for example, how they react to a good athlete making a home run and to a poor athlete.
- Show and discuss the film *A Plain White Envelope.*
- Have four or five pupils observe situations on the playground and discuss their various reactions and comments. What really happened?
- Have the pupils discuss issues where there are two sides that are not necessarily right or wrong, for example, favorite food, color, and subject.
- Show and discuss the film *Barbara (To Conform or Not To Conform).*

How We Think and Feel About Our Families

A. Mother, father, and siblings
B. Step-parents or foster parents
C. Living with relatives
D. Others living in the home

- Compare family life in colonial times with family life today, and compare the changes in the roles of each family member.
- Read and discuss books like *Secret of the Andes. Caveman to Spaceman.*
- Show and discuss the film *The Family.*
- Read and discuss stories like *Stepsister Sally. A Place for Johnny Bill.*
- Have each pupil write a story describing his family and telling about

any significant changes in family composition.
- Read and discuss stories like *The Beech Tree. Adopted Jane. A Home for Penny. Here's a Penny.*

The Effect of Status in the Family

A. The responsibilities and privileges of an oldest child or an only child

B. The advantages and disadvantages of being an only boy in a family of girls, or an only girl in a family of boys

- Have the pupils tell about their families and their position among their siblings. Ask them to tell what they feel are the privileges and responsibilities as a result of this position.
- Read and discuss stories like *The Middle Moffat. A Brother for the Orphelines. Benito.*
- Show and discuss the film *Family Life.*

Responsibilities to One's Family

A. Doing chores
B. Being considerate of others
C. Helping brothers and sisters

- Act out situations to emphasize the contributions and interdependencies of members of the family.
- Show and discuss the film *Family Teamwork and You.*
- Have pupils discuss situations in which they were especially considerate and helpful.

Making a Happy Family

A. Trying to understand one another

- View and discuss one of the many films on families in other cultures, such as *Mexican Children. Spanish Children.*
- Assign small groups of pupils to develop reports on family life in other cultures, bringing out the roles and functions of the families.
- Examine and discuss the book *The Family.*

B. Appreciating the differences between the members of the family

- Have the pupils make illustrated booklets showing what each member does or can do to improve his family group.
- Have a class panel discussion on such topics as (1) reporting vs. tattling, (2) helping vs. cheating, (3) borrowing vs. stealing, and (4) relating news vs. gossiping.

C. Planning together

- Discuss in class how pupils can contribute to plans for a family party.

D. Not making unreasonable demands on one's family

E. Taking pride in the family

- Dramatize family activities, for example, family picnics, dinner, and getting ready for breakfast.
- Have each pupil ask his parents to list three things that he does that interfere with maintaining a happy home, and have parents suggest ways of correcting these differences.
- Discuss the generosity of a father (when a child gets a new bicycle or some other item). Discuss reasons why fathers sometimes cannot be generous in this particular way.
- Have pupils write and read to the class paragraphs on the topic, "What My Home Means to Me."
- Have the pupils describe some of the special events in their family's life.

1. Am I proud to introduce my friends to members of my family?
   - Act out the etiquette of introductions.
   - Have each pupil make a list of the special qualities of each member of his family.
2. Do the accomplishments of other members of my family make me happy?
   - Have pupils recall and discuss their feelings when a sibling was rewarded for something special.
3. What can I do to help?
   a. Help keep the home neat.
   - Discuss how pupils can help with the household chores in everyday living. Discuss the differences between assuming a responsibility and waiting to be told or asked.

   b. Make decorations for the home.
   - Have the class make simple decorations for the home, for example, pictures and waste baskets.

Family Beginnings

A. The factors necessary for having a family, that is, mother, father, home, and affection

- Ask the pupils to tell about the birth of a baby brother or sister; about a new family of pets.
- Review materials covered in earlier grades [see especially page 66].

B. Family resemblances

- Have a committee trace the pedigrees (heredity and family tree) of famous racehorses, sheep, cattle, and dogs.

1. What are your family traits, that is, build, features, and eye, skin, and hair color?
   - Have the pupils ask their parents about their family traits and then discuss them in class the next day.

2. Do family traits sometimes skip a generation?

- Discuss with the class the meaning of *heredity.*
- Read and discuss the book *All About Heredity.*
- Have the class discuss environment vs. heredity in relation to a specific trait in which they are interested.

C. Understanding the miracle of reproduction

1. Terminology
2. Fertilization
3. Growth of the embryo
4. Birth of a baby

- Review what was learned in earlier grades about human reproduction. Clarify misconceptions that may have occurred. Continue to develop and expand the correct vocabulary.
- Show and discuss the film *The Miracle of Reproduction.*
- Read and discuss the book *The Wonder of Life.*
- Read and discuss the book *The Human Story: Facts on Birth, Growth and Reproduction.*

D. The greater dependence of a human baby than of an animal baby

- Discuss some of the things a human baby can do the first month of life.
- Study the care of pets at home, in school, at a neighbor's house, in the zoo, in pet shops, and in a museum.
- Discuss how animal babies compare to human babies in the ability to meet their needs.
- Have some of the pupils tell about the behavior of a baby brother or sister.

Acceptance of Sex as a Basic Life Function

A. Some girls will be beginning their growth spurt.

B. Many boys "catch up" to the girls in size at about age 15.

- Have pupils write a paragraph on "What Kind of a Person I Am."
- Discuss the comments made on sex role identity.
- Discuss the difference in growth patterns for boys and girls as they enter puberty.
- Provide opportunities for boys and girls to play and work together to foster their understanding of and appreciation for each other.
- View and discuss the film *Growing Up—Preadolescence.*

Resources

Books

Alexander, Arthur, *The Hidden You: Psychology in Your Life*. Englewood Cliffs, N.J.: Prentice-Hall, 1962.
Buck, Pearl S., *The Beech Tree*. New York: John Day, 1955.
Bulla, Clyde R., *Benito*. New York: Thomas Y. Crowell, 1961.
Burden, Shirley, *I Wonder Why*. Garden City, N.Y.: Doubleday, 1963.
Carlson, Natalie S., *A Brother for the Orphelines*. New York: Harper & Row, 1959.
Clark, Ann N., *Secret of the Andes*. New York: Viking, 1952.
Daringer, Helen F., *Adopted Jane*. New York: Harcourt, Brace & World, 1947.
——, *Stepsister Sally*. New York: Harcourt, Brace & World, 1952.
Estes, Eleanor, *The Middle Moffat*. New York: Harcourt, Brace & World, 1942.
Friskey, Margaret, *Caveman to Spaceman*. Chicago: Children's Press, 1961.
Hark, Mildred, and Noel McQueen, *A Home for Penny*. New York: Franklin Watts, 1959.
Haywood, Carolyn, *Here's a Penny*. New York: Harcourt, Brace & World, 1944.
Hofstein, Sadie, *The Human Story: Facts on Birth, Growth and Reproduction*. Glenview, Ill.: Scott, Foresman, 1967.
Juline, Ruth, *A Place for Johnny Bill*. Philadelphia: Westminster, 1961.
Levine, Milton I., and Jean H. Seligman, *The Wonder of Life*. New York: Golden, 1952.
Mead, Margaret, and Ken Heyman, *Family*. New York: Macmillan, 1965.
Randal, Judith, *All About Heredity*. New York: Random House, 1963.

Films

Barbara (*To Conform or Not To Conform*), Interlude Films, color, 6 min. Barbara, a little girl, is shocked to discover that everybody is pretty much the same. She decides to distinguish herself by being a leader, only to find out that too many others have the same idea. She decides to be different too. She takes her problem to her tough old uncle, who wisely solves her dilemma by convincing her that she is most distinctive when she is herself.

The Family, Du Art Film Labs, b/w, 20 min. Presents a true-to-life family situation that calls for understanding and a willingness to work and share.

Family Life, Coronet Films, color, 11 min. Illustrates that proper management of schedules, responsibilities, privileges, and finances leads to a happier home.

Family Teamwork and You, Charles Cahill & Associates, color, 13 min. Presents a visual comparison of two families—one that works together and one that is disorganized—and shows how each accomplishes its goals.

Growing Up—Preadolescence, Coronet Films, color, 11 min. Nicky and Peggy illustrate variations in the normal growth process that occur with age and that differ between boys and girls. The role of the endocrine glands in controlling growth is explained.

Learning from Disappointments, Coronet Films, color, 11 min. When children are not chosen for the roles they wanted in the school history pageant, they overcome their disappointment through good sportmanship, by choosing another goal and trying again.

Mexican Children, Encyclopedia Britannica Films, b/w, 11 min. Shows two Mexican children at home, at play, at school, and at work in the fields. Includes scenes of a fiesta with its displays and unusual Aztec dances.

The Miracle of Reproduction (rev. ed.), Sid Davis Productions, color, 15 min. Presents similarities in the growth and development of fish, chickens, cows, and human beings. Shows scenes of the growth of the baby within the mother's body.

A Plain White Envelope, Film Associates of California, color, 20 min. Tells the story of a boy who, wanting very badly to win a spelling contest, accidentally finds a white envelope with the contest words inside and faces the problem of cheating.

Spanish Children (rev. ed.), Encyclopedia Britannica Films, color, 16 min. Provides a visit with a rural family of southern Spain showing representative aspects of Spanish life. Follows a boy and his father through characteristic landscape to a city marketplace.

Fifth Grade

Instructional Objectives

The pupil:

1. Develops an understanding of the age of puberty.
2. Continues to develop an appreciation for the uniqueness and also the similarities of individuals.
3. Continues to develop constructive ways of expressing his own sexuality.
4. Is able to assume more responsibility for his own care and the well-being of others.
5. Is developing a realistic image of his talents and limitations.
6. Continues to develop respect for and acceptance of all family members.
7. Continues to develop skill in interpersonal relationships.

Content	Suggested Learning Opportunities
What Happens When You Grow?	• Have the pupils bring in pictures for the bulletin board illustrating the variety of sizes of fifth graders.

A. Puberty

1. Physical changes that take place during puberty

- Have the pupils discuss the meaning of *puberty,* from the Latin verb *pubescere* meaning "to become hairy."
- Show and discuss the film *The Story of Menstruation* and the sound filmstrips *Especially for Boys* and *Especially for Girls.* Do not separate the boys and the girls; the class as a whole should see both films.
- Clarify any misconceptions that occur about seminal emissions, masturbation, and menstruation.
- Read and discuss the pamphlets *Your Years of Self-Discovery. A Boy Today, A Man Tomorrow.*

2. Secondary sex characteristics

- Discuss the secondary sex characteristics illustrated in the films and the increased need for attention to physical fitness and cleanliness.

B. Role of the endocrine glands in the growth cycle

1. Endocrine glands
2. The dependency of normal growth and development on properly timed action of the hormones

- Have some of the pupils prepare and give an oral report on the pituitary gland.
- Discuss the role of the endocrine glands as portrayed in the films.
- Read and discuss the book *Growth.*
- Discuss how the change in glandular functioning affects changes in personality and interests.

C. Emotional development

1. Ways of showing emotions
2. How emotions may affect our physical growth

- Have the pupils discuss ways of showing emotions, and evaluate for constructiveness.
- Discuss the different ways boys and girls express emotions.
- Arrange a bulletin board of pictures of people expressing different moods. Label and discuss.
- Explain how moods can change and why.
- Discuss how if we are unhappy we may not eat our dinner or we may overeat.
- Have the class discuss and/or act out situations showing slow development of emotional control, for example, hurt feelings, shyness, and showing off.

What Are Interpersonal Relationships?	• Discuss with the class the meaning of interpersonal relationships.
A. Relationships at home 1. How talking things over with parents helps relieve anger, worries, and fears and helps solve problems	• Have selected pupils make reports on books like *The Popular Crowd. Only Child. Bittersweet Year. Freckle-Face Frankel.* Follow up with discussion. • Use a "Question Box" and have the pupils submit anonymous problems that they are having with family relationships. • Divide the class into small discussion groups. Have them apply the problem-solving techniques learned in the fourth grade, and pose resolutions to selected problems from the Question Box. Have a reporter from each group give a brief summary of his group's discussion to the reassembled class.
2. How family relations shape our lives	• Have some of the pupils describe their feelings when they were recipients of parental disapproval, sibling rivalry, or "unjust" punishment. • Have the pupils dramatize ways of handling the situations listed above.
B. Relationships at school 1. General	• Have each student anonymously list three things he likes and three things he dislikes about the classroom and the activities. Compile and discuss with the class. • Have a committee of pupils observe and report on relationships noted on the playground during recesses.
2. Boy–girl relations	• Have the class discuss the statement "In our class, most girls are more interested in boys than boys are interested in girls." • Take an anonymous poll to determine the validity of the statement for the class.
a. Mixing socially	• Have the class plan an outing or field trip. • Survey the community resources for the availability of mixed group activities for fifth graders. • Have the pupils plan for a party to

be held in their home. Act out situations of host, hostess, guest, and chaperone.

b. Competitiveness

- Discuss the stereotype roles in our society in regards to male–female competitiveness; for example, boys are better at athletics; girls may play baseball but boys may not play dolls.
- View and discuss films like *Developing Friendships. Feeling Left Out? How Friendly Are You? Making Friends.*
- Read and discuss books like *Little League Heroes. Worst Room in the School. Robert E.*

c. School manners and relationships

- Dramatize situations showing positive and negative behavior, for example, new student in school, class actions while a pupil recites, teacher giving instructions.
- Read and discuss the pamphlet *Getting Along in School.*

C. What we need to help us grow in our relations with people

- Have each pupil make a list of the basic requirements for effective interpersonal relationships, that is, friendliness, respect, interest, responsibility, enjoyment, acceptance, and others. Compile and discuss.

What Kind of a Person Am I?

A. How well do I know myself?

B. How responsible am I?

C. Do I kid myself?

- Have the class design a self-rating scale on personal qualities, such as happy-go-lucky, considerate, generous, reliable, reads a lot, good sport, does things quickly, makes friends easily, leader, follower, quick-tempered, talkative, adventurous, studious, and serious.
- Administer the scale and discuss with the class the qualities that the pupils want to discuss.
- Ask the pupils (1) to write a sentence describing a conflict (e.g., a mother reminds a pupil of his homework assignment; a pupil's sister will not let her watch her favorite TV program)

and then (2) to propose for evaluation by the class three or four ways that a person faced with that situation might behave.

- Construct a self-rating test by compiling the items written by the students and administer it to the class. Discuss the answers: Was the most constructive and responsible form of behavior chosen?
- Have the pupils describe some of their daydreams and relate them to reality and effective action.

Resources

Books

Bishop, Curtis K., *Little League Heroes.* Philadelphia: Lippincott, 1960.
Dickson, Marguerite, *Only Child.* New York: David McKay, 1952.
Emery, Anne, *The Popular Crowd.* Philadelphia: Westminster, 1961.
James, Norma W., *Bittersweet Year.* Ontario, Canada: Longmans, 1961.
Keir, Leota H., *Freckle-Face Frankel.* New York: Coward-McCann, 1959.
Muehl, Lois B., *Worst Room in the School.* New York: Holiday House, 1961.
Musgrave, Florence, *Robert E.* New York: Hastings House, 1957.
Tanner, James M., and Gordon R. Taylor, *Growth.* Morristown, N.J.: Silver Burdett, 1965.

Pamphlets

Hayes, M. V., *A Boy Today, A Man Tomorrow.* St. Louis, Mo., 4494 Lindell Blvd.: Optimist International, 1961.
Neugarten, Bernice, and Paul J. Miser, *Getting Along in School.* Chicago: Science Research Associates, 1951.
Your Years of Self-Discovery. Neenah, Wis.: Kimberly-Clark, 1968.
The Pleasures of Femininity. Neenah, Wis.: Kimberly-Clark, 1968.

Films

Developing Friendships, Coronet Films, color, 11 min. Shows that it is vitally important that young people understand how real friendships are developed and maintained.

Feeling Left Out? Coronet Films, color, 13 min. Attempts to develop sympathy and understanding for the socially isolated by offering suggestions for overcoming this condition.

How Friendly Are You? Coronet Films, color, 11 min. Shows that the ways young people cultivate friends are often obscured by the artifical bonds of belonging to a clique or school crowd. Discusses some of the values of being friendly and encourages the broadening of one's range of friends.

Making Friends, Encyclopedia Britannica Films, color, 11 min. Considers three types of friendships—casual acquaintances, special friends, and family friends. Uses the problems of three high school boys to point out ways people can make and keep friends.

The Story of Menstruation, Association Films, color, 10 min. Shows in animation what happens during the menstrual cycle, and explains how this process prepares the body for the possible beginnings of the childbirth cycle. Produced by Walt Disney Studios.

Sound Filmstrip

Especially for Boys, Henk Newenhouse, color, 12 min. Animated drawings describing the pubescent growth and development of boys.

Especially for Girls, Henk Newenhouse, color, 12 min. Animated drawings describing the pubescent growth and development of girls.

Sixth Grade

Instructional Objectives

The pupil:

1. Understands what helps him grow up in his relationships with others.
2. Has knowledge of and accepts the physical and emotional changes of puberty.
3. Continues to develop constructive ways of handling emotions.
4. Understands better how his sex identity is affected by the way the roles of men and women change as they grow older and by the way society changes technologically.
5. Realizes that making choices involves acceptance of consequences.
6. Understands that it takes time and effort to become physically, emotionally, and socially mature.
7. Is able to discuss sex in an honest dignified fashion without embarrassment.

Content	Suggested Learning Opportunities
Solving Problems of Growing Up in Relationships with Others	• Have the pupils submit questions on relationships for class or small group discussions.
A. How can I make and keep good friends?	• Have the pupils analyze the difference between a friend and an acquaintance.
1. Attitudes and behavior	• Dramatize and discuss situations such as how to make a new student in the class feel he's welcome; how to agree or disagree with one another and still remain friends.
2. Attitudes and feelings	• Have the class list qualities that boys and girls like in each other; discuss. • Read and discuss books like *Henry and the Paper Route. Cristy at Skippinghills. Judy's Summer Friend.* • Discuss the result of "chopping"[1] another person. How does it affect you? How does it affect him?
B. What can I do to feel comfortable in social situations?	• Act out many social situations, such as introducing girls and boys, friends, and family correctly.
1. Know the right thing to do (manners)	• Read and discuss the book *Manners for Minors.* • Use a "Manners Quiz Box" for anonymous questions to be answered by the class or a small group.
2. Be interested in others and show it	• Discuss the statement "Blowing out someone else's candle never makes yours burn brighter." • Act out situations to illustrate what to do and say when first introduced. • View and discuss films like *Shy Guy* and *The Show-off.*
C. How can I make a good first impression?	• Discuss the importance of one's appearance, including posture and facial expression. • Have the girls make a list of "Hints for Boys" on clothes, cleanliness, and

[1] Vernacular for deliberately making remarks designed to make another person uncomfortable and to enhance the speaker's status with the "crowd."

hair care. Have the boys make a list for the girls.
- Have a committee observe a popular classmate and list the traits and actions that make him popular.

D. How can I have good family relationships?

1. With parents

- Have a small group discussion on the topic "What Can I Do When I Think My Parents' Rules Are Too Strict?"
- Have a panel of parents discuss the same topic.
- Have a panel of students discuss the topic "How We Show Our Parents That We Appreciate Them."

2. With siblings

- Have some of the pupils report on how they settled a difference with an older brother or sister; with a younger one. Have the class discuss the effectiveness and constructiveness of the manner of the settlement.
- Have the pupils make a list of things they do to help younger siblings.
- Have the pupils give ideas on how they can make their families proud of them.
- Read and discuss the book *How To Deal with Parents and Other Problems.*

E. What are some basic rules for good relationships?

- Discuss the idea that certain situations call for special "know-how." Etiquette makes life easier.
- Discuss the idea that good relationships develop from our *doing,* not just *knowing.*
- Review the concept that love and respect for others presupposes love of self.
- Dramatize situations that demonstrate the need to be able to communicate to others and to listen to others' communication to us.
- Have the class list some of the signs that one is growing up in relationships, for example, is friendly, is considerate, is understanding, respects himself and others, is interested and interesting.

Changes Undergone During Puberty

- Review the fifth-grade material on puberty.

A. Physical
   1. Body size and shape
   2. Menstruation
   3. Nocturnal emissions

- Have the class bring in full-length pictures of themselves at an earlier age. Discuss the changes in size and shape.
- View and discuss the film *Human Growth.*
- Use a Question Box for anonymous questions to be answered by the teacher.
- Read and discuss the book *Human Growth.*

B. Emotional

- Have the class list some of the emotional needs of humans.

   1. Moodiness

- Have some pupils tell about some of their recent moods; discuss.
- Discuss how changes in glandular functioning affect emotions.
- Read and discuss the pamphlet *All About You.*

   2. Love

- Review prior material on love, especially pages 54 and 56. Have the class give their ideas on love, and compare with earlier ideas.

   3. Boy–girl relationships
      a. Friendship

- Read and discuss books like *What Boys Want To Know About Girls* and *What Girls Want To Know About Boys.*

      b. Dating

- Have a panel discussion on the question "At what age am I ready to date?"
- Have a panel of parents discuss the topic of dating for sixth graders.
- Use the Question Box for anonymous questions about dating for the class to answer.
- Dramatize dating situations, such as asking for a date and saying good night.
- Review fifth-grade material on boy–girl parties.

Standards of Conduct

- Have the class list what they think are good standards of conduct; discuss.

- Read and discuss *The First Book of Ethics.*
- Have each student write out a code of behavior or standard of conduct and keep it for reference.

A. Conformity

- Define and discuss *conformity.*
- Have each pupil submit anonymously situations illustrating "going along with the crowd"; discuss and evaluate them as constructive or destructive in reference to the code of behavior each student has just written.
- Discuss the question "Is obeying the law conformity?"

B. Alternatives of behavior

- Read and discuss some of the stories in *Profiles in Courage.* Speculate on how different history might have been if the person in the story had compromised his principles.
- Have the class list the areas in which they make the major decisions. Select some for discussion and assess the values and consequences of the various behaviors that might be selected. Use the problem-solving technique.
- Have the class discuss where they might receive help in assessing the values and consequences of a choice, that is, from parents, an older sibling, a teacher, the school nurse, a counselor, or a relative.
- Have a panel discussion on the question "What happens to me if I break my own code of behavior?"

Resources

Books

Beck, Lester F., *Human Growth.* New York: Harcourt, Brace & World, 1949.
Black, Algernon D., *The First Book of Ethics.* New York: Franklin Watts, 1965.
Cleary, Beverly, *Henry and the Paper Route.* New York: Morrow, 1957.
Hunt, Mabel Leigh, *Christy at Skippinghills.* Philadelphia: Lippincott, 1958.
Kennedy, John F., *Profiles in Courage,* Young Readers Edition. New York: Harper & Row, 1961.

Ladd, Elizabeth, *Judy's Summer Friend.* New York: Morrow, 1958.
Loeb, Robert H., Jr., *Manners for Minors.* New York: Association Press, 1964.
Menninger, William C., *All About You.* Chicago: Science Research Associates, 1955.
Miller, Claire G., *What Boys Want To Know About Girls.* New York: Grosset & Dunlap, 1962.
Osborne, Ernest G., *How To Deal with Parents and Other Problems.* New York: Grosset & Dunlap, 1966.
Unger, Arthur, and Carmel Berman, *What Girls Want To Know About Boys.* New York: Grosset & Dunlap, 1966.

Films

Human Growth (2nd ed.), Henk Newenhouse, color, 19 min. Shows a seventh-grade class as they view and discuss an animated film that traces human growth from conception to adulthood. Differences in male and female structural development are emphasized.
The Showoff, McGraw-Hill, b/w, 12 min. The story of a smart-aleck high school boy. Designed to provoke thoughtful discussion of the effects upon the individual and those surrounding him.
Shy Guy, Coronet Films, color, 13 min. Friendliness to shy guy demonstrated by better adjusted fellow students helps the shy adolescent to improve social relations.

Pamphlet

Menninger, William C., *All About You.* Chicago: Science Research Associates, 1955.

part **III**

suggested content for junior high school

chapter **7**

suggested content for the seventh grade

Introduction: Junior High School

Junior high school students show a great range of maturity. Some are still in the pre-adolescent stage, while others are fairly mature adolescents. Despite these individual variations, however, the students have many common needs. They are growing up, and they all need love, understanding, and guidance. They need to develop into healthy individuals who will not only satisfy themselves in life but contribute to society as well.

With their increasing maturity students can take more responsibility in achieving better self-understanding, in designing their destiny, and in realizing their purposes.

This is a period of rapid growth. Girls are usually taller and proportionately heavier than boys. Voice changes occur, most noticeably among boys. Poor posture and awkwardness become increasingly evident, and pimples and excessive perspiration are two common physical phenomena that distress students at this time. Some girls are already physically quite mature; the development of breasts and hips becomes noticeable, and menstruation begins. Some boys will have begun to have nocturnal emissions. Many students are bewildered and frightened by these mysterious changes. Even students who have been well prepared may pass through a period of considerable emotional disturbance and exaggerated concern over their health.

Adolescence is a period when the student faces uncertainty, difficulty, and serious conflicts. The period is characterized by flux and change, commonly called "adolescent turmoil," and is the crucial transitional phase of character development. "The conflict is between the instinctual drives, which in adolescence are biologically strengthened, and the external demands that are made upon the child as he enters adolescence."[1] Ideally, the student emerges from adolescence with a stable, socially acceptable character.

Much has been said and written about the communication problems that exist between adolescents and adults, particularly parents. According to Dr. Rhoda L. Lorand, a practicing psychotherapist, "It is natural and healthy development of teenagers to be reluctant to discuss sexual matters with their parents; in a sense, talking about sex is sharing a sexual experience. At this time of life teenagers become much more self-conscious about even verbal intimacy with the parents."[2]

The school must approach the instructional areas of family life and sex education in a positive and objective manner. The students need help to determine their solutions to problems in the light of their own goals and philosophy, within the context of the community's goals and values. They need opportunities to develop effective interpersonal relations and attitudes to serve as a specific basis for making meaningful moral judgments. Above all, the students must be taught to think in advance of the consequences of their decisions. They need to learn that a correct or moral decision creates increased trust among people, greater integrity in relationships, the dissolution of barriers separating people, cooperative attitudes, enhanced self-respect, and an appreciation of the worth of personality. They also should learn that an incorrect or immoral decision creates increased distrust, deceit and duplicity in relationships, barriers between persons and groups, resistant, uncooperative attitudes, and diminished self-respect.

To develop constructive attitudes the students must be given the opportunity to participate in the dialogue in the classroom. The students must be given an opportunity to question adult beliefs about what is moral, to examine the reality of adult behavior, and to discuss their own beliefs with their peers. The teacher serves as a catalyst, creating a classroom where honest communication can take place between students, supplying materials from many sources, and making the students aware of the various beliefs that are relevant to our society. Each student must also be given the time to synthesize what he learns from the dialogue and written materials, to consult with his family, and to develop his own moral standards. The

[1] Sandor Lorand and Henry Schneer, eds., *Adolescents: Psychoanalytic Approach to Problems and Therapy* (New York, Dell, 1965), p. 2.

[2] Rhoda Lorand, *Love, Sex, and the Teenager* (New York, Macmillan, 1965), p. 79.

teacher who truly believes in the worth of students as embryonic adults, and who can create a classroom climate in which honest communication between students exists, can teach an effective family life and sex education class.

The following curriculum outlines are adapted from units in the Anaheim Union High School District *Family Life and Sex Education Course Outline*, which was developed under the leadership of Superintendent Paul W. Cook. The units are designed to be taught in mixed classes of both sexes for a five-week period during the physical education or health education classes. The teacher should be a regular member of the faculty assigned to the Family Life and Sex Education Department. The class size should be approximately twenty-five students or less with a balance between boys and girls. It is also important that the classes be grouped heterogeneously, not homogeneously, with respect to the I.Q. scores or other mental indices of the students. In classes grouped homogeneously, and particularly in classes made up entirely of slow achievers, the family life and sex education program fails in its purpose.

The general aim of the family life and sex education program during the junior high school years is succinctly stated in the Anaheim *Guide:* "The program is designed to supplement and support the home that is doing a good job and to make up for the shortcomings of the homes where parents have not accepted their responsibility."[3]

Overview: The Seventh-Grade Unit

Junior high school students must be oriented to their new school and to the manner in which the family life and sex education course will be presented for the next six years. The students will probably also need instruction in their roles in small group discussions and role playing.[4]

After this orientation the students begin to study personality development. They discuss ways to improve their personalities if they so desire. They also study the kinds of values of friendships and the qualities that one seeks in friends.

From the study of friendships the students pass to a study of physical growth and adolescent development. The basic list of terms (Document 7-2) found in the Background and Teaching Materials section at the end of this

[3] Anaheim Union High School District, *Family Life and Sex Education Course Outline: Grades Seven Through Twelve* (Anaheim, Calif., 1965), p. x.

[4] The small group discussion and role playing techniques are discussed in Chapter 13.

chapter includes the words and definitions that students will need to understand in order to discuss the maturation of the reproductive system.[5] Copies of the list should be made and distributed to the class. To evaluate how well the students have learned the terminology and to expedite the learning process, a "word game" can be played. A few meetings after the list has been distributed, divide the class into two teams and use the words and definitions from the Basic Terminology List as the basis for a competitive quiz, in the style of television's College Bowl. The game atmosphere tends to reduce the initial embarrassment in the use of the terms, because the incentive to win overrules the emotional reaction to some of the words.

Teacher-constructed tests will serve the students' best interests. It is best to have a minimum of right and wrong questions; it is more effective to describe a problem in a paragraph and ask the students to write a brief solution. The answers should not be graded as correct or incorrect but rather as satisfactory or questionable solutions to the hypothetical problem. Class discussion of the test answers can serve as an additional learning opportunity.

It is generally not considered appropriate for the family life and sex education class to label the parts of the male and female anatomy on a diagram. This activity tends to create embarrassment and negate the major task of the unit, which is to develop constructive attitudes toward the role of sex in the life of the individual.

The final area of study in this unit focuses on the role and functions of the family in society today.

The recommended basic texts are Landis and Landis' *Building Your Life* and Beck's *Human Growth*.

Curriculum Outlines

Instructional Objectives

The student understands that:

1. He and other persons are individuals with varying capacities and abilities for living and working together, and he accepts himself in these terms.

[5] Since the terms "sexual intercourse" and "masturbation" cannot be satisfactorily defined in a few words, they are omitted from the list. The terms are discussed in Documents 7-3 and 7-4 and should be taken up with the class at the point indicated by the Curriculum Outline, or when brought up by the class.

2. An important part of a healthy personality is a realistic understanding of oneself.
3. The family is the basic unit of our American society.
4. Normal individuals differ in patterns of physical growth and development.
5. A healthy moral adjustment to the adolescent sex drive is essential to individual development.
6. There is correct and scientific terminology to describe human anatomy and the physical functioning of the human body.
7. The role of the family changes as society changes.
8. Some functions of the family remain relatively static throughout history.

Content

Introduction

A. Orientation to junior high school

B. Orientation to the junior high family life and sex education class and to some of its basic procedures, such as the small group discussion and role playing

Suggested Learning Opportunities

- Ask students to recall and volunteer statements regarding their feelings on the first day of junior high school.
- Distribute the class text *Building Your Life,* and assign Chapter 1.
- Show and discuss the film *Junior High—A Time of Change.*
- Ask students to consult their parents about their own birth weight and length. The class can analyze whether the longest babies are still the tallest in the class.
- Ask students to interview their parents for information pertaining to their physical and personal–social development during early childhood.
- Ask students to bring in one of their baby pictures. Post them on bulletin board and let the class try to identify the babies. Discuss how students change as they grow.

Resources

(S) Landis, Judson, and Mary Landis. *Building Your Life*. Englewood Cliffs, N.J.: Prentice-Hall, 1964, ch. 1.

(S) Film: *Junior High—A Time of Change,* McGraw-Hill, color, 10 min. Defines some of the problems that will arise as boys and girls enter junior high school, and encourages students to look at themselves and their place in junior high.

Content

Suggested Learning Opportunities

Learning To Know Yourself

A. Why is it important to know yourself?
1. Interests
2. Aptitudes
3. Personal preferences
4. Character traits
5. Physical and emotional health
6. Behavior patterns

- Have each class member list what he thinks he should know about himself. List and group the items and discuss their relative importance.
- Have the class write a description of an ideal friend. Discuss the items listed.
- Have the class discuss each item listed in the content area and its importance.
  Note: Discretion should be used before considering any group evaluation that might embarrass the individual student.

B. What is personality?
1. Your physical build
2. The way you walk, dress, and talk
3. The way you think
4. Your feelings
   a. Fears
   b. Hopes
   c. Interests
5. The way you get along with others
6. The way other people affect you

- Have a student report on the definition of personality in the dictionary.
- Have students evaluate the personality of a famous person.
- Demonstrate how persons tend to react in a positive manner to attitudes of friendliness and courtesy and in a negative manner to expressions of hostility.
- Discuss how attitudes of acceptance are expressed (facial expression, quality of voice, approach, friendliness). Instruct students to test this hypothesis by recording the initial reactions of students whom they meet during the day.
- Have students read and discuss *All About You,* pp. 11–20.

C. What factors influence your personality? Every human being started life with the same basic human qualities, but each evolves a unique personality. Some factors are:
1. Environment
2. Family

- Divide the class into small groups. Ask each group to list as many ideas as they can in ten minutes with reference to the topic, "What I Think Contributes to a Mature Personality." Have student recorders report their group's ideas to the class; discuss.

3. Heredity
4. School
5. Friends
6. Maturity

- Assign Chapters 2 and 3 in *Building Your Life.*
- Ask class members to list five characteristics they admire in a person. Appoint a committee to prepare a self-rating scale, utilizing the characteristics mentioned most often. Have the students use the scale as a self-administered checklist. Document 7-1 at the end of the chapter, a "Personality Rating Scale," suggests one way that such a list may be organized.

D. What are some practical ways to improve your personality?

1. Understanding your needs

- Have the class suggest and describe common personality problems. Use small group discussions to search for possible resolutions to these problems.
- Choose a typical excuse for not handing in required homework and use it as a basis for role-playing. Analyze and discuss the excuse, and then turn to a more general discussion of the ways in which we try to escape the consequences of our behavior.

2. Trying to understand other persons
3. Having emotional control

- Role-play situations to interpret how it feels to be considered different and use as a basis for a discussion of how we should treat others who differ from us in race, beliefs, and customs.
- Discuss the meaning of maturity of judgment. Appoint students to devise role-playing situations that exemplify both immature and mature judgment.
- Have students write and perform a skit illustrating typical adolescent behavior.

Resources

(S) Landis, Judson, and Mary Landis, *Building Your Life.* Englewood Cliffs, N.J.: Prentice-Hall, 1964, chs. 2 and 3.

(S) Menninger, William C., *All About You.* Chicago: Science Research Associates, 1955.

(S) Document 7-1, "Personality Rating Scale."

(T) Lorand, Rhoda, *Love, Sex, and the Teenager.* New York: Macmillan, 1965, ch. 8.

Content

Friendships

A. Values
1. Share your experiences, thoughts, troubles, and good times.
2. Friendship helps develop social skills.
3. A variety of friendships helps develop your personality.

B. Qualities that can help improve your friendship rating
1. Be interesting.
   a. Be dependable and loyal
   b. Have a sense of humor but do not use it at the expense of others
   c. Accept criticism graciously
   d. Be modest, not boastful
   e. Maintain good sportmanship and control of temper
2. Be interested.
   a. Be a good listener
   b. Emphasize the favorable qualities of other people, not their faults
   c. Cooperate rather than compete
   d. Be poised and self-confident

Suggested Learning Opportunities

- Have students develop rating charts of traits that make good friends.
- Have students use the rating chart developed for self-evaluation.
- Show the filmstrip *How To Make and Keep Friends.* Discuss.
- Role-play the introduction of a new person to friends, how to meet a new group of girls and boys.
- Discuss the difference between "belonging to" and "being on the outside of" the group.
- Discuss or debate the following topics: (1) Some people are born with the ability to make friends. (2) Beauty and brains count most in winning friends. (3) Having plenty of spending money is a sure way to win friends. (4) One of the best ways to win popularity is to follow the ads, use the "glamor" products recommended, and wear the latest fashions pictured.
- Discuss ways that your family helps you to become a friendly person.
- Show and discuss the filmstrip *Learning About Popularity.*
- Assign Chapter 7 in *Building Your Life.*
- Have students write a paragraph describing an ideal friend. Compile and discuss the common traits mentioned.
- Assign *Making and Keeping Friends.* Have selected students report on their reading.

Resources

(S) Filmstrip: *How To Make and Keep Friends. Learning About Popularity,* Society of Visual Education, color, 33⅓ r.p.m. record, 9 min. and 9½ min., respectively. Answer many teenage questions. Show teens how to get along with people of different temperaments and how to understand a teen's role in society.

Several alternatives are presented for each topic to stimulate discussions and independent thinking.
(S) Landis, Judson, and Mary Landis, *Building Your Life*. Englewood Cliffs, N.J.: Prentice-Hall, 1964, ch. 7.
(S) Menninger, William C., *Making and Keeping Friends*. Chicago: Science Research Associates, 1952.

Content

Physical Changes; Maturation of the Reproductive System

A. What do we really mean when we talk about "growing up"?
1. Stages of development
   a. Infancy
   b. Childhood
   c. Adolescence
   d. Adulthood
2. Changes related to interests
3. Changes related to responsibilities
4. Determination of individual characteristics
   a. Color of hair and eyes
   b. General body build
   c. Facial features
   d. Sex
   e. Capacity to develop intellectually
   f. Family setting, which affects realization of inherited potential

Suggested Learning Opportunities

- Have the class discuss the term "growing up" and compose a definition.
- Discuss the words pre-adolescence, maturity, and adult.
- Distribute Document 7-2, "Basic Terminology List."
- Play a word game to help learn the new terminology.
- The discussion should bring out what this particular class would like to know about the growing-up process and should provide a springboard for individual and class exploration of the various problems confronting them.
- Read and discuss Chapter 5 in *Building Your Life*. Discuss the pamphlet *Finding Out About Ourselves*.
- Read and discuss Chapter 4 in *Building Your Life*.
- Have students ask their parents to comment on family resemblances. Compare the heredity factor in class.
- Read and discuss Chapter 6 in *Growth*.
- Introduce the Question Box, and request each student to place a written question or blank paper into the box. The teacher should consult with the school nurse for appropriate answers and should answer the questions the next day.

B. What are the important physical changes that occur during adolescence?

- Show the films *Boy to Man* and *Girl to Woman*.

1. Changes in body size and shape; secondary sex characteristics
2. Development of the endocrine glands
3. Maturation of the reproductive system.

- Distribute the textbook *Human Growth.*
- Assign Chapters 1 and 2 in *Human Growth.* Discuss.
- Use anatomy charts from the science department for review and to answer some student questions.
- Ask the school nurse to assist in answering the technical questions.

C. What are some special problems that may concern us as we are growing into maturity?

1. Seminal emissions
2. Menstruation
3. Masturbation
4. Size of genitalia

- Ask each student to again place a question or blank paper in the Question Box. Plan to devote one class session to answering the questions from the Question Box and those the students ask orally. Ask the school nurse to attend and answer some of the questions that relate to abnormalities.
- When appropriate, discuss the ideas contained in Document 7-3, "Sexual Intercourse."
- Discuss ideas contained in Document 7-4, "Masturbation."
- Complete this segment of the unit with the showing of the film *The Miracle of Reproduction.*

Standards of Conduct

A. Right vs. wrong
B. Making a moral judgment

- Define the word *moral* and discuss in class.
- Discuss the ideas contained in Document 7-5, "Basis for Moral Judgments." Care must be exercised to have the students think through what their moral standards are; they should not parrot the teacher.
- Ask the students to interview their parents regarding the meaning of right vs. wrong.
- View and discuss the film *Right or Wrong—Making Moral Decisions.*
- Give a hypothetical situation and have the students write their solutions to the problems and justify their choice. Follow up with class discussion.

Resources

(S) Document 7-2, "Basic Terminology List."
(S) Landis, Judson, and Mary Landis, *Building Your Life.* Englewood Cliffs, N.J.: Prentice-Hall, 1964, chs. 4 and 5.
(S) Kirkendall, Lester A., *Finding Out About Ourselves.* Chicago: Science Research Associates, 1956.
(S) Tanner, James M., and Gordon R. Taylor, *Growth.* Morristown, N.J.: Silver Burdett, 1965.
(S) Film: *Boy to Man,* Churchill Films, color, 17 min. Film for boys, dealing candidly with secondary and primary sexual changes of adolescence in the male.
(S) Film: *Girl to Woman,* Churchill Films, color, 16 min. Describes the male and female reproductive system. Traces the human growth pattern in the change from girlhood to womanhood. Uses extensive animation.
(S) Beck, Lester F., *Human Growth.* New York: Harcourt, Brace & World, 1948, chs. 1 and 2.
(S) Document 7-4, "Masturbation."
(S) Film: *The Miracle of Reproduction* (rev. ed.), Sid Davis Productions, color, 15 min. Presents similarities in the growth and development of fish, chickens, cows, and human beings. Shows sciences of the growth of the baby within the mother's body.
(S) Document 7-5, "Basis for Moral Judgments."
(S) Film: *Right or Wrong–Making Moral Decisions,* Coronet Films, color, 11 min. Tells the story of a boy who is caught breaking into a warehouse. Considers the moral decisions of the watchman, the boy's mother, the property owner, the police sergeant, a social worker, and the boy himself.
(T) Document 7-3, "Sexual Intercourse."
(T) Montagu, Ashley, *Helping Children Develop Moral Values.* Chicago: Science Research Associates, 1953.
(T) Kirkendall, Lester A., *Understanding Sex.* Chicago: Science Research Associates, 1947, particularly p. 17.

Content

Functions of the Family

A. The functions of the family change as society changes. Traditional family functions
1. Father was the head of the household, taskmaker, teacher, minister, decision maker.
2. Mother was subservient to her husband, did the household chores, and worked the land.
3. Children worked with parents,

Suggested Learning Opportunities

- Have the class list the functions of the family during colonial times. Refer to history texts if necessary.
- Discuss the ideas in Document 7-6, "Functions of the Family."
- Have students discuss which responsibilities belong to the family and which may be delegated to other agencies, that is, church, school, health department, and law enforcement agencies.

were "seen not heard," and provided the additional hands for work.

B. Families today
   1. Families sell their labor for money and have moved from rural to urban areas.
   2. Father is still the head of the household by law and the major breadwinner.
   3. The major functions of the family are reproduction, child rearing, emotional support, and decision making.

- Use role-playing to dramatize the roles of the various family members in the traditional family compared to the family of today.
- Read and discuss Chapter 20 in *Building Your Life*.
- Have small discussion groups list and report to the class the changes they have noted in family organization.
- Discuss the ways the student can contribute to his family stability when his mother is employed.
- Have the students compile a list of household tasks appropriate for them to assume full responsibility for.
- Have students make up a daily schedule of their activities and evaluate its effectiveness in terms of time allowed for schoolwork, recreation, and family responsibilities.

Family Relationships

A. Family "conflicts"
   1. Personal conflict—a struggle within oneself, for example, family beliefs or standards vs. group standards
   2. Personality conflicts
   3. Dualism—action vs. standards
   4. Antagonism
   5. Social pressure

- Have students list areas of family conflict. Divide the class into small discussion groups. Choose the conflicts most frequently listed and assign each group a conflict situation to discuss and propose resolutions for. Report to the class for further discussion.
- Discuss a current movie, play, or literature assignment to illustrate consequences of revenge, retaliation, or dictatorial actions.
- Have each student list the things about which he usually worries. Compile a master list and discuss in class. Have the class suggest ways to eliminate and avoid worries.
- View and discuss the film *The Story of Debbie*.

B. Parent–child conflicts
   1. Disagreement about child's friends
   2. Child's physical habits, for example, dress, eating, grooming, cleanliness

- Show the filmstrip *Learning To Understand Your Parents*.
- Discuss factors that contribute to healthy family relationships. What type of respect should exist between parents in order to strengthen the

3. Responsibilities to home, church, and school
4. Allowance and use of money
5. The independence of the child

family unit? between parents and children? between grandparents and children? between brothers and sisters?

- Have students discuss the extent to which they should be involved in family decision making. Request that they list the decisions in which they believe they should have a part, those which they should be allowed to make by themselves, and those which are none of their concern.
- Role-play some of the problems suggested by the students.

C. Brother and sister relationships
   1. "We did not choose each other."
   2. External duty conceals hostilities.
   3. There is competition within the family.
   4. Achieving good fellowship between family members will prepare the student for living in the world, since skillful management of relationships is part of the task of successful living.
   5. The home can be an effective proving ground for democracy.
      a. Parents should have patience and understanding.
      b. Children grow to enjoy each other because of differences in personalities, interests, and abilities.

- Show the filmstrip *Living with Brothers and Sisters.*
- Ask students to tell about a situation where as an older brother or sister they had the advantage or disadvantage in their family. Do the same for a younger brother or sister.
- View and discuss the film *Jamie—The Story of a Sibling.*
- Assign the reading of *Life with Brothers and Sisters.*
- Have class write and/or discuss: "The problems that would be caused if I were the only child."
- Have the class write and/or discuss: "The problems that would be eliminated if I were the only child."
- Arrange for the school nurse or school psychologist to discuss with the class conflicts and their effects on the individual.
- Role-play a family council discussing one of the problems listed by the class.

Resources

(T) Document 7-6, "Functions of the Family."
(S) Landis, Judson, and Mary Landis, *Building Your Life*. Englewood Cliffs, N.J.: Prentice-Hall, 1964, ch. 20.
(S) Film: *The Story of Debbie,* Education Films, b/w, 25 min. Debbie, who has lived with relatives and in foster homes and institutions for 11 years, is shown

at the Children's Baptist Home in Los Angeles as she attempts to adjust to life while awaiting a reunion with her family and a return to a more normal life.

(S) Filmstrip: *Learning To Understand Your Parents. Living with Brothers and Sisters,* Society of Visual Education, color, 33⅓ r.p.m. record, 7½ min. and 8½ min., respectively. Show the importance of good family relationships. Several answers are presented to help the teenager arrive at his own best solution.

(S) Film: *Jamie—The Story of a Sibling,* McGraw-Hill, b/w, 25 min. Considers how sibling rivalry can affect personality patterns and family relations.

(S) Ullman, Francis, *Life with Brothers and Sisters.* Chicago: Science Research Associates, 1952.

(T) Rodman, Hyman, *Marriage, Family, and Society: A Reader.* New York: Random House, 1965.

Background and Teaching Materials

Document 7-1 Personality Rating Scale

_ _
Student's Name Date

Personality Traits	Ratings*								
	A Friend			A Parent			Self		
	1	2	3	1	2	3	1	2	3
Shows interest in others									
Stays calm									
Controls temper									
Holds no grudges									
Acts friendly									
Acts promptly									
Lives with reality									
Faces facts realistically									
Accepts responsibility									

* 1 Occasionally
2 Usually
3 Always

Document 7-1, *Personality Rating Scale,* is from *Teachers Guide in Health Education for Secondary Schools,* Sacramento, California, Bureau of Health Education, Physical Education and Recreation, California State Department of Education, 1952, p. 29. It may be reproduced by teachers for use in connection with their own family life and sex education classes.

Document 7-2 ***Basic Terminology List***

abdomen the part of your body below the chest; that part of the body containing the stomach, intestines, liver, and internal sex organs of the male and female.

acceptable O.K.; agreeable; worthy of being approved.

adolescence the time when boys and girls grow into men and women, as indicated by the appearance of body hair, change in voice and, in girls, menstruation.

adolescent one who is in the process of changing from a child to an adult.

adult a grownup; a man or woman who has reached maturity.

anxiety worry; mental distress or uneasiness caused by apprehension of danger or misfortune.

biological about the science of life; about how things grow, especially with reference to their origin, growth, reproduction, and structure.

birth being born; coming out of the mother's body into the outside world.

bowels an internal part of the body below the stomach; the intestines; the lower part of the intestines, where fecal material is stored until you go to the bathroom.

breast the upper front part of the body, below the neck and above the waist; in women, where milk is made for the baby.

characteristic something about a person that makes him different from other people; a distinguishing feature or quality.

childhood the time when one is a child, that is, a boy or girl.

chromosome the part of a cell that carries the things you get (inherit) from your family; a tiny structure, found in cells, that carries the family resemblances. Each body cell, except the sex cells, contains forty-six chromosomes. The sperm and the ovum contain only twenty-three chromosomes each.

conflict (*noun*) disagreement, controversy, quarrel, fight; a battle or struggle; (*verb*) to come into collision or be in opposition with.

constipation difficulty in expelling fecal material from the body.

development growing, evolving; the act of becoming more advanced.

economy taking care not to waste your money; the wise management of one's resources, especially money.

egg cell the female sex cell or ovum; the cell that, combined with a male cell (sperm), grows eventually into a human being.

---

ejaculation the discharge of semen by the male reproductive system, through the penis.

emotion any of the feelings of joy, sorrow, fear, hate, love, etc.

endocrines the name applied to the glands that make hormones that reach the blood supply. Examples are the pituitary, the testes, and the ovaries; also, the hormones produced by these glands.

environment everything that is around you, including buildings, a hill, cold weather, and other objects, conditions, and influences.

erection the condition of the male penis when it becomes hard and straight.

fallopian tube the slender tubes inside a female that go from the ovaries to the uterus. These tubes carry the egg cell to the uterus.

fecal material the brown-colored material that comes out of the rectum when you go to the bathroom; body waste material expelled from the bowels.

female a girl or woman.

feminine like or typical of a female; womanly, ladylike.

fertile the condition of a man or woman who is able to have children. An egg cell that is capable of developing into a living thing—that is, an egg cell that has been joined by a sperm cell—is also said to be fertile.

fertilization when the sperm enters the egg cell (ovum) and starts the growth of a human being.

genes the tiny chemical units that make up a chromosome and that cause members of a family to resemble one another; the carriers of inherited traits.

genitals the reproductive or sex organs on the outside of the body.

gland an organ of the body that makes a juice or chemical substance. The glands help in the regulation of growth and body activities. The sweat glands, for example, help to regulate body temperature, whereas the pituitary gland affects the rate of growth.

heredity the passing of physical traits and characteristics from parents to children. Some of these inherited physical qualities have a lot to do with the way a person looks, so children often tend to look like their parents, and brothers and sisters tend to look like each other. Other traits (the kind of brain one has, for example) make it likely that children will share some mental characteristics with their parents. This adds to the chances that a child will resemble his parents, and his brothers and sisters, in how smart he is and how he thinks, as well as in how he looks.

hormone a chemical that is made by a gland and that travels in the blood to other glands or parts of the body to help you grow.

infancy the time when you are a baby; early childhood.

male a boy or man.

masculine like or typical of a male; manly.
maturity adulthood, complete development or full growth—physically, socially, emotionally, mentally.
menstruation the normal flow of blood from the uterus through the vagina, occurring about once a month for most women.
morality doing what is good for us and others; obeying good rules about how to act; acting in ways that do not harm others or oneself or good relationships between people.
motive the reason people do things or act in a certain way.
ovaries the two female organs inside a woman's body that produce egg cells or ova and also certain hormones.
ovulation the time the ripe egg cell (ovum) leaves an ovary.
ovum the female sex cell; the egg cell. If joined by a sperm cell, the egg develops into a baby.
penis a man's sex organ that is on the outside of the body. The sperm cells move out of the body through the penis. It is also used to pass urine out of the body.
pituitary a small gland, located in the brain, that makes the growth hormone and helps regulate body activities.
puberty the time when a person becomes reproductively mature; when a person is physically able to become a father or a mother.
pubic region the lowest part of the abdomen where the outside sex organs are found.
physiological about how the body works.
psychological about the mind, or how people think; mental.
rationalize to have an excuse or to invent a reason for acting some way; to justify behavior.
realistic concerned with what is real and practical; things as they really are.
rejection the act of refusing to accept, of rebuffing, or of throwing away.
religion what a person believes about God; a particular system in which the search for the values of the ideal life is conducted.
scrotum the pouch of skin that is below the man's penis and contains the testes.
semen the white-colored liquid that carries the sperm cells from the man's body through the penis during ejaculation.
seminal emission wet dream, nocturnal emission, the normal discharge of semen from the penis when a man or boy is asleep, often accompanied by a dream about girls.
sex the character of being either male or female.
sex cell the sperm in the male, or the ovum in the female. These cells combine to start a new life.

social of or about the life and relations of human beings in a community.
sperm the male sex cell, which, by joining with an ovum, starts a new life.
spermatozoa another name for sperm.
spiritual of or about the spirit or soul, as distinguished from physical nature.
testes the male organs that produce sperm cells and certain hormones. They are two small oval-shaped glands inside the man's scrotum.
tolerant fair and patient toward people who are different or who have different ideas.
uterus the organ inside the lower part of the woman's body where a baby lives and grows until it is ready to be born; the womb.
vagina the passage from the uterus to the outside of a woman's body through which babies are born; the birth canal; the place where sperm cells are deposited by the man.
womb another name for uterus.

Document 7-3 ***Sexual Intercourse***

Students need a more comprehensive definition of sexual intercourse, mating, or coitus than the old definition in terms of a sexual connection, the placing the male penis in the female vagina. To create or change attitudes towards the role of human sexual intercourse in life, the teacher must give students a realistic answer to this question: What *is* sexual intercourse? One of the keys to establishing honest communication between students and teachers is the ability to give a mutually satisfactory answer to this important question. The following answer has been evolved as a guide and serves to answer the original question without inviting more questions relating to technique.

Sexual intercourse can be the most intimate experience a husband and wife can share. Combined with love and consideration it is a basic part of a happy marriage.

It is a topic of great interest to everyone, but it is a very personal one. It is something everyone should understand, for what could be more important than to know about the way babies start?

Some couples may have sexual intercourse several times a week, others once or twice a month. Intercourse may take anywhere from a few minutes to a half hour or more. The couple come together and usually kiss, embrace, caress, or pet each other. They tell of their love for each other. After a time the woman's mind and body become prepared for the act of intercourse. The vagina becomes soft and moist. Meanwhile, the man's penis has become erect or hard so that it may enter the vagina easily. At the time of intercourse the urinary passage is closed. The friction caused by the movements of the partners helps create a pleasurable sexual climax, or orgasm, in both of them. During the climax the semen containing the sperm of the male is ejected or released into the upper part of the woman's vagina. This is known as ejaculation. When sperm cells are released into the vagina they try to move into the uterus and fallopian tubes. If a live ovum or egg cell is found by the sperm, the two unite, and a new life is begun. After the climax of intercourse, the couple feel close, loving, and relaxed. When two married people, deeply in love, have intercourse, they communicate their love in this intimate and joyous way.

Document 7-4 **Masturbation**

Most students have had some experience with masturbation before puberty, although many of them are unfamiliar with the word "masturbation." They have heard it called "touching yourself," "playing with yourself," "self-abuse," or, more commonly among the boys, the slang term "jacking off."

Authorities tell us that it is an almost universal practice among healthy boys and is also a common, though not so frequent, behavior in girls. People learn it by themselves or else from their youthful friends. Masturbation may begin at any age. It has been observed in children under three years of age. It may be started again in the adolescent years and re-occur in adult life during times of stress or sexual deprivation.

The dire consequences that are commonly believed to follow from masturbation are almost entirely fictitious. Masturbation will not impair the mind. It will not interfere with the successful performance of the sexual function in marriage. Many fears, superstitions, and unfounded attitudes have been handed down from generation to generation that implied that masturbation would have very dangerous consequences for the boy in his teens and for the man he is going to be. Actually, any harm resulting from masturbation, according to the best medical authorities, is likely to be caused by worry or a sense of guilt due to misinformation. While doctors do not encourage the practice, they urge young people and their parents to accept it as a natural part of growing up, like nocturnal emissions.

Some families and churches believe that masturbation is morally wrong. Each student must consider these beliefs when deciding what behavior is best for him or her. Most religious and medical counselors now take the position that masturbation is a normal way-station in the maturation process.

Document 7-5 ***Basis for Moral Judgments***

What is moral and what is immoral?

"Those actions, decisions, and attitudes are

Right-Moral
which produce

1. increased trust among people
2. greater integrity in relationships
3. dissolution of barriers separating people
4. co-operative attitudes
5. enhanced self-respect
6. an appreciation of the worth of personality

Wrong-Immoral
which produce

1. increased distrust
2. deceit and duplicity in relationships
3. creates barriers between persons and groups
4. resistant, unco-operative attitudes
5. diminished self-respect
6. exploitive behavior toward others"[1]

"The right and moral consequences are those which eliminate confusion and allow you to move toward love and understanding of others. Sometimes you will be called upon to make decisions of the moment that will have long-range ramifications. Sometimes these decisions will require you to stand up for your broader principles, to be co-operative with more people, even at the expense of losing the friendship of one or a few persons. Loyalty to your group is important; but when your group is in conflict with the broader aspirations of mankind as a whole, you should have the courage of your convictions and point out to the members of your group

---

Document 7-5, *Basis for Moral Judgments:* see the footnotes for information about copying.

[1] Adapted by Alice L. Call from Lester A. Kirkendall and Irving Tebor, *Syllabus and Reading Guide for Courses in Marriage and Family Relations* (Dubuque, Iowa, Wm. C. Brown, 1957). William C. Brown Company, Publishers, grants teachers permission to make copies of this paragraph for use in connection with their own family life and sex education classes. On each reproduction the following copyright notice must be given: © 1957 by Lester A. Kirkendall and Irving Trebor.

that they are wrong—even if it means breaking down the solidarity of the group."[2]

[2] Alice L. Call, *Toward Adulthood* (Philadelphia, Lippincott, 1964), p. 9. Address requests for permission to copy this paragraph to J. B. Lippincott and Company, East Washington Square, Philadelphia, Pa. 19105.

Document 7-6 ***Functions of the Family***

The family is the only social institution other than religion that is formally developed in all societies. Family duties are the direct role responsibility of everyone in the society, with rare exceptions. The family is the fundamental instrumental foundation of the larger social structure, in that all other institutions depend on its contributions. The family is the socially approved means for production, nurture, rearing, and socialization of children.

In the United States the family has changed from a producing unit to a consuming unit. The transition from a domestic work group to a domestic group in which the individual members of the family are dispersed at work and at school has taken place gradually over the last one hundred years. As the business function of the family changed, the individual family members' roles have also changed. Although the family home remains the center of activity, the nature of the work and its division between husband and wife is different.

In colonial times all members of the typical free family worked to supply all necessities. The father was the undisputed head of the household. He was the taskmaster, teacher, and minister. He made all decisions of consequence. The mother was subservient to the husband. She performed practically all the household chores and sometimes helped farm the land with her husband. The role of the child was strictly defined. Children were "to be seen not heard," and they were expected to work along with their parents. The larger the family, the more hands to do the necessary work.

Today the family sells its labor for money, and most families have moved from rural to urban areas. The father is generally still the head of the household, but he is no longer the educator and minister. He still influences the development of ideals, moral and spiritual habits, and values in his children. He sometimes helps his wife with household tasks. The mother usually has more equality. She participates in decisions of consequence and is both wife and companion to her husband. The wife may work outside the home. The children are still expected to help with household tasks but are primarily concerned with their schoolwork.

Other organizations have taken over the direction of economic production that was formerly exercised by the family, and they have assumed some of its financial and educational responsibilities as well. The mass media, peer groups, hospitals, and voluntary associations have all assumed functions formerly performed by the family. The family has therefore become a much more specialized group, and now it concentrates its functions on the socialization of the child and the emotional support and affection that are exchanged among its members.

Many families are operating as true partnerships of husbands and wives. Others enjoy a more traditional relationship between spouses. Families choose the form that is most expedient, necessary, and workable for them. The important thing is for the family to be comfortable with its role arrangements and for all its members to derive the benefits that variety makes possible.

chapter **8**

suggested content for the eighth grade

Overview

In this unit the students study how to get along in school and the purposes of going to school at all. Eighth-grade students are as concerned with popularity, parent and sibling conflicts, and other personal problems as they are with their academic work, and so the unit will not simply focus on "How to Study" but will give suitable emphasis to the personal problems that are important to individual students. The teacher fills the role not of the students' natural enemy but of a counselor to students who have major problems.

A second focus of the eighth-grade unit is on the many changes, some curious and some puzzling, that occur in the bodies of children of this age. These changes should be discussed with the accurate terminology and the physiological concepts taught in the seventh grade. (To make sure that the students remember the seventh-grade content, compose a test based on the Basic Terminology List [Document 7-2] and administer it to the class. If the test reveals certain weaknesses, the teacher can review the old material or shape his presentation of the new unit to correct them.) Major emphasis should be placed on genetics. Continued use of a Question Box is very helpful because it allows the students to obtain the information they need without having to display their ignorance to their peers.

The problem of the double standard is present in the eighth grade.

Most boys are aware of a pressure to prove their masculinity by participating in sexual intercourse, but at the same time they know that there is a community pressure or condemnation against their doing so. They are often further confused because they are not sure that they even *like* girls. It is sometimes helpful to schedule a separate class session for each sex. The school nurse can work with one group, the teacher with the other; they can encourage the students to discuss in depth some of their concerns about their bodies and the feelings that they are reluctant to pursue in the presence of peers of the opposite sex. They may also wish to decide on questions they would like to have the opposite sex answer as a group.

Problem solving is an important technique that has many practical applications in the lives of eighth graders. You may wish to discuss this technique first in the abstract and then apply it to areas of philosophy of life and parent–child conflicts.[1] The students should also be aware that a great many adult problems of utmost personal importance—career choice, mate selection, size of family, and marriage–divorce problems, for example—can be solved more satisfactorily by using an objective problem-solving technique than by giving free play to the confused emotional processes that so often prove decisive in these matters. Several aspects of problem solving are reviewed again in the eleventh grade.

The unit concludes with a study of dating. Although many students in this grade are not dating, they are very concerned about dating etiquette, the age to start dating, how to be a good date, and what to do on a date. The opportunity to discuss these pressing concerns, to share ideas, and to learn that most other students are equally concerned about the process of dating serves to reassure each student.

The recommended basic texts are Landis and Landis' *Building Your Life* and Johnson's *Love and Sex in Plain Language,* with extensive use of the supplementary pamphlets and books mentioned in the Curriculum Outlines.

Curriculum Outlines

Instructional Objectives

The student understands that:

1. A person needs a set of sound ethical and moral values as a guideline for directing his own behavior.

[1] Problem solving is discussed in Evelyn M. Duvall's book *Family Development* (Philadelphia, Lippincott, 1967), p. 140.

2. A healthy moral adjustment to the adolescent sex drive is essential to individual development.
3. Normal individuals differ in patterns of physical growth and development.
4. The schools attempt in various ways to educate students for citizenship in a democracy.
5. The problem-solving approach may be used to help find realistic, socially acceptable solutions to personal problems.
6. In early adolescence boys and girls become increasingly interested in being together and learning adult skills.
7. People need successful social relationships with others to develop personal social maturity.

Content

Getting Along in School

A. How does the school help a person develop a pleasing, healthy personality and maintain good mental health? Consider the contribution of:

1. The "Climate" or atmosphere of the total school environment (physical and emotional)
   a. Recognition of and respect for individuals
   b. Regard for physical, emotional, and social needs of students
2. Leadership and "followership" roles of the school faculty and the students
3. Curriculum and teaching methods
4. Student government and extracurricular activities
5. Health services and staff
6. Guidance and counseling staff
7. School–community relationships

Suggested Learning Opportunities

- Discuss the extent to which the school serves as a socializing agency. Request the students to name the duties and responsibilities required of teenagers by the school. Obtain a copy of the school motto or rules, and examine with students the extent to which the values expressed are promoted by teachers and students. To what degree do the goals and expectations of the school agree with those of the family?
- View and discuss the filmstrip *Making the Most of Yourself.*
- Have several students interview relevant members of the school's central office staff about their duties related to helping students maintain mental health. Or, invite the staff to participate in a panel discussion about the mental health objectives of the total school program and the roles each one of them plays in meeting these objectives.
- Have class committees survey the school plant and the kinds of services offered to students to help them de-

velop into mature individuals. The findings of this survey may be used as a basis for discussions, possibly leading to recommendations of changes or expansion of school services.

- Discuss reasons why students sometimes believe that they have too little independence. Organize a panel discussion on the topic "How Much Independence Should a Junior High Student Have?"
- Cite examples that demonstrate how students are growing in the ability to deal with abstractions, generalizations, and ideas. Illustrate how a person's attention span increases with maturity.
- Cite district standards on homework time allotted at each grade level.
- Have the students organize committees to discuss the values of school clubs and other extracurricular activities. Do these activities help students develop a feeling of adequacy or self-confidence in interpersonal relations?

B. Why do we go to school?
   1. Courses one should or should not take
   2. Worrying about school to the point that it affects one's work
   3. Quitting school and getting a job
   4. Why some students fail a course when most other students don't

- Read and discuss the ideas presented in *Make Your Study Hours Count.*
- In consultation with the guidance counselor, arrange for the students to take a study-habits inventory. The students may start by recording in a diary just what they do each day, and then they can draw up a typical schedule. The schedule notations might include time spent on recreation, meals, house chores, classes, homework. Are there gaps in a student's day when he is doing "just nothing" (as opposed to relaxation and recreation)? Real lassitude may be a symptom of a beginning physical illness or the lack of a commitment to living.
- Read and discuss Chapter 11, "In-School Problems," in *Points for Decision.*

- View and discuss the film *You're No Good.*
- Have the class or a committee formulate criteria that may be used to evaluate the total educational program of the school for its strengths and weaknesses in developing and maintaining the abilities of students to get along in school.
- Discuss with the class the necessity and value of first knowing as much as possible about a subject or problem before attempting a solution or plan of action. For example, if a student is named to a committee, he should find out what job is to be done, which people can do certain jobs, and what steps can be taken to accomplish the objective. A parallel can be drawn between this situation and the need to carry on the business of living well.

C. Are teachers and pupils natural enemies?

1. "Mrs. Smith is always picking on me."
2. "Are teachers people?"

- Discuss some rationalizations for poor student performances and the failure to get the desired grade that are commonly heard in school.
- Have students observe specific teachers work to learn about the ways they help individual students; report to the class.

D. Where can you get money for school expenses?

- Make a survey of the kinds of part-time jobs at which students in your school work. Are jobs available?
- Arrange a poll in your class. Ask students to indicate on an unsigned slip how much money they have available to spend each week. Also ask them whether they earn all, part, or none of their spending money. Compile the data. Do boys have more money than girls? What percent earn all or part of their spending money? Discuss the results with the class.

Resources

(S) Film: *You're No Good,* McGraw-Hill, b/w, 28 min. Dramatizes feelings of a high school dropout, his frustrations, drives, and fantasies.

(S) Mahoney, Harold J., and T. L. Engle, *Points for Decision.* New York: Harcourt, Brace & World, 1961, pp. 385–423.
(S) d'A Gerken, C., and Alice Kemp, *Make Your Study Hours Count.* Chicago: Science Research Associates, 1956.
(S) Filmstrip: *Making the Most of Yourself,* Society of Visual Education, color, 33⅓ r.p.m. record, 8 min. Shows teens how to get along with others. Several alternatives are presented to stimulate discussions and independent thinking.
(T, S) Smart, Russell, and Mollie Smart, *Living in Families.* Boston: Houghton Mifflin, 1965.

Content

Physical Changes

A. Review of seventh-grade materials about reproduction
B. Human reproduction
   1. Sexual maturity
      a. What is it?
      b. How do we know when we have reached reproductive maturity?
      c. How do we tell our parents we have matured reproductively?
   2. The fetal stage
   3. How birth occurs
   4. Heredity
      a. Chromosomes and genes
      b. Current research and progress in the study of hereditary abnormalities

Suggested Learning Opportunities

- Prepare and administer a pretest to evaluate the level of class knowledge of terms and concepts.
- Issue the class text, *Love and Sex in Plain Language.*
- Show again the seventh-grade films *Girl to Woman* and *Boy to Man* if the class desire to see them.
- Show the film *Human Reproduction.*
- Class discussions of human reproduction should be centered around the above films and text.
- Make use of the Question Box to implement class discussion and indicate misconceptions.
- Make two books, *Attaining Manhood* and *Attaining Womanhood,* available for student supplementary reading.
- Show and discuss the pictures of the developing fetus in *Growth.*
- Have the class discuss the care of a newborn baby and the effect of environment and attitudes of parents and siblings toward the infant.
- Read and discuss the book *A Baby Is Born.*
- View and discuss the Dickenson Birth Models.
- Show the film *Human Heredity.*
- Read and discuss *Finding Out About Ourselves.*

- Arrange for the school nurse to explain and discuss the growth of the fetus and the birth process.
- Discuss some of the problems of hereditary abnormalities, for example, mental retardation, blindness, and deafness.

Resources

(S) Johnson, Eric W., *Love and Sex in Plain Language*. Philadelphia: Lippincott, 1967.
(S) Film: *Human Reproduction*, McGraw-Hill, b/w, 23 min. Uses animation to explain the reproductive systems of both men and women, and to show the process of normal human birth.
(S) Tanner, James M., and Gordon R. Taylor, *Growth*. Morristown, N.J.: Silver Burdett, 1965.
(S) Maternity Center Association, *A Baby Is Born*, 3rd ed. New York: Grosset & Dunlap, 1964.
(S) Dickinson Birth Models (series of six polystyrene models), Cleveland Health Museum, Cleveland, Ohio.
(S) Film: *Human Heredity*, Henk Newenhouse, color, 22 min. Explains how characteristics such as color of hair or skin and type of body are inherited. (*Note:* The reference to the number of chromosomes is no longer correct. This outdated fact may be used to illustrate the changing nature of science.)
(S) Kirkendall, Lester A., *Finding Out About Ourselves*. Chicago: Science Research Associates, 1956.
(S) Corner, George W., *Attaining Manhood*. New York: Harper & Row, 1952.
(S) ——, *Attaining Womanhood*. New York: Harper & Row, 1952.
(T) Kirkendall, Lester A., *Understanding Sex*. Chicago: Science Research Associates, 1947.

Content

Philosophy of Life
A philosophy of living refers to any pattern of thought that enables us to answer life's problems for our own satisfaction.

A. Ideas of right and wrong
   1. Our personal conduct demonstrates our code of ethics.

Suggested Learning Opportunities

- Compare values of Western philosophies to those of other peoples, for example, Buddhists and Moslems.
- Discuss how spiritual values differ from intellectual and emotional values.
- Issue the class text *Building Your Life*, and assign Chapter 18.
- Role-play situations involving moral decisions.

2. Doing what is right is not always easy.
3. We must understand the consequences of breaking our moral code.

B. The meaning and purpose of life
1. The major purpose of a code of ethics is to give us a pattern of action that adds meaning and purpose to our lives.
2. Your personality, conscience, religion, and culture contribute to your purpose in life.

C. A philosophy of life and environmental influences
1. A philosophy of life or code of ethics is not suddenly acquired when a crisis occurs, but is built up through previous experiences.
2. Basic principles of right and wrong change very little, but attitudes of right and wrong change from group to group or within a particular group to meet new conditions.
3. The Golden Rule and the Ten Commandments have come down through the centuries and have survived the interpretation of many great cultures.

- View and discuss the film *Big Man on Campus.*
- Read and discuss Document 8-1, "Erasing a Mistake."
- Devise a situation involving the concept of conformity. Develop and administer a list of multiple-choice questions with several responses, each of which is correct. Poll the class by a show of hands to find out how many students chose each response, and record results on the chalkboard. Permit the students to change their answers and poll the class again. Evaluate the role of conformity in influencing the students' decisions to change original answers.
- Ask students to discuss with their parents their family philosophy. (It would be well to discuss this assignment at a prior P.T.A. or orientation meeting.)
- Have students develop their own philosophy of life or code of behavior. The teacher must be careful that the students do not parrot his prior remarks on the subject.
- Have students describe experiences that have contributed to developing their philosophy of life.
- View and discuss the film *Moment of Decision.*
- Discuss the following topics: personality—character conscience—appreciation of right and wrong—religion—belief in something greater than human resources—culture—social order
- Assign *Building Your Philosophy of Life.*
- Have the class discuss the idea that obeying the law is a necessary part of a mature code of ethics.
- Have the class discuss the concept that we do not live in a vacuum; what we do has an effect on others.

- Have the class discuss the following: John says he does not care what other people think of him; his standards of conduct are his own.
- Assign *Ethics for Everyday Living.*

Resources

(S) Landis, Judson, and Mary Landis, *Building Your Life.* Englewood Cliffs, N.J.: Prentice-Hall, 1964, ch. 18.

(S) Film: *Big Man on Campus,* Sid Davis Productions, color, 10 min. Tells the story of Jerry Warner, junior high school student who finds himself in trouble with the authorities and realizes that it is his own attitude and behavior that have caused his predicament.

(S) Document 8-1, "Erasing a Mistake."

(S) Film: *Moment of Decision,* Sid Davis Productions, color, 10 min. Tells the story of four boys who are faced with a decision whether or not to steal a car and take a joy ride. Shows that even though a boy's decision may be colored by his background, the responsibility is his.

(S) Smith, T. V. *Building Your Philosophy of Life.* Chicago: Science Research Associates, 1953.

(S) Neff, Mary V., *Ethics for Everyday Living.* Chicago: Science Research Associates, 1958.

(T) Juvenile Justice Commission, *Laws for Youth.* Orange County, Calif., 1967.

(T) Montagu, Ashley, *Helping Children Develop Moral Values.* Chicago: Science Research Associates, 1953.

(T, S) Smart, Russell, and Mollie Smart, *Living in Families.* Boston: Houghton Mifflin, 1965, pp. 180–86.

Content

Problem Solving

There are various methods of approaching a problem.

A. How can we meet our problems?
   1. Direct attack
   2. Detour
   3. Retreat
   4. Scientific problem-solving technique

B. How can we use our abilities well?

Suggested Learning Opportunities

- Assign Chapter 23 in *Building Your Life.* Discuss the problem-solving method for clarification and applicability.
- Have students write descriptions of their two most common problems and submit them anonymously. Have a committee tabulate the results and report to the class. Assign a problem to each small group and have them ap-

What habits of thought can hinder us?

1. Facing reality
2. Rationalizing
3. Projecting
4. Daydreaming
5. Identifying
6. Sublimating

C. What steps are involved in solving our problems constructively?

1. Efficiency
2. Release from tension

ply the problem-solving technique to suggest a resolution of the problem.[2]

- Show the film *Facing Reality* and discuss it in class.
- Have students anonymously write their most common fears and follow the above procedure.
- Have students give illustrations of the various types of behavior listed in this content area.
- Use stories to identify problem-solving techniques. (You may use the Scholastic Literature Unit *Family.*) List five steps involved in meeting problems constructively.
- Discuss how some people try to use their emotions to solve problems, for example, making fists, crying.
- List sources they may seek for help with their problems.
- Assign *Your Problems: How To Handle Them.* Discuss in class.
- Read Chapter 2, "How To Solve a Moral Problem," in the pamphlet *Ethics for Everyday Living* in class, and discuss.
- Ask students to react to problems listed in Chapters 3 and 4 of the same pamphlet.
- Assign small committees to write up a problem similar to the ones listed in the pamphlet, and have the class discuss it.
- Plan a panel discussion on developing self-confidence. Why is the formulation and accomplishment of attainable goals important in building self-confidence?
- Ask students to analyze the statement "I'll wait until I get to high school before trying to do my best."

[2] Some of the problems based on the reasons for parent–children conflicts suggested in the next section can be taken up here.

Resources

(S) Landis, Judson, and Mary Landis, *Building Your Life*. Englewood Cliffs, N.J.: Prentice-Hall, 1964, ch. 23.
(S) Film: *Facing Reality*, McGraw-Hill, b/w, 12 min. Examines the common ways in which people escape from reality—daydreaming, identification, suppression, and malingering. Shows how a sympathetic instructor helps a high school boy to change his negative attitudes.
(S) *Family*, Scholastic Literature Unit. Englewood Cliffs, N.J.: Scholastic Book Services.
(S) Remmers, Hermann H., and Robert H. Bauernfeind, *Your Problems: How To Handle Them*. Chicago: Science Research Associates, 1953.
(S) Neff, Mary V., *Ethics for Everyday Living*. Chicago: Science Research Associates, 1958, chs. 2–4.
(T) Strang, Ruth, *Helping Children Solve Problems*. Chicago: Science Research Associates, 1953.
(T) English, O. Spurgeon, and Stuart M. Finch, *Emotional Problems of Growing Up*. Chicago: Science Research Associates, 1951.
(T, S) Smart, Russell, and Mollie Smart, *Living in Families*. Boston: Houghton Mifflin, 1965, p. 179.

Content

Parent–Children Conflicts
Disagreements may arise because a parent

A. Expects too much of us.
B. Refuses to let us grow up.
C. Worries unnecessarily about our affairs.
D. Lacks confidence in our judgment.
E. Clings to old-fashioned ideas.
F. Has ambitions for us that are different from our own.
G. Shows favoritism to a brother or sister.
H. Has more experience than we do and so can see that the consequences of our proposed course of action will not be what we think.

Suggested Learning Opportunities

- Discuss factors that contribute to healthy family relations.
- Assign Chapter 19 in *Building Your Life*.
- Have each student make an anonymous list of things that bother him most about his parents. Have a committee compile the results, and use small group discussion techniques to discover possible resolutions of the problems.
- Show and discuss filmstrip *Learning To Understand Your Parents*.
- Ask the class to discuss the extent to which they should be involved in family decision making. Request them to list the decisions in which they believe they should have a part, those which they should be allowed to make themselves, and those which are none of their concern.

Resources

(S) Landis, Judson, and Mary Landis, *Building Your Life*. Englewood Cliffs, N.J.: Prentice-Hall, 1964, ch. 19.

(S) Filmstrip: *Learning To Understand Your Parents,* Society of Visual Education, color, $33\frac{1}{3}$ r.p.m. record, $7\frac{1}{2}$ min. Helps teenagers understand the importance of good family relationships.

Content

Dating

A. Values
   1. Helping one to understand himself and others
   2. Understanding and accepting variations
   3. Learning social skills
   4. Getting acquainted with members of the opposite sex
   5. Learning what type of people fit one's personality needs

B. Considerations for dating
   1. Age
      The proper age to start dating is a matter of individual interpretation. The personality of each student and the kind of home in which he has grown up play a major part in determining the age at which boys and girls become interested in each other.
   2. Types of dates
      a. Party dating
         Boys and girls get together

Suggested Learning Opportunities

- Assign Chapters 10 and 11 in *Building Your Life*.
- Have the class design and use a dating customs survey. Have a committee compile the results and report to the class. See Document 8-2, "Dating Customs Survey," for a model.
- Have students collect clippings from the newspapers and magazines about current dating attitudes. Then have them write a short report giving their opinion about these materials.
- Report on dating customs in foreign countries based on library research.
- Show and discuss the filmstrip *Ready for Dating*.
- Have the class design a survey instrument to obtain the opinions of adults and students regarding the age to start dating. Be sure to define the term *dating*. Compile the results.
- Show and discuss the filmstrip *What To Do on a Date*.
- Assign a committee to do a survey of the school on the question, "Should girls ask boys for a date?" Compare their findings with the survey on p. 87 of *Building Your Life*.
- Arrange a panel discussion with both students and parents to discuss "The Role of the Chaperone at a Party."

in one home, school, or church. There is no specific pairing of boys and girls attending.

b. Group dating
Several couples participate in an activity, for example, a beach party under parental supervision.

c. Double date
Two couples attend a function together.

d. Single date.

3. Etiquette
   a. Asking for a date
   b. Accepting a date
   c. Calling for your date
   d. Meeting her parents
   e. Manners on a date
   f. Frequency of dates
   g. Inviting a boy in after a date
   h. How to say goodnight
   i. Breaking a date

C. How to be a good date
   1. Personal appearance
   2. Responsibilities of the boy on a date
   3. Responsibilities of the girl on a date
   4. Where to go and what to do

D. Factors in choosing a good date
   1. Personality
   2. Appearance
   3. Companionship
   4. Consideration and versatility of person

E. Family and dating
   1. Do your parents approve of dating?

- Discuss the problems of group dating in your community.
- Discuss the advantages and disadvantages of each type of date listed under the content section.
- Have the class list the various kinds of dating activities available to them in the community.
- Have class discuss the problems and benefits of boy–girl parties in individual homes.

- Role-play situations where the boy asks the girl for a date.
- Have the class role-play situations illustrating the various activities under the content section.
- Have the class list ways a student can be introduced to someone whom they think they might like.
- Read and discuss Chapter 12 in *Building Your Life.*
- Show and discuss the filmstrip *Getting a Date.*
- Have the class discuss the statement, "Kissing a boy goodnight is just a way of saying 'thank you.'"
- Have the class list the qualities they would like a date to have.
- Have students make a survey of students in the school on factors they consider in choosing a date; then have students summarize and report to the class.

2. Should your parents meet your date?
3. Should your parents know where you are going?
4. What time should you be in?
5. What do you do for transportation?

- Arrange a panel discussion with students and parents to discuss parent–youth conflicts regarding dating.
- Have the class discuss the practice of "secret dating."
- Have the class discuss ways parents can meet their child's date.
- Use small group discussions to resolve the problems of transportation in dating.

Resources

(S) Landis, Judson, and Mary Landis, *Building Your Life*. Englewood Cliffs, N.J.: Prentice-Hall, 1964, chs. 10–12.

(S) Document 8-2, "Dating Customs Survey."

(S) Filmstrip: *Ready for Dating,* Society of Visual Education, color, 33⅓ r.p.m. record, 8 min. Illustrates the proper way to ask for, accept, or refuse a date and tells how to get parental approval.

(S) Filmstrip: *What To Do on a Date,* Society of Visual Education, color, 33⅓ r.p.m. record, 8 min. Describes the responsibilities the boy and girl have toward the date.

(S) Filmstrip: *Getting a Date,* Society of Visual Education, color, 33⅓ r.p.m. record, 6½ min. Presents factors in choosing a date—future effects—and tells how to share date experiences with parents.

Background and Teaching Materials

Document 8-1 ***Erasing a Mistake***

Keeping a dating relationship within comfortable, mutually acceptable bounds is no easy task. Many people make mistakes while they are learning how far they should go and how to stop. It is particularly important that young people know how to redeem themselves once they have made a mistake, gained a bad reputation, or shocked their own sense of what is right.

Document 8-1, *Erasing a Mistake,* is taken from Evelyn M. Duvall, *The Art of Dating* (New York, Association Press, © 1958), pp. 211–12. Reprinted with permission. May not be copied without the written permission of the Association Press, 291 Broadway, New York, N.Y. 10007.

The first step in the process of righting things again is to face your mistake honestly and admit you were wrong. If you can take responsibility for what you did without blaming someone else, the battle is half won.

The second step is to try to make amends to the person you may have hurt or wronged. The boy who steps out of bounds on a date should apologize for his behavior as soon as possible. The girl in the case should admit that some of the responsibility was hers. And both should avoid further situations in which there may be a reoccurrence of the unfortunate behavior.

If the incident has been noised about, there may be the problems of erasing a bad reputation. This involves avoiding any repetition of the regrettable behavior and leaning over backward, if necessary, to regain the trust of your associates. It means throwing yourself into socially acceptable work and producing well enough so that others can respect you as a person again. This takes time but it can be done.

Andy is a case in point. When he was a sophomore in high school, his girl became pregnant, dropped out of school, and left the community. He was allowed to stay in school but he was forbidden all extracurricular privileges. He had to leave the ball team. He was not allowed to attend school dances. He was avoided by many of the fellows and most of the girls. He talked his unpleasant position over with his principal and his religious advisor, and they suggested that if he applied himself wholeheartedly to his work, his situation might improve in time. During his junior year, by dint of hard work and extra hours in the library, he made the best grades he'd ever had. He stayed out of mischief, got over his rebellious attitude toward his teachers, and began treating them with respect. He slowly regained the acceptance of both the adults and young people in his school. He never was elected the most popular boy in his class, but when he graduated, he felt that he belonged. Most of the people who knew him looked upon the early unfortunate incident as something that was over and done with. It was a long hard pull, but Andy made it. He feels it was worth the effort now to be able to walk down Main Street and feel he belongs and is accepted.

Document 8-2 Dating Customs Survey
[*A suggested survey form*]

Dating Customs in Our Community

Please answer the following questions with a check mark or by supplying the information required.

Do you date? **Yes** ☐ **No** ☐

If your answer is no, skip to the last question. If your answer is yes, please fill in the following information:

Type of Date	Yes	No	How Often
Attend school, church, or organization parties, dances, sport events in group	☐	☐	________
Attend school, church, or organization parties, dances, sport events as couple	☐	☐	________
Attend movies as a couple	☐	☐	________
Attend movies in a double date	☐	☐	________
Have "home dates" as a couple	☐	☐	________
Have "home dates" as a double date	☐	☐	________

What is your own real preference about whether or not to date and what kind of date to have, if any? What are your reasons?

[*Processing the survey results*]

Number of students responding ______

Number who date ______ Percentage ______

Number who have each type of date: 1 ______ 2 ______ etc.

---

chapter **9**

suggested content for the ninth grade

Overview

By the ninth grade many students have begun to assume that the word "immaturity" is their label. A study of maturity gives them an opportunity to find out what this label really means, for they learn that there are various kinds of maturity and various levels of maturity and that we all are immature at certain times.

The major portion of the class sessions will be needed for the study of dating standards and sexual behavior during adolescence, since these are bound to be topics of great concern to the class. The unit is designed to give the students an opportunity to give serious thought to dating standards in relation to their personal philosophy or code and to give them a firm foundation for their dating years. The family life and sex education units for earlier grades have prepared the students to study their own behavior in a meaningful way.

The problems created by the divergence between actual behavior and personal and societal moral codes, and an increasing awareness of the double standard, confuse many ninth-grade students. They also feel that they are very close to adulthood and that they want adult experiences. Tape recordings of youths involved in premarital sexual relationships and illegitimate pregnancies form a very effective means of giving students some of the information that they are seeking. The tape recordings give them a basis for small group discussions of the consequences of breaking society's code of behavior.

Many ninth-grade students are already facing the great debate concerning sexual intercourse before marriage. The family life and sex education class should provide the framework that enables them to thoroughly discuss their problems with their peers and formulate their own decisions. The problem-solving method should be used to help them resolve some of the problems.

The film *Dance Little Children* illustrates the pressures of mass media and various adult attitudes toward sexual intercourse before marriage, but it also brings in the topic of venereal disease. The course in family life and sex education is approached from a positive angle, but a brief discussion of venereal disease is appropriate. The health and science classes, however, should retain the major responsibility for the study of venereal disease in their communicable disease units. They should also take primary responsibility for the topics of smoking, drinking, and drug abuse. While these topics cannot be omitted from family life and sex education classes because of the attitudes of adults toward them, their study in depth should be in science or health classes.

The students again need the opportunity to investigate the problem of conflicts with their parents and other family members and to apply the steps of the problem-solving method to help in the resolution of these problems.

The recommended basic text is Duvall's *Love and the Facts of Life.* Extensive supporting materials are printed at the end of this chapter.

Curriculum Outlines

Instructional Objectives

The student understands that:

1. Dating requires a person to develop an understanding of social mores.
2. Going steady may limit his own personality development.
3. A good moral decision creates trust, confidence, and integrity in relationships. It increases the capacity of individuals to cooperate and enhances the sense of self-respect in the individual.
4. The greater a person's emotional maturity, the better he is prepared to solve problems.
5. Individual dating experiences vary according to personal maturity and the influence of the community and family.

Content

Becoming More Mature

Maturity is a word commonly used today. It is often used in a way that implies that each person can be labeled definitely as mature or immature. Such use overlooks the fact that in the same person there may be many different "ages" or levels of maturity and that the different types of maturity may proceed at different rates of speed in the same person.

A. What are the qualities of a good emotional maturity adjustment?

1. Is not dominated by moods. Has learned constructive ways of working out feelings.
2. Is cooperative.
3. Reduces tendencies to be jealous.
4. Is not easily hurt.
5. Is generous in judgment of others.
6. Works to be adaptable.
7. Holds positive attitudes about sex in life.
8. Can make reasonable decisions.
9. Is able to meet problems constructively.
10. Has realistic life expectations.
11. Knows the kind of person he is and what he wants to be.
12. Is able to meet responsibilities.
13. Uses good judgment in earning and spending money.
14. When required, can sacrifice his own preferences for the good of others.

B. Do we have these qualities? People who are making good progress

Suggested Learning Opportunities

- Give the "Test of Social Maturity" suggested in *Growing Up Socially,* pp. 13–16. Discuss results and findings.
- Discuss how one person may have several different ages.
- Invite the school nurse in to discuss the difference between chronological age and bone age.[1]
- Use small group discussion to react to the frequent admonishment "Act your age!"
- Assign Chapter 8, "Growing into Maturity," in *Dating Tips for Teens.*
- Have the class use Document 9-1, "Self-Evaluation Test of Social and Ethical Maturity." The instructions on the test ask the student to identify the areas in which they think they are relatively superior, above average, average, below average, or low. Each student should indicate why he is rating himself as he is by citing on the back of the form one or more specific examples of his own behavior that would justify this rating.
- Assign Chapter 1 ("How Do You Feel?") in *Love and the Facts of Life.* Read and discuss.
- Have the class compile their own list of the qualities of a mature person.
- Assign *Growing Up Socially* for reading and discussion.
- Have students complete Document 9-2, "How Self-Confident Am I?" Compile the results and discuss in class.
- Have students complete Document 9-3, "How Self-Reliant Am I?"

[1] Bone age is determined by x rays and is one factor in determining a person's biological age.

toward the maturity that will enable them to make a success of marriage and parenthood will gradually achieve consistent levels of maturity in all phases of their development.

Compile the results and discuss in class.

- Discuss the ideas contained in Document 9-4, "Some Problems That Trouble Teenagers." Have small group discussions to suggest ways of resolving some of these problems or other problems offered by the class.

Resources

(S) Weitman, Ellis, *Growing Up Socially*. Chicago: Science Research Associates, 1949, pp. 13–16.
(S) Kirkendall, Lester A., and Ruth Farnham Osborne, *Dating Tips for Teens*. Chicago: Science Research Associates, 1962, ch. 8.
(S) Document 9-1, "Self-Evaluation Test of Social and Ethical Maturity."
(S) Duvall, Evelyn M., *Love and the Facts of Life*. New York: Association Press, 1963, ch. 1.
(S) Document 9-2, "How Self-Confident Am I?"
(S) Document 9-3, "How Self-Reliant Am I?"
(S) Document 9-4, "Some Problems That Trouble Teenagers."

Content

Review of Dating
A. Values
B. Etiquette
C. Family attitude toward dating

Suggested Learning Opportunities

- Assign Chapters 11, 12, 14, and 15 in *Love and the Facts of Life*.
- Show and discuss the film *Are You Popular?*
- Have the students use the evaluation "How Do You Rate?" on pp. 17–18 in *Dating Tips for Teens;* discuss.
- Read and discuss Chapter 5, "Parents and Dating," in *Dating Tips for Teens*. Read and discuss Chapter 16 ("Caught Between Your Parents and Your Dates?") in *Love and the Facts of Life*.

Resources

(S) Duvall, Evelyn M., *Love and the Facts of Life*. New York: Association Press, 1963, chs. 11–16.
(S) Film: *Are You Popular?* Coronet Films, color, 12 min. Gives examples of how

to be popular and welcome by being friendly, considerate, and interested in other people.

(S) Kirkendall, Lester A., and Ruth Farnham Osborne, *Dating Tips for Teens.* Chicago: Science Research Associates, 1962, ch. 5, pp. 17–18.

Content

Going Steady

A. Reasons
   1. Provides security in social situations
   2. Offers status with peers
   3. Relieves parental pressure

B. Advantages
   1. Gives a feeling of belonging
   2. Provides companionship
   3. Insures dates
   4. Requires less effort

C. Disadvantages
   1. Limits knowledge of other persons
   2. Limits personality development
   3. Makes sexual relationship more difficult to control
   4. Makes it difficult to break up and become available again

D. Breaking Up

The problem of how to break up a "steady" relationship is difficult to resolve without hurting the other's feeling.

   1. Let your steady know how you feel about staying together.
   2. Try to make sure that your steady still feels that he or she is an attractive person but that your relationship just isn't working.
   3. Recognize that friendships change and shift.

Suggested Learning Opportunities

- Have the class compile a list of the advantages and disadvantages of going steady.
- Select students to debate the question "The Pros and Cons of Going Steady."
- Design a survey instrument on the subject of going steady. (See Document 9-5, "Dating: Going Steady," for an example.) Have the students use the survey to obtain the opinions of other teenagers and parents about the subject.
- Discuss the ideas contained in Document 9-6, "Going Steady."
- Read and discuss Chapter 6 in *Dating Tips for Teens.*
- Show and discuss the filmstrip *What About Going Steady?*
- Discuss the ideas contained in Document 9-7, "The Physical Aspects of Necking and Petting." Have the class discuss the meaning of necking and petting.
- Read and discuss Chapter 17 ("Is Going Steady a Good Idea?") in *Love and the Facts of Life.*
- Ask the students to list as many points as they can regarding the right way and then the wrong way to break up, remembering that no one likes to be hurt. Discuss the points listed in class and evaluate their possibilities.
- Have the class discuss "ways of get-

4. Help each other get back into circulation.

ting back into circulation" quickly and easily.

- Use role-playing situations on how to break up tactfully.

Resources

(S) Document 9-5, "Dating: Going Steady."
(S) Document 9-6, "Going Steady."
(S) Kirkendall, Lester A., and Ruth Farnham Osborne, *Dating Tips for Teens.* Chicago: Science Research Associates, 1962, ch. 6.
(S) Filmstrip: *What About Going Steady?* Society of Visual Education, color, 33⅓ r.p.m. record, 9 min. Tells what it means to go steady; gives the advantages and disadvantages.
(S) Document 9-7, "The Physical Aspects of Necking and Petting."
(S) Duvall, Evelyn M., *Love and the Facts of Life.* New York: Association Press, 1963, ch. 17.

Content

Dating Standards

A. Standards, and why they are important
B. Expression of affection
C. Personal standards and popularity
D. Reasons for society's moral code
   1. Premarital relations
   2. Nonmarital pregnancies
   3. Teenage marriages
   4. Personality development
   5. Mental health
   6. Family stability
E. Standards of behavior
   1. Actions, decisions, and attitudes in everyday activities should enhance:
      a. the dignity and worth of man
      b. the freedom of man
      c. equality of men
   2. Sex standards of the past remain yet are tested to a greater extent now.

Suggested Learning Opportunities

- Have the class identify and discuss their greater freedom to set their own standards.
- Have the class discuss the following ideas regarding public demonstrations of affection: (1) indicates insecurity of one of the couple; (2) indicates overpossessiveness of one of the couple; (3) indicates poor taste; (4) is harmful to the girl's reputation.
- Play the tape recording "Personal stories by young people involved in premarital pregnancy, nonmarital intercourse, and teenage marriages."
- Develop a chart of moral judgment as a self-evaluation technique. Use the ideas contained in "Reasons for a Basic Moral Code" in Landis and Landis, *Personal Adjustment, Marriage, and Family Living,* pp. 90–91, as a guide.
- Show and discuss the film *Early Marriage.*
- Discuss the ideas contained in "Facts

a. The girl usually entertained her boyfriend at home.
b. Young people go on single dates more today.
c. Under the traditional old double standard the boy can sow wild oats with "bad girls" but every man expects to marry a "good girl."
d. More responsibility is placed on young people because of more freedom; young people are pushed to have fun; parents are too often not home to supervise.

and Fiction About Sexual Intercourse Before Marriage" on pp. 52–59 in Duvall's *Before You Marry.*

- Ask the students to develop a list of ways to draw the line tactfully and effectively. (See Landis' *Building a Successful Marriage,* p. 71.
- Discuss the ideas contained in Document 9-8, "Discussion of Premarital Sex Relationships." Use small group discussions.
- Read and discuss Chapter 13 ("What's the Harm in Petting?") in *Love and the Facts of Life.*
- Have one student report on "Sex Standards," pp. 7–14 in *Why Wait Till Marriage?*
- Read and discuss the pamphlet *Sex and Our Society.*
- Distribute the book *Why Wait Till Marriage?* Assign specific chapters to a group of students to read and present orally to the class.

Resources

(S) Tape Recording: "Personal stories by the young people involved in premarital pregnancy, nonmarital intercourse, and teenage marriages." (Produced in the individual school district by an expert interviewer. When the purpose of the tape is made known, you will not lack volunteers who sincerely want to tell their story to help other students realize the ramifications caused by premarital relationships and teenage marriages.)

(T) Landis, Judson, and Mary Landis, *Personal Adjustment, Marriage, and Family Living.* Englewood Cliffs, N.J.: Prentice-Hall, 1966, pp. 90–91.

(S) Film: *Early Marriage,* E. C. Brown Trust, color, 26 min. Deals with marriage, high school counseling, and classroom teaching of marriage preparation.

(S) Duvall, Sylvanus M., *Before You Marry.* New York: Association Press, 1959, pp. 52–59.

(S) Landis, Judson, and Mary Landis, *Building a Successful Marriage.* Englewood Cliffs, N.J.: Prentice-Hall, 1963, p. 71.

(S) Document 9-8, "Discussion of Premarital Sex Relationships."

(S) Duvall, Evelyn M., *Love and the Facts of Life.* New York: Association Press, 1963, ch. 13.

(S) ——, *Why Wait Till Marriage?* New York: Association Press, 1965, pp. 7–14.

(S) Kirkendall, Lester A., and Elizabeth Ogg, *Sex and Our Society.* New York: Public Affairs Pamphlets, 1964.
(T) *Early Marriage: A Film Guide for Teachers and Discussion Leaders.* Portland, Ore., E. C. Brown Trust, 1961.
(T) Duvall, Evelyn M., and Sylvanus M. Duvall, *Sex Ways—In Fact and Faith: Bases for Christian Family Policy.* New York: Association Press, 1961.

Content

Sexual Behavior During Adolescence
A. The great debate—sexual intercourse before marriage
  1. The double standard
  2. Personal values
  3. Interpersonal relationships
  4. Family relationships

Suggested Learning Opportunities

- Assign a few students specific chapters to read; have them prepare a report for the class from the book *Letters to Jane.*
- Discuss the ideas contained in Document 9-9, "Discussion Guide: The Double Standard."
- Show the film *Dance Little Children.* Discuss the adult attitudes portrayed.
- Plan a debate on the topic "Is Sexual Restraint Bad for You?" Be certain your debators are well prepared with facts.
- Read and discuss Document 9-10, "The Great Debate: Sexual Intercourse Before Marriage."
- Discuss the topic "Sex Conduct Cannot Be a Private Affair."
- Discuss the idea that physical union before marriage is rarely a preview of sexual love within marriage.
- Read and discuss Chapter 9 ("What About Those Sex Problems?") in *Love and the Facts of Life.*

Content

B. Masturbation: is it harmful?
C. Sexual deviation
  1. Homosexuality
  2. Exhibitionism
  3. Rape
D. Drinking
  1. To drink or not to drink
  2. Drinking and dating

Suggested Learning Opportunities

- Review the ideas contained in Document 7-4, "Masturbation."
- Discuss Document 9-11, "Homosexuality," and Document 9-12, "Exhibitionism."
- Discuss ways a student may handle the situation if an incident does occur.
- Show and discuss the films *Boys Beware* and *Girls Beware.*
- Assist the class to use the problem-

solving method to consider the question of drinking. (See Chapter 23 of the eighth-grade text, *Building Your Life.*)
- Discuss the ideas contained in Document 9-13 "Drinking."
- Have the class compile their own list of "Tips for Nondrinkers" (see Document 9-14 for an example).

E. Venereal disease
   1. Mode of transmission
   2. Treatment

- Discuss the material contained in Document 9-15, "Venereal Disease."
- Review Chapter 9 in *Love and the Facts of Life.*

F. Drug abuse
   1. Our drug society
   2. Teenage drug abuse: a social activity
   3. Drug use and dating

- Analyze the TV drug commercials. List the reasons given for the use of drugs. Have a committee chart how often the commercials appear.
- Discuss the topic "Our Drug-Oriented Society."
- Have the class write answers to "Dear Abby" letters (see Document 9-16 for samples), and discuss the answers in class.
- Have the class bring in newspaper and magazine articles on the abuse of drugs to discuss in class.

Resources

(S) Shultz, Gladys Denny, *Letters to Jane.* Philadelphia: Lippincott, 1960.
(S) Document 9-9, "Discussion Guide: The Double Standard."
(S) Film: *Dance Little Children,* Calvin Productions, color, 28 min. The question is raised as to how much of the blame for the increased incidence of V. D. in adolescents can be placed on the teenager and how much is the fault of the adults. Graphic portrayal of current adult attitudes toward premarital sexual relations.
(S) Document 9-10, "The Great Debate: Sexual Intercourse Before Marriage."
(S) Duvall, Evelyn M., *Love and the Facts of Life.* New York. Association Press, 1963, ch. 9.
(S) Document 7-4, "Masturbation."
(S) Document 9-11, "Homosexuality."
(S) Document 9-12, "Exhibitionism."
(S) Film: *Boys Beware,* Sid Davis Productions, color, 10 min. Tells in good taste the problems of the homosexual. Four case histories are dramatized, showing various approaches the homosexual may use to develop a relationship with

a young boy. The pattern and danger signs are pointed out so they can easily be detected.

(S) Film: *Girls Beware,* Sid Davis Productions, color, 10 min. Explains the problem of young girls falling prey to the molester in four case histories. Covers do's and don't's in babysitting situations. Develops the problem of the "pick up" and the girls who go with boys who are too old.

(S) Landis, Judson, and Mary Landis, *Building Your Life.* Englewood Cliffs, N.J.: Prentice-Hall, 1964, ch. 23.

(S) Document 9-13, "Drinking."

(S) Document 9-14, "Tips for Nondrinkers."

(S) Document 9-15, "Venereal Disease."

(S) Document 9-16, "Dear Abby."

(T) Duvall, Evelyn M., and Sylvanus Duvall, *Sense and Nonsense About Sex.* New York: Association Press, 1962.

(T) Kirkendall, Lester A., *Premarital Intercourse and Interpersonal Relationships.* New York: Julian, 1961.

(T) Lorand, Rhoda L., *Love, Sex, and the Teenager.* New York: Macmillan, 1965.

(T) Nowlis, Helen H., "Drugs on the College Campus," NASPA Drug Education Project, 110 Anderson Tower, University of Rochester, N.Y. 14627.

Content

How Members of the Family Can Adjust to Problems and Seek Solutions

A. Problems can be resolved.
1. The problem must be identified.
2. Each person should be able to state his feelings.
3. Every solution should be mutually examined.
4. In finding a solution both parties may have to compromise.

B. Sometimes common sense can resolve a problem.
1. An honest mistake may have been made.
2. Children and adults are not infallible.
3. The other person might be right.

Suggested Learning Opportunities

- Role-play a family council that considers a problem and reaches a solution on the basis of the following principles:
  (1) Earning the right to adult freedom
  (2) Necessary allocation of authority
  (3) Maintenance of mutal respect and courtesy
  (4) Maintenance of health and well being of all
- Ask the class to submit their most irritating problem anonymously in the Question Box. Use these problems for the bases of small group discussions.
- Have the students read *How To Solve Your Problems.*
- Ask students to describe anonymously a problem and to suggest its solution;

4. One's own motives should be analyzed:
   a. selfishness
   b. spite
   c. jealousy
5. Was the problem that important in the first place?

discuss in small groups the appropriateness of the solutions.

- Assign some students to read and review the paperback book *How To Deal with Parents and Other Problems.*
- The teacher may describe serious family problems and ways in which people have solved them. Have the class discuss the appropriateness of the solution.
- Have the class bring in newspaper articles for discussion.

Resources

(S) Seashore, Robert H., and A. C. Van Dusen, *How To Solve Your Problems.* Chicago: Science Research Associates, 1950.
(S) Osborne, Ernest G., *How To Deal with Parents and Other Problems.* New York: Grosset & Dunlap, 1966.
(T) Strang, Ruth, *Helping Children Solve Problems.* Chicago: Science Research Associates, 1953.
(T) Lawton, George, *How To Be Happy Though Young.* New York: Vanguard Press, 1949.

Background and Teaching Materials

Document 9-1 Self-Evaluation Test of Social and Ethical Maturity

This test is meant to help you decide what your own relative strengths and weaknesses are. *Put two X's in each column.* The two *X*'s you put in the "Low" column do not mean that you rank low on these items compared to anyone else, only compared to your own strengths. The meaning of the two *X*'s in each other column is relative to yourself in the same way.

	Superior	Above Average	Average	Below Average	Low
A. Willingness to sacrifice selfish interests for the welfare of others.					
B. Regular practice of a worthy code of right and wrong.					
C. Readiness to stand up for what is believed to be right.					
D. Persistence at unpleasant tasks.					
E. Honesty in relationships with other teenagers.					
F. Honesty in relationships with parents and other adults.					
G. Accent on the positive instead of the negative qualities in environment.					
H. Sense of personal responsibility for behavior.					
I. Attitude of tolerance for the opinions of others.					
J. Wise use of time and energy.					

Document 9-2 ***How Self-Confident Am I?***

Answer the following items true or false.

_______ 1. Starting a conversation with a stranger is usually easy for me.

_______ 2. I dislike getting up stunts to put life into a party.

_______ 3. I never become extremely excited about a situation.

_______ 4. Making up my mind is usually hard for me.

Document 9-2, *How Self-Confident Am I?,* is taken from John and Dorathea Crawford, *Better Ways of Growing Up, rev. ed.* (Philadelphia, Fortress Press, 1964), pp. 77–78. Reprinted with permission. Fortress Press grants teachers permission to make copies of this questionnaire for use in connection with their own family life and sex education classes. On each reproduction the following copyright notice must be given: © 1964 by Fortress Press.

________ 5. I like to meet important persons.
________ 6. I think I am a shy person.
________ 7. The presence of important people does not make me self-conscious.
________ 8. Criticism usually makes me feel bad.
________ 9. I rarely feel nervous.
________10. It does not take much to make me blush.
________11. Seldom do I feel just miserable.
________12. When others disagree with me I feel discouraged.
________13. It takes more than praise to convince me I am succeeding.
________14. I often go out of my way to avoid meeting someone.
________15. I usually solve my problems without help.
________16. Others seem to want to take advantage of me.
________17. I do not experience feelings of inferiority.
________18. A good sales talk makes it hard for me to say "No."
________19. My feelings are not easily hurt.
________20. Many times I have ups and downs of mood.
________21. I would not mind making an important speech in public.
________22. I get stage fright easily.
________23. Having someone watch me work does not disturb me.
________24. Scoffing and teasing make me uncertain of myself.
________25. I think I am fairly self-confident.

Document 9-3 ***How Self-Reliant Am I?***

Answer the following items true or false.

________ 1. I enjoy spending a few hours by myself.
________ 2. My most difficult problems I prefer to study out by myself.
________ 3. I try to match the success of other people.
________ 4. In a difficult situation I do not like to take a chance alone.

Document 9-3, *How Self-Reliant Am I?*, is taken from John and Dorathea Crawford, *Better Ways of Growing Up*, rev. ed. (Philadelphia, Fortress Press, 1964), pp. 78–79. Reprinted with permission.

_______ 5. When I am ill I prefer to get along without company.
_______ 6. When I feel "down" I do not seek someone to cheer me.
_______ 7. I welcome advice when I make plans or work on hard jobs.
_______ 8. I often seek company when I feel sad.
_______ 9. I prefer not to share my responsibilities with others.
_______10. If I feel I am needed, I am always inclined to help.
_______11. I often feel a need to be with other people.
_______12. I do not like to make important decisions for myself.
_______13. I do not need close supervision to keep me hard at work.
_______14. My political and social views are a result of my own reading and thinking.
_______15. I usually seek advice when in difficulty.
_______16. I much prefer to work with others than by myself.
_______17. I usually need less outside help and advice now than I used to need when thinking through important plans and decisions.
_______18. My best qualities are not brought out by being part of a group.
_______19. Games and sports interest me much more than books.
_______20. I have difficulty in becoming completely absorbed in my work.
_______21. Generally I can get more ideas from books than from discussion.
_______22. Asking questions of the speaker at a meeting does not embarrass me.
_______23. Working very long in a solitary place would bother me.
_______24. A group party entertains me much more than books or movies.
_______25. I would not mind assuming responsibility for a companion while traveling.

Document 9-4 ***Some Problems That Trouble Teenagers***

1. Shyness: Do I keep to myself too much? Am I afraid to meet people? Would I rather not go to parties?
2. Nervous habits: Do I feel jittery at times? Do I often feel keyed-up? Do I play with jewelry or other things to reduce the tension when I am talking?

Document 9-4, *Some Problems That Trouble Teenagers,* is taken from John and Dorathea Crawford, *Better Ways of Growing Up,* rev. ed. (Philadelphia, Fortress Press, 1964), pp. 37–38. Reprinted with permission. Fortress Press grants teachers permission to make copies of this questionnaire for use in connection with their own family life and sex education classes. On each reproduction the following copyright notice must be given: © 1964 by Fortress Press.

3. Nail biting: Do I fuss with my nails or bite them? Does a rough nail make me want to bite it smooth right then?
4. Speech defects: Do I stutter at times? Do certain words make me feel that I will stutter on them when I have to talk?
5. Feelings of differentness: Do I feel too different from others? Am I too tall, too fat, too short, too thin? Do I feel my clothes are too shabby? Am I embarrassed about my family?
6. Feeling of inferiority: Do I secretly think I am not as good as others in some way? Do these feelings stay with me long?
7. Sense of shame: Do I have guilty feelings about myself? Do I think I am a bad person? Am I secretly ashamed of myself?
8. Jealousy: Am I jealous of anyone? Does the green-eyed dragon trail me around very often?
9. Worry and anxiety: Am I a worrier? Do I lie awake thinking about my problems? Do tough problems disturb my appetite?
10. Unfriendliness: Do I have few real friends? Do I feel that friends are a waste of time? Do I like to be alone much of the time?
11. Discouragement: Do I seldom seem to get a break? Do many of the things I want in life seem beyond my power to attain?
12. Loneliness: Do I often feel lonely? Do I sometimes feel strangely alone even when I am with others?
13. Daydreaming: Do I spend much time daydreaming? Do I spend too much time building castles in the air about my plans for the future?
14. Bragging: Do I brag? Do I think I am better than other people in certain ways and let them know it?
15. Moodiness: Do I have gloomy spells? Do I often feel depressed? Do my moods seem to swing rapidly?
16. Fear: Do I fear certain things so much that even thinking about them for awhile makes me feel afraid?
17. Irritability: Do I lose my temper easily? Am I easily moved to tears or anger? Do I have many grouchy spells?
18. Pouting: Do I remain angry long? Do I hold grudges? Do I pout about things that do not please me?
19. Sense of failure: Do I feel that I have been a failure? Do I think there is little chance of success in life for me?
20. Sensitivity: Are my feelings too easily hurt? Am I too sensitive about certain things? Do I blush too easily?

Document 9-5 **Dating: Going Steady**

Before you start to work define your terms. What do you mean when you talk about "going steady"?

Let's find out if people differ in their definitions of "going steady." Make your own survey, asking two girls ages 14–15, two boys ages 14–15, two girls ages 17–18, two boys ages 17–18, and two parents besides your own, for their definitions.

14–15-year-old girls:

14–15-year-old boys:

17–18-year-old girls:

17–18-year-old boys:

Parents:

My own parents:

My conclusion:

Document 9-6 **Going Steady**

Going steady usually means dating only one person exclusively. Various reasons are given by young people as to why they go steady:

1. *Date Insurance.* If you go steady you are sure of a date when you want one. You are sure of having a date on Saturday night. You are sure of having a date for the school dances.
2. *Group Acceptance.* Everybody goes steady if they can. Going steady is the thing to do.
3. *Social Pressure.* If you date the same person twice, the crowd says

---

you are going steady. They won't believe you when you say you are not, so it's easier just to go steady.

4. *Personal Security.* Going steady is a lot easier than going out with different people. You know how to talk with your steady. Your parents know who your steady is and let you date more often. If you date often you are popular.
5. *Mutual Preference.* You like each other and don't want to date anyone else.
6. *Mature Adjustment.* When you go steady you get to know the person very well and it helps you learn how to adjust and understand people.
7. *Less Expensive.* When you go steady you don't always have to go someplace special. You can just go out for a coke or hamburger instead of going for dinner. You don't have to impress each other by going to fancy places. You go where you want to just because you like to be together. It's easier for a boy and a girl to split the cost of a date if they go steady. On an ordinary date the boy is expected to pay for everything.

Some of the problems that may be caused by going steady may be:

1. Going steady limits your social contacts.
2. Going steady interferes with your schoolwork and takes up a lot of time.
3. Going steady sometimes gets you into trouble sexually.
4. It is hard to break up with your steady.

Document 9-7 **The Physical Aspects of Necking and Petting**

When you're out on a date you generally have to cope with the fact that you're a girl and he's a boy. It starts with kissing . . .

There are lots of kinds of kisses, as Shakespeare observed. There are the simple affectionate greetings you give your family and friends. There are the tentative, shy good-night kisses that come with early dating; the warm kiss that says, "I like you very much" to a boy you've dated often.

It seems you've hardly gotten straightened out about how you feel about this kind of kiss—the simple "I like you, I hope you like me" kiss—when you've got another kind to worry about. This is the "I like to kiss you, and I want to kiss you more" kind of kiss.

The emotions that this kind of kiss stirs are not simple and straightforward and uncomplicated. This kiss evokes more than a simple exchange of pleasant thoughts; it is an exchange of physical feelings, and it leads quite naturally to a big subject: kissing and petting.

A boy is "aroused" or stirred physically by a great many things; his body was designed that way. He can be stimulated by such indirect things as smell or sight. Even an intangible thing like a dream has the power to arouse his sex organs to physical release.

A girl is built differently—it usually takes a good deal of direct physical contact to create in her an urgent need for complete sexual union. "Now, wait a minute," you say. "How did we get so quickly from a subject like 'kissing and petting' to 'intercourse?' "

We're not being too hasty, really. Because kissing and petting are physical contacts perfectly designed to arouse both a boy and a girl. They are the first steps in intercourse. And that's why they have to be kept under constant and firm control.

If kissing stopped at kissing, if petting stopped at petting—there'd be no problem. You could kiss your steady date for hours, or until bored; keep things at a kissing level for the months or years you were "going steady," and have a nice, warm, friendly time of it.

The trouble is, your body has a hundred different signals for "go ahead" and not many for "let's stop." Your mouth has nerves which are stimulated by kissing; your tongue has more. It's natural to embrace someone when you kiss—and when you hold someone, it's natural to touch them, to stroke them, and to fondle them. When your emotions are involved in he–she thoughts, the fondling turns naturally to the he–she areas of the body. You are no longer expressing a simple "I like you." You are now saying, "I like your body." This is physical love-making—and everything about it prepares your bodies for the union which is the climax of physical love-making.

Just as a first, light kiss led to one with greater meaning, and then to petting, so petting urges you on to the next step.

There's another factor involved. It often urges you *at a different rate* from the urgency the boy is feeling.

You may think you have everything under control. You're enjoying the pleasure of petting, and feeling very mature and womanly—when suddenly you realize again that in boy-and-girl relationships *two* people are involved, and it takes *two* to keep control. The boy you're petting with is aroused faster—and loses control faster. His need for physical release is stronger than his concern for you, or his own desire for self-control. You've petted too far and it takes all your strength to get things back on an even keel.

Don't underestimate your own capacity for passion. Once stirred, a woman has a physical urgency that rivals a man's in its single-minded drive toward completion. You're a big girl now, if you're petting, and you must know yourself. You're playing with fire if you're telling yourself, "I can go so far—and no farther—any time, without trouble."

For sooner or later, the girl who is aroused and excited by petting will be faced with a choice. She must make up her mind about an old-fashioned-sounding word that is as modern as today: chastity.

The teen years, in some ways, might be called the chip-on-the-shoulder time of your life. You're testing all the theories you've learned in childhood, and weighing the standards of the adult world against your new-grown maturity. Your restless body and mind lead you to question everything you hear and read and learn and see; you question politics and religion and your parents and sex. And you find that most of your skepticism leads only to a new appreciation of accepted standards.

Take cheating, for instance. In grade school you learned not to cheat, and you didn't cheat, because your parents and the teacher said not to. Somewhere in your early teens, you noticed that there were some kids who cheated with what seemed nonchalance, and who seemed to profit by it. But sooner or later you noticed that not only did they lose out in the long run—because they never did learn a subject for themselves—but they lost the respect of their classmates. By observing, and learning, you learned *for yourself* that cheating doesn't make sense. Perhaps you even tried a little cheating yourself, only to learn that it pays off in the bitter coin of self-disappointment and the humiliating fear of "being caught."

Earlier in this book we talked about some things that were worth questioning and knowing about—but which could and should be learned by observation or by example *only*—things where actual experience, instead of helping your knowledge, would only hurt *you*.

We called them the *permanent* mistakes, the mistakes whose effects are felt long after your teen years; too much alcohol and the use of drugs were the two mistakes we meant when we said there are some things you should learn just on say-so, not by experience. (Sitting on a hot stove to learn if you'd really get burned is another example!)

At some point during your dating years, if you're a reasonably active teen-ager, you can make another permanent mistake—the kind you live with all your life, the kind that leads not to growth but to trouble. The mistake is the loss of chastity.

Well, aren't we *stuffy*, you may be thinking. Here we are, practically thrown together with boys, alone in parked cars and petting-pit drive-ins—perfect setups for the loss of chastity. Ads and magazines and books plug sex; they suggest that life isn't life if it isn't filled with sex activity; sex feels good, and besides isn't a teen supposed to drink of life to the full and try every new experience? Go back to the dark ages, with your talk about *chastity*. That word hasn't been used in years.

Well, we've got news for *you*. The word may be dated, but the principle isn't.

Refraining from sexual union before marriage is, in this age of sex-absorption and individual freedom, a disturbingly difficult assignment. Our society is set up so that marriage usually isn't possible until *after* the teens. Most young men and women can't accept the responsibility of marriage until they have their first job although—and this is what makes for the strain and difficulty—their bodies are ready for marriage while they are still in high school.

But let's go back to what we learned about intercourse. You'll remember that men and women had their sex drive built in, in order to insure the world enough babies to go around. Nature's purpose for intercourse is the conception of a child—the continuity of the human race. We don't deny the tender, the poetic, the haunting emotional accompaniments of the act of love. But nature, in this instance, is no respecter of poetry. Nature takes no chances and sees to it that the physical drive, once under way, is difficult to reverse! This means that after the first steps of intercourse (you call it petting) a woman's body is driving toward union with a male; it *wants* complete fulfillment.

If petting is stopped at this point, there is both physical and emotional frustration. The glands were getting themselves all worked up—and suddenly there's a let-down. Not only is there a physical reaction, but an emotional one as well—and that's why steady daters who pet frequently are often filled with strains and tensions. By working themselves up to fever pitch and then applying the brakes, the couple produce their own misery. Repeated over and over, this builds up tension to a degree that is hard for a teen-ager to handle.

Sooner or later if you date a boy steadily and frequently, and pet enthusiastically, one of the petters won't want to apply the brakes, and will demand the next stage—actual intercourse up to the point of climax but no actual union—either because the male sperm is ejected outside the body or because a physical device is used to prevent conception.

We would make quite a case for chastity right here by pointing out that despite the wonders of modern science, despite your own faith in your self-control and ability to stop at a given point, you are by no means "protected" from pregnancy by such methods of "controlling" intercourse. Many a girl who considered herself "smart" in her indulgence in sex finds, too late, that she has made a permanent mistake.

Pregnancy outside marriage is a mistake because it hurts you and the child, your family, and the man who is the father of the child. Only a very irresponsible or immature person can ignore these responsibilities; only a selfish teen could pretend that such a pregnancy "didn't matter." So perhaps one of the most practical arguments for chastity is simply this: any *one* act of intercourse (even if it's your *first* mistake) can lead to the permanent mistake of an unplanned and unwanted pregnancy outside of marriage.

Document 9-8 ***Premarital Sexual Involvement Levels***

I. Transitory Relationship—No Affectionate Involvement

Transitory relationships are generally formed to satisfy curiosity or to achieve personal satisfaction and do not take into account the other person's needs. The relationships may be with a prostitute or a casual pickup. With boys in early or mid-adolescence, the significant relationships usually involve sexual curiosity. The sexual partner is simply a person with whom they became involved while satisfying their curiosity. Also, boys may engage in intercourse for the purpose of impressing others, since they are often very reluctant to admit that they have not had intercourse. There may be a disturbing degree of crassness in such relationships, and they may be very unsatisfying sexually. Guilt may easily result from conflict between the boy's behavior and his basic values.

Sexual curiosity is less frequent among girls because of culture inhibitions and because chances of severe disapproval are greater than for boys. Girls are more likely to engage in casual sexual intercourse in an effort to attract and hold a boy. If the behavior of a person, either male or female, remains at the transitory level, it probably reflects some emotional problem, particularly a difficulty in forming permanent, deep heterosexual relationships.

II. Relationship with Acquaintance

If a sexual relationship at this level occurs when the partners are fifteen or sixteen, there is likely to be minimal emotional involvement. As it occurs at later ages, the likelihood of emotional involvement is increased. Boys often enter into relationships at this level for pleasure and for group prestige. Girls are more likely to enter intercourse to please the boy and to

---

Document 9-8, *Premarital Sexual Involvement Levels,* is based on findings reported in *Premarital Intercourse and Interpersonal Relationships,* by Lester A. Kirkendall (New York, Julian Press, 1961). Dr. Kirkendall grants teachers permission to make copies of this document for use in connection with their own family life and sex education classes.

insure the continuation of the relationship. The girl's eagerness to have a boyfriend and get married predisposes her to "fall" in love before the boy is ready for this depth of involvement. The consequence is a one-sided attachment, the breaking of which is often traumatic.

III. Relationship Based upon Deep Emotional Involvement

Generally speaking, individuals who engage in intercourse at this level are in their late teens or older. The couple is frequently concerned with expressing their affection, and intercourse provides this opportunity. They may also be testing their sexual adjustment. With younger couples a limited capacity for communication, an inability to handle criticism, or other possible negative consequences may make it difficult, even impossible, to maintain stability in their relationship. Since strong physical attraction is assumed to be characteristic of deeply affectionate couples, they must communicate freely about their sexual feelings and the circumstances they face. Otherwise sexual involvement may place too great a strain on their relationship, causing it to break.

Document 9-9 ***Discussion Guide: The Double Standard***

Under the traditional double standard, more sexual freedom is given to men than to women. Men are permitted to have sexual intercourse before marriage and are not criticized, but women are sharply criticized for this behavior.

The developing equality and independence of women in America has caused the traditional double standard to be weakened. The double standard has also been weakened by a growing awareness that while the sexual drive does have a biological basis, the method of its expression is learned. Men and boys now realize that they do have a choice of sexual expression, that they may remain chaste or virginal before marriage if they so desire.

The notion that our sexual problems would disappear by completely eliminating the double standard and having a standard of complete freedom is frequently suggested. But consider the impact of complete freedom.

> Think how different it would have been for you if your father had felt free to take up with any woman he wanted, and your mother to sleep with any man she found attractive! How would this have affected your whole family living? What would it have meant in the love and affection shown you by your parents? How different would your father's attitude have been toward any of your brothers or sisters if he had not been sure that they were

---

his children? How different would you have felt toward your parents if you were not quite sure who they really were?

Consider, not only your own family, but your world. Suppose that overnight most of our present standards were to disappear. For one thing, you teenage boys at once would be in terrific competition with older men who have been around more, have more money, can do more things, and are still attractive. They would quickly take over the most attractive girls of your age group. As to the women, long before they were forty most of them would be ditched in favor of the "Newer models." Need we go on? Would you like to live in that kind of world? What kind of world does your own sex conduct help to build?[1]

According to M. B. Loeb, a sociologist who conducted a study of sexual behavior among junior and senior high school students,

> Teenagers who trust themselves and their ability to contribute to others and who have learned to rely on others socially and emotionally are least likely to be involved in irresponsible sexual activity.
>
> Teenagers who have learned to be comfortable in their appropriate sex roles (boys who like being boys and wish to be men, and girls who like being girls and wish to be women) are least likely to be involved in activities leading to indiscriminate sexuality."[2]

[1] Evelyn M. and Sylvanus M. Duvall, *Sense and Nonsense About Sex* (New York, Association Press [Reflection Book], 1962), p. 105.

[2] Lester A. Kirkendall and Arthur E. Gravath, "Teen-Agers' Sex Attitudes and Behavior," in Evelyn M. and Sylvanus M. Duvall, eds., *Sex Ways—in Fact and Faith: Bases for Christian Family Policy* (New York, Association Press, 1961) p. 122.

Document 9-10 ***The Great Debate: Sexual Intercourse Before Marriage***

It should be easy to give a categorical answer. The devout of any religious faith can reply without hesitation. Our grandfathers had two answers, "Yes" for boys and "No" for girls. In their day and in their own grandparents' time boys were expected to "sow their wild oats" before they married and settled down—with wives who came to the altar virgins, never with partners in oat-sowing.

When you come to think of it, they had something! They did not confuse sexuality with love and marriage. Now that woman has discovered that she too is capable of sexual desire and sexual enjoyment, everything has

---

become tangled up. New methods believed to avert pregnancy and the great scientific strides recently made in the cure of those twin deterrents—syphilis and gonorrhea—have added to the confusion.

In this chapter, therefore, we will take a look at the problem on all sides and present the information now available, so that boys and girls can make for themselves the decision which they feel is right.

First of all, let us accept this fact: sexual appetite can and does exist without love. Physical union is a wonderful and satisfying part of a happy marriage but marriage is not successful merely because a wife is seductive or a husband is a competent lover. In marriage love comes first. With love sexual adaptability and adjustment is possible even for the totally inexperienced.

The human being is unique among all living things; man alone knows the lofty emotion of love, and he is also the only being capable of sexual activity without regard for its procreative purpose. In other creatures there is a season when the female is receptive and the male is then—and only then—stimulated. But woman is always capable of physical receptivity and man's sexual desire is sparked by many different forces—a strain of music, a special fragrance, a passing embrace, or merely uninvited and unexpected thoughts. His response is complicated by religious training, moral codes, the attitudes of his associates, his ideas about its relation to his lifelong virility and health, and its part in love and marriage. Without any of the simple directed forces established by Nature for the other species, people have to decide to what extent they should satisfy their sex drives, why, and for what purpose.

Physical union before marriage is very, very seldom a preview of sexual love within marriage. When it is one of many promiscuous encounters, to the boy it is merely an exciting sensual episode during which he is interested only in his own satisfaction. It has no other meaning, no past, no future. It does not involve present liking or future friendship. To some boys it is comparable to gulping a long drink of water when they are thirsty. In others, especially younger boys, it may leave an after-taste of shame or disgust or worry about inadequate technique or abilities. This can affect their sexual relations for years, even for life.

Document 9-11 ***Homosexuality***

In sexual development, as in many other areas of a person's life, difficult problems may arise. One of the most common problems is homosexuality.

"What is homosexuality?" and "Who is homosexual?" are not easy questions to answer because the opinions of experts and the evidence from scientific research vary. It is, however, commonly agreed that homosexuality refers to sexual attraction to a person of the same sex and includes relations between females as well as between males. We may define homosexuals, therefore, as adult individuals, male or female, whose sexual interests are predominantly directed toward members of their own sex, in contrast with normal heterosexuals, individuals who are sexually interested in members of the opposite sex. The term "lesbian" is commonly applied to homosexual females, while the term for homosexual males is simply "homosexual." To call a person homosexual who has had a few homosexual experiences is false and can be harmful to him.

Homosexuality has been known throughout human history and occurs in many societies. There is evidence that homosexuality is relatively widespread in our society, although it is not approved, condoned, or encouraged for males or females of any age. It is often stated that homosexuality is increasing in our society. There is no evidence on which to base such a statement. It is not known whether homosexual behavior has actually increased, is increasing, or has merely become more obvious. Certainly an increase in numbers of homosexuals is to be expected as the population increases, but whether this is reflected in an increasing rate of homosexual behavior, or even possibly in a decreasing rate, cannot be determined without more accurate scientific data than are now available. Under present social conditions it is very difficult to obtain such data.

Can homosexuals be easily identified? The answer is no. It is a common misconception that men who appear physically feminine or girlish, women who appear physically mannish, and generally any persons who have characteristics usually attributed to the opposite sex are homosexuals. Scientific studies have demonstrated that most real homosexuals do not differ in physical appearance or manner from individuals with normal sexual impulses.

What causes homosexuality? There is no single cause. Many psychological, social, cultural, and biological conditions have been investigated in scientific studies in an effort to discover the combinations that cause homosexuality. The causal effects of heredity (genetics), constitutional, glandular, or other biological factors in producing homosexuality have not been demonstrated, but some of the evidence suggests that they may have an indirect influence. Homosexuality is not innate; no person is born with homosexual characteristics. Scientific studies have shown that combinations of psychological, social, and cultural conditions appear to be the primary causal factors. Many authorities in the field state that disturbed parent–child relationships are the primary causes, but scientific studies have not provided the necessary proof for this statement. The most commonly stated theory is that the combination of a dominant, controlling, and possessive mother and a detached, hostile, or indifferent father will cause their son to become homosexual or to have homosexual problems. This same parent–child relationship is found in the family background of normal adults.

Occasional sexual interest in others of the same sex or periods of great interest frequently occur in adolescents who do not become homosexuals in adult life. If you are troubled by such interests or fear that they may develop, it would be wise to talk with a trustworthy adult such as a parent, counselor, teacher, or school nurse, who can help you to understand your feelings and to develop effective methods of coping with your concerns. During adolescence, boys and girls may also be troubled if approached by homosexuals because they fear that a contact or an overt sexual experience with a homosexual may cause them to become homosexual. Authorities agree that such fears have little basis in fact. Normally developing students will not be seriously affected by isolated experiences. However, if approached, the best policy is to indicate firmly that you are not interested and walk away from the situation. Boys may feel especially threatened and want to display their masculinity by attacking homosexuals. Violent physical actions are unnecessary. If lack of interest is made very clear, homosexuals will not persist in their attentions.

Can homosexuality be cured? Not all authorities agree that homosexuality is a disease. Thus, the question should be stated: "Can homosexuals be changed?" Yes. A certain number have been changed by individual and group psychotherapy. In adolescence, individuals may prematurely believe that they are homosexual and accept that as fact because of intense interest in members of their own sex and overt sexual practices with them. Thus, they may believe that efforts to change are useless. Such pessimism is unwarranted; but psychotherapy is more effective in younger age groups. The prognosis, or success prediction, for adult homosexuals with a long-established pattern of exclusive homosexual behavior is not too encouraging at the present time. The Wolfenden Committee (a committee of experts appointed by the British Parliament some years ago) concluded that homosexuality is not a symptom of mental illness. Some homosexuals are mentally ill, but the evidence indicates that the illness may be caused not only by the strains and conflicts brought about by the homosexual condition, but also by repressive legal and moral laws.

What are the laws regarding homosexuality? Homosexual acts are legally classified as crimes in all states except Illinois. The Wolfenden Committee in England, and in the United States the American Law Institute (a high-level body of legal scholars that concerns itself with theoretical law), have recommended that private sexual behavior between consenting adults should be removed from the list of crimes, regardless of how it is morally considered. Although church opinion is divided, a number of churchmen support these recommendations. Such a revision has been made in Illinois law and is under consideration in other states.[1] The arguments for change in the law are: (1) the exposure of the homosexual to blackmail and other forms of harassment; (2) the encouragement of unfair enforcement procedures; and (3) the effect on the homosexual himself: the demoralizing and humiliating behavior into which he is pushed. The arguments for maintaining the laws against homosexual acts are: (1) it is "unnatural" and immoral; (2) relaxation of laws may lead to greater sympathy for homosexuality and result in a serious threat to the role of the family in society. It is generally agreed that laws against homosexual acts do not prevent homosexuality.

How can homosexuality be prevented? An excellent summary of the major recommendations by two research experts in the field is provided by Dr. Isadore Rubin.[2] According to Dr. Evelyn Hooker, "Preventive efforts should focus on: (1) creating a climate of opinion that will allow homosexuality to be openly and reasonably discussed and objectively handled; (2) providing for adequate sex education of both parents and children, so that the homosexual can understand himself better and the community can free itself of its punitive attitudes toward all sexuality; and (3) increasing efforts to provide family counseling and child guidance services designed not only to promote healthy family life, but also to provide specific help for parents whose children show early signs of developmental difficulties, before these become fixed." According to Dr. Edwin Schur, "It seems likely that major alterations of social structure and culture would be necessary in order to reduce homosexuality to any significant degree."

[1] Isadore Rubin, *Homosexuality* (New York, Sex Information and Education Council of the United States, 1965).
[2] *Ibid.*

Document 9-12 **Exhibitionism**

Another sexual deviation a young person may encounter is exhibitism. Exhibitionists are adult men or adolescents who show their sex organs to women or girls. The exposure is most commonly made at a distance, and the great majority do not molest or harm anyone. The urge to exhibit oneself in this way is a symptom of mental illness. The most common variety of

---

exhibitionists repeat the behavior again and again in compulsive fashion.[1] In about half of the cases studied, the repetitive exhibitors began between sixteen and twenty-five years of age.

If an adolescent boy discovers that he has such urges or impulses, he should seek counsel with a trustworthy adult so that he may have help in coping with the problem. If a girl should see an exhibitionist, she should leave immediately and report the event so that the man may be found and be given psychiatric treatment. It would also be helpful to her to discuss the situation, and her own feelings about it, with an adult in whom she has confidence.

[1] P. Gebhard, et al., *Sex Offenders* (New York, Harper & Row, 1965).

Document 9-13 **Drinking**

Whether to drink or not to drink is a serious decision faced by many young teenagers. If a person has been reared in a family that considers alcohol in any form immoral and sinful, he either accepts these beliefs or deliberately goes against his parents' wishes. If he is reared in a family that includes an untreated alcoholic he will have seen the effects of uncontrolled drinking and most likely will never touch liquor. These are extremes. In many homes alcoholic beverages may be served to adults on special occasions or they may have them frequently in moderation. Attitudes toward the serving of alcoholic beverages vary within families, social groups, and churches.

Unfortunately many people believe that liquor is a stimulant. This is not true. Liquor is a depressant—more like an anesthetic. Liquor depresses the nervous system, particularly the part of the brain that acts as a restraint on good judgment. The reason some persons may feel better after a drink is that some of their shyness or uncomfortable feelings have been dulled. For instance, one boy who would not ask a girl to dance because he was afraid she would laugh at his lack of skill took a drink and found that he could walk right up to a girl and ask her for a dance. The boy's dancing skill was not improved but he was no longer self-conscious about it. He was no longer afraid the girl might laugh at him. If he had more than one drink he would probably have felt sleepy and not wanted to dance or talk. How valid is courage that comes out of a bottle? Does it enhance personal growth?

Nowadays everyone is aware that drinking affects your nervous system and your physical coordination. The newspapers have almost daily articles about tragic automobile accidents caused by drivers who have been drinking. It is a serious highway safety problem in our society today. Even a small quantity of alcohol will interfere with your attention, concentration, and judgment.

Most teenagers know that liquor slows down physical efficiency. Drinking and sports do not go together. Professional athletes who want to be in top form do not drink.

Dating and drinking also can cause problems. While alcohol does not make the sexual urge stronger, as you may have been led to believe, it does reduce your self-control. Even a couple who have discussed the problems of petting and have agreed not to risk engaging in it because their desires might be so aroused that they would be carried too far should not risk drinking. The effects of liquor could cause the girl to become relaxed and her judgment dulled, while at the same time the couple may forget about their agreement regarding the risks of petting. The lost of self-control on the part of the boy will cause him to make his demands for sexual intercourse very insistent. This happens frequently. The other problem caused by drinking while dating is the fact that while excessive drinking may render a boy sexually incapable while he is under the influence of liquor, the girl only needs to become submissive; the more she drinks, the more likely she is to accept sexual intercourse. The emotional situation gets out of hand and causes serious problems for the boy and the girl.

People drink for a number of reasons. The most common reason for beginning to drink is social pressure. If everyone else seems to be doing it, it is easier to conform than to be different. While many people continue to drink to conform to the friends' actions, others may continue to drink to escape from problems or to help them overcome shyness in social situations.

Use of alcoholic liquors is legal for adults in almost all states, and social drinking is a widespread custom in America. But the decision whether to drink or not to drink is an individual matter that usually is decided during the teenage years.

Document 9-14 ***Tips for Nondrinkers***

Whether you wish to drink or not, as a teenager, you will encounter a great many situations where your "dry" status is put to a strong test. But there are also more good reasons for not drinking than ever before.

"My church is opposed to my drinking. Please excuse me." "Too many calories. I'll never fit into my new formal." "You're so much fun to be with, who needs it?" "I'll have a rum-and-coke without the rum please." "Maybe some other time. I'm in training." (You could hint it's for the Olympics. It's unpatriotic to lead an Olympic contender astray.) "No thanks. The guide book says it's safe to drink the water here." "I'm allergic to the stuff . . . Break out in hideous hives." (Hint that it is contagious.) "When they make beer taste better than strawberry malteds, I'll switch." As long as you don't go around smashing bottles and chopping up saloons with your hatchet, your friends will respect your decision.

The drinkers who won't let you alone are the ones who feel there really is something wrong about what they're doing. They're the ones who tell you that you must, because everybody's doing it. And they fervently wish everybody would, so they'd have more people to hide behind when the finger points.

Document 9-15 **Venereal Disease**

What are the venereal diseases? First, they are infectious diseases. Syphilis and gonorrhea are the two common venereal diseases in this country. All are contracted almost exclusively by sexual intercourse. The old belief that VD could be caught in public wash basins or toilets or by handling dishes, bed linens, or other personal items used by an infected person is virtually untrue. The germs that cause syphilis and gonorrhea die very quickly when they are exposed to the air. They also die immediately when touched by soap and water. They require the special conditions inside the human body to survive and multiply, so that only the most unusual combination of circumstances make it possible for VD to be transmitted except through very intimate sexual contact.

What are the symptoms of syphilis and gonorrhea? In the early stages of both diseases, shortly after the germs have entered the body, a few minor symptoms may occur. If the symptoms are recognized and given medical attention immediately, both diseases can be cured. BUT—and this is a big but—the diseases are made more dangerous because these few early symptoms can be very minor or, worse, may not appear at all. After the first stage—from three to six weeks—the germs go into hiding for as long as twenty years, gradually multiplying and destroying body cells. Eventually, damage to the body becomes evident and disability, if not death, may result.

Venereal disease is not, as so many people think, limited to prostitutes. Nor is it limited to such groups as the uneducated. A venereal disease can be carried by anyone.

Few young people recognize the dangers or know that a cure—in the early stages—is available. It can't be too strongly emphasized that prompt detection and medical attention can bring complete and permanent cure.

Any unusual soreness or discharge from the genital organs (outside sex organs) should be shown to a doctor immediately. The genital area is quite susceptible to other infections which occasionally show symptoms that look like VD, but are actually minor infections. An examination, along with a simple test, will show if they are symptoms of syphilis or gonorrhea. Shame and embarrassment often stop a young person from seeing a doctor. But doctors are, after all, trained to fight disease, not to stand in judgment. They are also trained, and can certainly be trusted, to protect the privacy of their patients.

Your local health department is equipped to diagnose and treat venereal disease. Most health departments will treat teenagers without parental permission or notifying the parent. This service is free and the privacy of the patient is protected. All records are also confidential. There is no reason for anyone to ignore possible danger signals of venereal disease.

Document 9-16 **Dear Abby**

Dear Abby,

I love my boyfriend very much. I don't know what to do. He keeps insisting that I smoke marijuana with him on our dates. How can I make him stop? I don't want to lose him.

Scared

Dear Abby,

I have had a bad trip. My girlfriend is mad at me. She says I can't be a father. Is it true? What can I do to get her back?

Worried

Dear Abby,

I don't drink but I do smoke pot now and then. It makes me feel good. I don't hurt anyone. Why do adults get so upset? My parents are threatening to have me busted. How can I convince them that I am not doing anything harmful?

Can't Understand

part IV

suggested content for senior high school

chapter **10**

suggested content for the tenth grade

Introduction: Senior High School

Senior high school students are approaching the end of the adolescent period of their lives. They will still seem immature and dependent in many situations, but at other times they will show increasing independence and often surprising maturity in thought and judgment. Wide variations in the maturity of individual students is to be expected in each class.

One of the biggest adjustments that senior high school students must make successfully is in response to the changes that are taking place within them. The boy should reach full acceptance of himself as a man, the girl should achieve acceptance of herself as a woman, and both should come to understand the roles they will play as men and women. They must discover their strengths and weaknesses, their interests and aptitudes, as they approach the time when childhood and its daydreams are replaced by the real possibilities of adult life.

High school students, either in pairs or groups, will talk long, earnestly, and heatedly about their interests and problems if given the opportunity. The dialogue-centered classroom is accordingly the major teaching technique available to the high school teacher. Student involvement—every student on every topic—is the key to the development of positive attitudes and behavior. Although the sex education materials are particularly sensitive, other topics that seem to be less emotionally charged for the group as a whole may have a special significance for some students. Such students may have to make a great effort to be able to join the rest of the class in an objective, rational study and discussion of the topics, but it is important that they take part.

The senior high school content is based on the foundation developed in the junior high school classes. The concepts discussed in previous classes should now be related and drawn together to focus on the concept of an *effective* family unit. The students should be encouraged to continue the use of the problem-solving method first introduced in the eighth grade. The method is examined in greater depth in the eleventh-grade unit.

The problems of achieving honest and effective communication form a thread that weaves throughout all the units and receives major emphasis in the eleventh grade.

High school students are still concerned with the problems of dating and want to study them further. Many more students will begin to date when they obtain their driver's licenses and access to a car. It is important to continue the study of human sexuality. Although most of the students' questions of a biological nature will have been answered in previous classes, they need to review their knowledge to clear up any misconceptions they may have. High school students are also still developing their own value system and moral codes, and they need additional opportunities to discuss and question the behavior they observe.

Young people make mistakes while learning, and it is important that they learn how to redeem themselves if they have broken their moral standards of premarital chastity. The classroom will serve as an effective laboratory for encouraging behavior that will improve interpersonal relationships if the teacher is sensitive to the opportunities.

The central themes of the senior high school units of study are: (1) Every individual is responsible for his own moral behavior. This behavior should be directed at creating effective interpersonal relationships in the home, the community, and the world. (2) Sex is a part of life, and it can be understood only within a framework of personal values. (3) Successful marriages are created, not conferred. The curriculum outlines come full circle when the twelfth-grade unit concludes with a section entitled "How To Teach My Child About Sex."

Obviously many classes will not have an opportunity to cover in depth each topic in the outlines to the satisfaction of each student; much depends on the number of sessions devoted to the family life and sex education program at each grade level.[1] The teacher must be continually alert to the

[1] In the Anaheim senior high schools, five weeks, that is, 25 class periods, were dedicated to the family life and sex education unit in each grade. More time is desirable, but there are many conflicting demands for time in every school, and the teacher must adjust his course to whatever time is finally allocated.

class's reactions and must be ready to move with the students to new topics of study.

The family life and sex education classes can be supplemented by other activities in the high school; for example, appropriate topics can be assigned for themes in English and for oral reports in speech, and the study of the population explosion can be undertaken in social studies. Close cooperation with all the school faculty will result in a vital, stimulating, and effective program in which the students' attitudes and behavior will be influenced to help them become more effective family members and citizens.

The following units are again adapted from the *Family Life and Sex Education Course Outline.*[2] The content and learning opportunities suggested are meant to be a realistic response to the challenge of the twentieth century. We feel that family life and sex education classes of this kind will help students become competent family members in our dynamic world, educate them so that their individual sexual natures contribute to their self-development and happiness, and make it possible for them to join in the task of conserving and advancing the welfare of American society, rather than striking out blindly and needlessly against it.

Overview: The Tenth-Grade Unit

In this unit the students are first oriented to the senior high school family life and sex education program. Dating is reviewed; some classes will be able to study it in depth, others will proceed quickly through this segment. Dating is now viewed as an aspect of mate selection as well as a social activity in its own right.

Choosing a marriage partner is one of the important decisions in life, and thus it is important to study the problem objectively. Marriage for most couples is a satisfying lifetime experience, but a successful marriage is the result of careful study before the wedding day and continued effort afterwards to make it work. Many facets of the marriage relationship have been identified by social science research. Knowledge of these research findings will help the student develop criteria about what attitudes and behavior to seek in a potential marriage partner. Our civilization is based on the stable family unit, yet the marriage failure rate has been steadily increasing, and, unfortunately, individuals who have failed once tend to

[2] Anaheim Union High School District, *Family Life and Sex Education Course Outline: Grades Seven Through Twelve* (Anaheim, Calif., 1965).

repeat their mistakes when they remarry. For this reason society has an important interest in seeing that young people are provided with the opportunity to become informed.

Sex manners and morals are included for study in greater detail. The concept that what each student does with his sex life matters to his family, his friends, his sex partner, and to himself should be emphasized. A section is included on learning from a mistake, because young people make many mistakes and they need to learn how to redeem themselves. The teacher is advised to discuss the most serious problems of individual students with the school counselor and jointly plan the most effective way to help these students.

Engagement is studied using the modern definition that it is a "testing period" rather than a "promise to marry." The factors to consider in choosing a marriage partner are also examined at this early grade, in recognition of the dropout problem. The unit concludes with the students assessing their readiness to marry and the characteristics of an ideal family.

Like all the high school family life and sex education units, the tenth-grade unit is designed to bring to the students' attention the current findings of research, to help them develop the ability to communicate honestly with the opposite sex, and to help you, their teacher, successfully guide their use of the scientific problem-solving technique to relate their sexuality to their total life. The students must be given the opportunity to question and seek answers to problems of living effectively, happily, and zestfully.

The basal text recommended is Landis and Landis' *Personal Adjustment, Marriage, and Family Living,* with extensive use of Duvall's *Why Wait Till Marriage?*, Bossard and Boll's *The Girl That You Marry,* and Boll's *The Man That You Marry.*

Curriculum Outlines

Instructional Objectives

The student understands that:

1. Understanding human sexuality helps one to live more effectively.
2. Selecting a marriage partner is one of life's important choices.
3. Our society has special laws and ceremonies to indicate the change of status from single to married life.
4. Being in love is more than being physically attracted to someone.
5. There are certain desirable characteristics of an effective family.
6. Male and female roles are constantly changing in our culture.

Content

Orientation and Review

A. Review briefly the material covered in the junior high school classes.

B. Begin the orientation to senior high school classes.

1. Goals and objectives
2. Concepts
3. Content
4. Method of presentation and operation of the class
5. Materials to be used

Suggested Learning Opportunities

- Ask students to write a brief review and evaluation of their junior high family life and sex education classes.
- Ask the class to list the topics they would like to discuss in class. Collect the lists, compile a master list, determine the priority of the topics, and submit the list to the class.
- Show the filmstrip *Values for Teenagers: The Choice Is Yours* to stimulate and reorient the class to small group discussion techniques.

Content

Dating

A. Dating becomes mate selection.

1. Dating is an education in the discovery of emotions and their control. Sexual urges, unruly tempers, and needs for affection come to the fore out of the new experiences of dating relations. Participants come to find that gestures of affection enrich their relations if tied in with the discovery of common interests and goals. Out of dating should come not only the ability to love and be loved, but constructive ways to show affection as well. Dating has value in training young people in the art of democratic give and take. Girls today are allowed more initiative in dating than they were in old-fashioned courting days. This equalitarian relationship carries over into later courtship, engagment, and marriage relations and makes for a more democratic marriage and family life.
2. Dating offers excellent oppor-

Suggested Learning Opportunities

- Assess the class interest in studying the problems of dating in greater depth than covered in the junior high school classes.
- Review dating etiquette and standards using role-playing and small group discussions.
- Ask students to estimate the cost of a date. Compare boys' answers with girls' answers.
- Hold small group discussions on the following statements or questions:
  - (1) The qualities considered desirable and undesirable in a date are the same as those considered desirable and undesirable in a mate.
  - (2) Girls are responsible for setting the limits in a dating situation.
  - (3) Should there be a "double standard"?
  - (4) There are feminine wolves as well as masculine wolves.
  - (5) A girl must always wait for the boy to ask her for a date.
  - (6) Dating and drinking do not mix.
- Have a panel discussion on the topic "The Problems of Dating in Our Community."

tunities for the young person to study himself and others for overly possessive attitudes and behavior. It must be remembered that no one of any age has achieved perfection in all attitudes and feelings; possessive tendencies, or urges to dominate, and some jealous feelings may occur at times in everyone's life. The important thing is that to achieve maturity and to build permanently happy and mutually satisfying relationships one must work to overcome undesirable tendencies in oneself and to be realistic about the characteristics of other people.

- Assign Chapter 5, "Dating," in *Personal Adjustment, Marriage, and Family Living.*
- Assign individual students to call the various community agencies that might provide activities for teenagers, ask what their facilities and programs are, and report back to the class.
- View and discuss the filmstrip *Date Behavior.*
- Assign Chapter 6, "Dating—Standards of Behavior," in *Personal Adjustment, Marriage, and Family Living.*
- Have the class discuss the important purposes to be accomplished during the dating stage of life.
- Have the class discuss the distinctions between *reputation* and *character.*
- Have the class discuss the statement: "Practically every hour of living is a more or less comfortable compromise between personal drives and social requirements."

B. Going steady is sometimes a trial engagement. Going steady is a good way to get to know each other. Moods and manners change as contacts multiply. Each member of the couple can see how the personality of the other reacts to the ups and downs of daily living far better when going steady than in more fleeting contacts.

- Have the class select teams to debate the pro's and con's of going steady.
- Have the class collect newspaper and magazine articles about current dating attitudes and then discuss and react to them.
- Have the class discuss and define what "going steady" actually means to them. What in particular is the commitment of each member of the couple to the other?

Resources

(S) Sound filmstrip: *Values for Teenagers: The Choice Is Yours,* Guidance Associates, color, Part 1, 18 min.; Part 2, 13½ min. Live interviews with a cross section of teenagers provide an eye-opening exposure to concerns of today's youngsters.

(S) Landis, Judson, and Mary Landis, *Personal Adjustment, Marriage, and Family Living,* 4th ed. Englewood Cliffs, N.J.: Prentice-Hall, 1966, chs. 5 and 6.

(S) Filmstrip: *Date Behavior,* Society of Visual Education, color, 9 min. Why proper dating behavior is important; qualities in dating partners.

Content	Suggested Learning Opportunities
Human Sexuality A. Sexuality and its place in our lives	• Discuss the ideas contained in Document 10-1, "Human Sexuality." • Discuss in small groups how your sex is an integral part of your life. • Have class members pose problems. Arrange the class into single-sex small groups and form solutions or resolutions to the problems posed. Have the recorders report to the class and compare the boys' solutions to the girls' solutions in the light of their sexual differences.
B. Masculinity and femininity C. The changing male and female roles	• Assign the books *The Man That You Marry* and *The Girl That You Marry* for individual reading. Have oral reports given on the first two chapters of each book, and discuss in class. • Divide the class into four groups. Group 1—all boys—will list characteristics of manliness. Group 2—all boys—will list characteristics of femininity. Group 3—all girls—will list characteristics of manliness. Group 4—all girls—will list characteristics of femininity. Re-form for class discussion of the various characteristics. • View and discuss the film *Psychological Differences Between the Sexes.*
D. Review of human reproduction	• Show and discuss the film *The Human Body: Reproductive System.* • Administer the Terminology Tests in Document 10-2 and use as a class discussion tool. • Use the book *Love and Sex in Plain Language* for review when necessary.
E. Sex manners and morals 1. Societies and cultures vary widely in what they expect and demand of people, but in no case has sex conduct ever	• Read and discuss Document 10-3, "What Is Moral and What Is Immoral?" • Have the class react to these statements:

been regarded as a strictly private affair.

2. In all known societies sex conduct is regulated as part of the total system, and absolute promiscuity has never been encouraged or supported by the moral codes.
3. The American culture approves of companionship of the sexes, socially and intellectually, but restricts sexual intimacies to married couples.
4. Sex is a powerful force in human society and needs controls.
5. What a person does about his sexual behavior is of concern to his family, his friends, his sex partner, and him personally.
6. A person's family bears the burden of his behavior.
7. A person's friends and associates care what he does. When he yields to the pressures of one group, he may find himself an outcast among others whose friendship over a period of time might mean more to him.
8. Future dates and marriage opportunities depend upon the reputation a person builds, the groups he relates himself to, and the standards of conduct he maintains.

(1) Cheating results essentially from a breakdown in communications or the inability of pupils and teachers to communicate with each other.

(2) Students do not cheat on something they believe is important to them and their well-being.

(3) Using the criteria given in Document 10-3, is cheating in the sexual area moral or immoral?

- Have students review their statement of values developed in the ninth grade.
- Discuss the idea that a person's sex manners and morals are shaped by his fundamental attitudes toward others, toward himself, and toward life itself.
- View and discuss the film *Phoebe—Story of a Premarital Pregnancy.*
- Pose the question: "What kind of person are you?" and discuss the following answers: (1) A person with a past, (2) a person in society, (3) a person among other persons.
- Review the ideas contained in the ninth-grade Document 9-9, "Discussion Guide: The Double Standard."
- Discuss: "How much responsibility does a teenager have for protecting his family's reputation and even improving it?"
- Distribute the book *Why Wait Till Marriage?* Assign students to give a brief summary of each chapter.
- Have the class discuss the meaning of conformity and peer pressures.
- Have the class try to evaluate how much they respond to peer pressures and discuss whether or not this is a problem with them.
- Have the class develop a list of techniques that could be useful in "Drawing the Line Tactfully and Effectively."
- Have a student report on "How To

F. Erasing mistakes

Keeping a dating relationship within comfortable, mutually acceptable bounds is no easy task. Many young couples make mistakes while they are learning how far they should go and how to stop. There should be no final tragedy in making mistakes. Everybody does—in some area of life. It is important that young people know how to redeem themselves once they have made a mistake in the sexual area.

Say No," from *Love, Sex, and the Teenager,* pp. 87–90.

- Have the class discuss what is meant by "reputation" and how one's reputation is developed.
- Invite a representative from the legal profession to answer students' questions on the laws designed to prevent sexual exploitation.
- Have students discuss the question: "What effect, if any, do modern contraceptives have on teenage sexual behavior?"
- Have the class discuss the following adult interpretation of America's twentieth-century sex code: "Go out and have a good time. Date whoever you want, as often as you want to. Go wherever you want and meet all sorts of interesting people. Fall in and out of love along the way, several times. Then, when you find the one person you want to spend the rest of your life with, enjoy a deeply meaningful courtship and get married when you are ready to settle down in a home of your own. Only one thing is required—that you reserve your full sexual intimacy for marriage with your marriage partner."
- Discuss the ideas contained in Document 10-4, "Learning from a Mistake."
- Have the class make suggestions concerning the most effective way to improve an individual's self-concept and reputation.
- Ask the school nurse to interpret the meaning of the term "abortion."
- Ask a representative of the local medical society to describe to the class his profession's stand on the state's laws defining legal abortions.
- Have the class discuss the importance of understanding their personal values to facilitate the prevention of mistakes.

Resources

(S) Document 10-1, "Human Sexuality."
(S) Boll, Eleanor S., *The Man That You Marry*. Philadelphia: Macrae Smith, 1963.
(S) Bossard, James H. S., and Eleanor S. Boll, *The Girl That You Marry*. Philadelphia: Macrae Smith, 1960.
(S) Film: *Psychological Differences Between the Sexes,* McGraw-Hill, color, 14 min. Dramatizes the way in which a girl and boy react to similar situations. Their diverse reactions exemplify some typical psychological differences between the sexes.
(S) Film: *The Human Body: Reproductive System,* Coronet Films, color, 13 min. Presents a clear and objective description of the human reproductive system. Shows similarities and differences between male and female reproductive organs, locates them in the body, and describes specific functions of each in the creation of new life.
(S) Document 10-2, "Terminology Tests."
(S) Johnson, Eric W., *Love and Sex in Plain Language*. Philadelphia: Lippincott, 1967.
(S) Document 10-3, "What Is Moral and What Is Immoral?"
(S) Film: *Phoebe—Story of a Premarital Pregnancy,* McGraw-Hill, b/w, 29 min. Dramatizes the mental and emotional reactions of a teenager who discovers she is pregnant.
(S) Duvall, Evelyn M., *Why Wait Till Marriage?* New York: Association Press, 1965.
(S) Lorand, Rhoda L., *Love, Sex, and the Teenager*. New York: Macmillan, 1965, pp. 87–90.
(S) Document 10-4, "Learning from a Mistake."
(T) Reiss, Ira L., "Sexual Codes in Teen-Age Culture," *Ann. American Academy of Political and Social Science,* vol. 338, November 1961, pp. 53–62.
(T) Kirkendall, Lester A., and Elizabeth Ogg, *Sex and Our Society*. New York: Public Affairs Committee, 1964, p. 10.

Engagement

A. Advantages of an engagement

Engagement is commonly thought to be important mainly for the woman. The formal aspects of engagements, the showers and parties and notices in the society pages of the newspaper, seem to emphasize the woman's good fortune and neglect the man. Actually, however, a modern version of betrothal has advantages for both people.

1. The engagement may save a man from being dazzled by

- Discuss this newer concept of engagement: "Today engagement is viewed as a 'testing period' rather than a 'promise to marry.' "
- Have the class read and discuss Chapter 12, "Engagement," in *Personal Adjustment, Marriage, and Family Living.*
- Discuss the advantages of an engagement.
- Discuss the ideas contained in Document 10-5, "Growing Toward Marriage: In What Stage Are You?"

the supposed glamor of his fiancée, since it gives him opportunities to see her in everyday clothes over a period of time.

2. The engagement enables the partners to become better acquainted with each other's families and to become accepted by them.
3. The engagement provides the opportunity to create an amorous monopoly in which "old flames" and rivals are eliminated as love objects.
4. The engagement provides insight for one into the relative responsiveness of the other. Even though there be a minimum of sex experimentation in the engagement, such deficiencies as frigidity, lack of capacity for demonstrating affection, and childhood fears about sex will show up in the engagement period.
5. The engagement provides many opportunities for a full and frank discussion of contraception and having children, child discipline, the woman's work plans as a wife, the handling of money, extramarital friendships, and other vital issues that often are inappropriate in the dating and courtship stages.
6. The engagement provides the couple time to arrange financial affairs and to gradually prepare for the economic burden of marriage, to talk over their business and occupational interests, and to discover similarities and differences in how they handle money.

- Have each student write a brief statement on his life goals and aspirations.
- Design a self-evaluation check form with your students. See Document 10-6 ("Are You Ready for Marriage?") for an example.
- View and discuss the film *Worth Waiting For.*
- Have the class discuss the following statements:
  - (1) In-laws are valuable assets, and their approval is a factor favoring marital success.
  - (2) If parents disapprove, they may act as a wedge to separate the pair when the first crisis develops.
- Have the class discuss ways that an engaged couple demonstrate their affection for each other.
- Have the class design and implement a survey to determine the number of times an average adult has been engaged and the age at the time of engagement.
- Have the class study some case histories of engagements that have been broken.
- Appoint several members of the class to conduct a survey of the community to identify agencies that provide premarital counseling.
- Have the class discuss the function of the dowry. What do we have today that fills this function?
- Have the class discuss and list reasons for maintaining pre-engagement sexual behavior standards.
- Have the class discuss the following statement: "Nothing succeeds like success, and the engagement enables the novices to succeed by starting them out with premarriage problems and inducting them slowly into the complications of married life."

7. The engagement also gives both persons a chance to occasionally assume some of the responsibilities of husband and wife and to learn some of the ropes while still in the engagement period.

B. Breaking an engagement

The following reasons would seem to justify a re-evaluation of an engagement, possibly leading to an agreement to sever the relationship: (1) recognition that fundamental feelings of alienation have arisen as a result of the more intimate relations of the engagement; not just doubts and misgivings, but strong feelings of incompatibility; (2) recognition that the engagement was made originally under pressure from relatives or circumstances and that the main reason for refraining from breaking the engagement is the fear of publicity; (3) recognition that either member of the pair is emotionally dependent on parents and too immature to stand the rigors of marriage; (4) changes in economic prospects due to loss of job, arrest for lawbreaking, or a serious accident affecting the ability to earn a living and carry on the functions of parenthood.

- Have the class discuss the statement: "A broken engagement is better than a poor marriage."
- Have the class list factors they believe would represent danger signals during an engagement. Compile and discuss.
- Write appropriate paragraphs for the students to evaluate. See Document 10-7, "When an Engagement Should Be Re-evaluated," for an example.
- Have the class discuss the relevancy of the four reasons for breaking an engagement listed at the left.

Resources

(S) Landis, Judson, and Mary Landis, *Personal Adjustment, Marriage, and Family Living*. Englewood Cliffs, N.J.: Prentice-Hall, 1966, ch. 12.

(S) Document 10-5, "Growing Toward Marriage: In What Stage Are You?"

(S) Document 10-6, "Are You Ready for Marriage?"

(S) Film: *Worth Waiting For*, Brigham Young University, color, 27 min. Describes the problems that arose for a high school couple when they decided to become engaged. Explores problems and pitfalls of early marriage.

(S) Document 10-7, "When an Engagement Should Be Re-evaluated."

Content	Suggested Learning Opportunities
Choosing a Marriage Partner A. Successful marriage 1. People approaching marriage are usually hoping for happiness as a pair; they are seldom aware that marriage affects and is affected by other people. 2. No absolute freedom exists for anyone, either outside of marriage or within it. But in marriage each partner gives up a measure of personal freedom in exchange for the close, personal, permanent relationship that marriage provides. 3. Choosing your marriage partner puts to the test everything you have learned about choosing friends and dates over many years. Choosing and being chosen are not new experiences. The difference in choosing a mate is in the finality of the commitment and the large number of people who care whether or not you make a good choice.	• Assign Chapters 9, 10, and 11 in *Personal Adjustment, Marriage, and Family Living.* • Discuss the ideas contained in Document 10-8, "Why Is Marriage Choice More Difficult Today?" • Have each student make a list of the personality traits he would consider most important in a person he would marry. Compile and compare to see (1) what are the most commonly desired traits in a mate; (2) how different persons seek different personalities in their marriage partners; (3) what traits are most commonly listed by boys; (4) what traits are most commonly listed by girls. • Have the class discuss: "How does our American culture influence mate selection?" • Discuss the factors listed in Document 10-9, "Predicting Success in Marriage—Premarital Factors." • Read and discuss Chapter 6, "The Right Mate for You," in *Looking Ahead to Marriage.* • Assign a student to report on Dr. Terman's studies of marriages on pp. 128–29 in *Personal Adjustment, Marriage, and Family Living.* • Ask students to assess, for their own information only, their own family background. Use the ideas in Document 10-10, "Discussion Guide: How To Assess Your Family Background."
B. Factors to consider 1. The capacity to give and receive permanent love 2. Mutual interests, companionship 3. Maturity 4. Ability to meet economic needs	• Discuss the relative importance of the following factors in choosing a mate: we share the same ideals and goals; he gets along with others; he feels affection for me; we have mutual friends; we have similar backgrounds; he likes children; he is outgoing and

5. Education
6. Ethnic and religious similarity or differences
7. Mental and physical health
8. Family approval
9. Mutual respect

friendly; he is honest; he can earn a living; he can handle money; he is good-natured; he is well mannered; he has sex appeal; he is tolerant; we have the same ideas about religion; he is intelligent; we have the same interests. Have the class form some conclusions.

C. Elements of growing in love
   1. Love does not come as a sudden answer to life's basic needs. We develop the capability to love gradually through years of interaction with other people.
      a. Love is not just an emotion but rather a complex relationship.
      b. Love is a relationship as distinguishable from a feeling.

- View and discuss the filmstrip *When You're in Love.*
- Discuss: "What is love?"[3]
- Have a student read and report on Erich Fromm's *The Art of Loving.*
- Have the class discuss the statement: "Love is not a rational basis for marriage."
- Review pp. 45–46, "The Great Romantic Fairy Tale," in *Love and the Facts of Life.*
- In small groups discuss the statement: "Learning to love and to be loved is certainly one of the most difficult tasks to accomplish."
- Discuss the ideas contained on pp. 40–41, "Differences Between Love

[3] Love is very difficult to describe. Love has been called "the most powerful force known to man"; "the greatest thing in the world." What love really is and is not vitally concerns students and, indeed, many other persons. The following resources are listed to enable the teacher to conduct meaningful discussions on the topic. You may wish to refer some of the better readers among your students to the references so that class discussion is not replaced by a lecture but continues to be student-oriented.

Womble, Dale L., *Foundations for Marriage and Family Relations.* New York, Macmillan, 1966, ch. 7 ("Building Love Enough for Marriage"). An excellent discussion on the developmental-task concept of love. Love is defined and studied; the various kinds and degrees of love are discussed. Womble discusses love after marriage; included is a comparison of low and high degrees of love as a relationship. A very comprehensive list of suggested readings follows this chapter.

Landis, Judson, and Mary Landis, *Building a Successful Marriage.* Englewood Cliffs, N.J.: Prentice-Hall, 1963, ch. 10 ("Love"). Lists some questions to think about in order to evaluate love.

Duvall, Evelyn M., *Family Development.* Philadelphia: Lippincott, 1957, pp. 355–58. Outlines some outstanding definitions and descriptions of love suggested by men and women of various orientations down through the years.

Lorand, Rhoda L., *Love, Sex, and the Teenager.* New York: Macmillan (Popular Library Edition), 1965, ch. 12 ("This Thing Called Love"). Discusses love at first sight, unconscious deception, and the love hungry. Dr. Lorand discusses the important question: "Is adolescent love real love?"

2. Love vs. infatuation:
   a. Infatuation is associated with immaturity, whereas love is associated with relative maturity.
   b. Infatuation is characterized by unsuitability, love by relative appropriateness.
   c. Infatuation is often mainly sex attraction, while love tends to involve the whole personality.
   d. Infatuation is marked by frustration, guilt, and insecurity more often than love.
   e. Infatuation is accompanied more often than love by a reluctance to face reality, to change, and to grow.
   f. Infatuation is, or can be, instantaneous, but love takes time to develop.

and Infatuation as Revealed by Contemporary Research Studies," in *When You Marry.*

- Have the class analyze the words of some popular songs. A study of 1,224 of the most popular songs in the U.S. for a 60-year period revealed that two thirds dealt with love.[4] The most frequent theme was the lonely or disappointed lover; second was unfulfilled love or longing, with a strong suggestion that marriage was the logical and inevitable outcome.
- Have the class discuss the following common misconceptions about love:
  1. Love is largely physical attraction.
  2. Love cannot change.
  3. Love happens at first sight.
  4. For each person there is one and only one possible love, and the two must keep looking until they find each other.
  5. Love leaps all barriers.
  6. Absence makes the heart grow fonder.
  7. If you're in love, nothing else matters.
  8. Out of sight, out of mind.
- Have each small group write up a "Test of Love." Compile and discuss in class.

Resources

(S) Landis, Judson, and Mary Landis, *Personal Adjustment, Marriage, and Family Living.* Englewood Cliffs, N.J.: Prentice-Hall, 1966, chs. 9, 10, and 11.
(T) Document 10-8, "Why Is Marriage Choice More Difficult Today?"
(T) Document 10-9, "Predicting Success in Marriage—Premarital Factors."
(S) Adams, Clifford R., *Looking Ahead to Marriage.* Chicago: Science Research Associates, 1949, ch. 6.
(T) Document 10-10, "Discussion Guide: How To Assess Your Family Background."
(S) Sound filmstrip: *When You're in Love,* Society for Visual Education, color,

[4] Norman Charles, doctoral study, University of Pennsylvania, Philadelphia, 1958.

33⅓ r.p.m. record, 9 min. How love develops from infancy to maturity. Difference between love and infatuation.
(S) Fromm, Erich, *The Art of Loving*. New York: Harper & Row, 1956.
(S) Duvall, Evelyn M., *Love and the Facts of Life*. New York: Association Press, 1963, pp. 45–46.
(S) Duvall, Evelyn, and Reuben Hill. *When You Marry* (high school edition). Boston: Heath, 1965, pp. 40–41.
(S) Kirkendall, Lester A., and Elizabeth Ogg, *Sex and Our Society*. New York: Public Affairs Committee, 1964.
(S) Duvall, Sylvanus, *Before You Marry*. New York: Association Press, 1959, pp. 40–41.

Content	**Suggested Learning Opportunities**
Am I Ready for Marriage? A. Legal requirements (Investigate your state marriage laws.)	• Assign Chapter 15, "Marriage Customs and Laws," and Chapter 16, "What It Means To Be Married," in *Personal Adjustment, Marriage, and Family Living.* • Discuss some of the legal responsibilities that accompany marriage. • Ask students to write a brief paper on "When is a person considered ready for marriage in our society?" Compile ideas and discuss in small groups. • Assign selected students to report on the marital customs in different countries. • View and discuss the filmstrip *And They Lived Happily Ever After?*
B. Life aspirations or goals 1. Individual philosophy 2. Economic responsibility 3. Readiness for a permanent relationship 4. Maturity	• Ask students to write a paper on "My Goals in Life," including their philosophy of life, their educational goals, and their individual contributions to national goals. • Have a clergyman explain the meaning of marriage vows in various faiths. • Review the eighth-grade section on Philosophy of Life. • View and discuss the filmstrip *Looking Ahead to Marriage.*

- Discuss the ideas contained in Document 10-11, "Outline for Self-Study: Maturity for Marriage."

Resources

(S) Landis, Judson, and Mary Landis, *Personal Adjustment, Marriage, and Family Living*. Englewood Cliffs, N.J.: Prentice-Hall, 1966, chs. 15 and 16.
(S) Sound filmstrip: *And They Lived Happily Ever After?* Guidance Associates, color, Part 1, 18 min; Part 2, 13½ min. Young people articulate their own experiences with economic handicaps, dependence on parents, personal immaturity, and other failure factors in premature marriage.
(S) Sound filmstrip: *Looking Ahead to Marriage,* Society for Visual Education, color, 33⅓ r.p.m. record, 9 min. Engagement period. Hardships of early marriage. What to give.
(S) Document 10-11, "Outline for Self-Study: Maturity for Marriage."
(T, S) Smart, Russell, and Mollie Smart, *Living in Families*. Boston: Houghton Mifflin, 1965, chs. 8 and 15.

Content

Characteristics of an Ideal Family

Love is given and received within families. Love is necessary for normal physical and personality growth.

Families teach their children ways of doing things, believing, and feeling. Later, a child learns that there may be several right ways of doing things. However, a person retains throughout life much of what he learned at home as a young child.

Families buy many goods and services and are important to business. It is possible to think of the work done at home as production of goods and services.

A. Your family is like other families. A family tends to resemble other families that live in similar neighborhoods, have about the same amount of money to spend, are of the same ethnic origin,

Suggested Learning Opportunities

- Ask the students to find out about the families their parents grew up in: How many brothers or sisters did each parent have? Were they older or younger? Were attitudes about the value of education, religious beliefs, and ancestry similar or dissimilar in the families of the two parents? Did they live in the same community? In similar neighborhoods?
- Have the students compare what their parents accepted when they got married with their ideas about what their children should do.
- Assign Chapter 1, "You and Your Family," and Chapter 8, "Family Understanding During Dating Years," in *Personal Adjustment, Marriage, and Family Living*.
- Ask the class to develop a list of responsibilities, achievements, aspira-

have comparable attitudes toward education and religion, and are in the same stage of development. Even if two families are similar in all these areas, however, they could not be exactly alike.

B. No two families are just alike. Families differ because of the number, sex, and ages of family members. Families differ in the responsibility they bear for their relatives and the help they receive from them. A larger family can be a real asset in giving its members added love and security. Families differ in their daily routines, in what they consider important, in hobbies and interests.

C. The student should decide what kind of family he wants to establish. Students should observe and reflect about the family behavior they see around them or have witnessed in the past. They should think through the processes underlying the behavior witnessed and draw conclusions that may help them when they establish a family of their own.

tions, and future roles usually expected of teenagers by the family.

- Discuss attitudes toward education. A person's attitude toward education means his point of view about whether it is better to know or to be ignorant, whether it is worth the effort to keep on learning or a waste of time. A person with the attitude that education is worthwhile is likely to be a well-educated person, even if he left school in the eighth grade, for this person will keep on learning wherever he is. A person who thinks education is unimportant is likely to be a poorly educated person, even if he went through college, for this person will take little advantage of his opportunities to learn.
- Assign Chapter 1, "Understanding Your Family," and Chapter 2, "Your Family Influences You," in *Living in Families.*
- Have the class list all the arguments they can to support the contention that people should receive special preparation for marriage.
- Discuss the statement: "I don't plan to get married for ten years; I'll read up on marriage when the time comes."
- Conclude the unit with a discussion of the statement: "The better we understand ourselves, the better we understand love."

Resources

(S) Landis, Judson, and Mary Landis, *Personal Adjustment, Marriage, and Family Living*. Englewood Cliffs, N.J.: Prentice-Hall, 1966, chs. 1 and 8.

(T, S) Smart, Russell, and Mollie Smart, *Living in Families.* Boston, Houghton Mifflin, 1965, chs. 1 and 2.

Background and Teaching Materials

Document 10-1 ***Human Sexuality***

Sex is only one element of your total personality. However, your sex has a direct relationship to your physical development, your emotional adjustment, and your thinking as an individual. Probably no other single fact about you influences your life as strongly as your membership in one or the other sex. Your ways of thinking, modes of behavior, social role, vocational choice, choice of friends, manner of dress, and other important factors are strongly conditioned by the biological fact of being male or female.

Physiologists are in general agreement that every cell of a male's body is slightly different from those of a female. In fact, it is said that if a small part of a body a hundred or more years old is exhumed, the sex of that particular person can easily be determined.

Girls are born female. Boys are born male. Nature endows girls with the physical potentialities of becoming women and boys with the physical potentialities of becoming men. Femininity is learned just as masculinity is learned. From the moment of your birth you are trained to develop masculinity or femininity according to your sex.

Human sexuality can never be understood simply in terms of physiological processes. Sex is not a function of the sex organs alone, nor of the body alone, but of the whole human being in relation to his world.

Document 10-2 ***Terminology Tests***

ANSWER KEY

Reproduction. 1, K; 2, O; 3, J; 4, D; 5, C; 6, F; 7, E; 8, G; 9, B; 10, A; 11, I; 12, M; 13, N; 14, Q; 15, L; 16, H; 17, P.

Sexual Intercourse. 1, D and H; 2, J; 3, P; 4, I; 5, C and N; 6, G; 7, E and O; 8, L; 9, A; 10, K; 11, M; 12, B; 13, F.

General Terms, Part A. 1, L; 2, I; 3, D; 4, G; 5, C; 6, B; 7, H; 8, A; 9, E; 10, J; 11, F; 12, K. *Part B.* 1, E; 2, A; 3, B; 4, C; 5, D; 6, G; 7, F.

In each space write the letter for the word that best matches the definition.

Reproduction

A. Abortion
B. Cesarean
C. Conception
D. Embryo
E. Endometrium
F. Fetus
G. Labor
H. Menopause
I. Miscarriage
J. Ovulation
K. Ovum (Ova)
L. Placenta
M. Pregnancy
N. Puberty
O. Sperm
P. Tuboligation
Q. Vasectomy

1.______ A woman's reproductive cell.
2.______ A man's reproductive cell.
3.______ The discharge of a woman's reproductive cell from the ovary.
4.______ The first stage of life of the fertilized cell in the womb.
5.______ Fertilization of a woman's reproductive cell from the ovary.
6.______ The second stage of life in the womb.
7.______ The lining of the uterus that nourishes the embryo.
8.______ The final stages of birth.
9.______ The birth of a baby by an abdominal operation.
10.______ The usually intentional loss or removal of a baby before it can live.
11.______ The usually unintentional delivery of a baby before it can live.
12.______ The condition of a woman from the time of conception until birth.
13.______ The stage of physical growth when rapid sexual development takes place and reproductive cells become active.
14.______ A surgical operation that makes a man unable to cause conception.
15.______ The organ in the uterus that nourishes the unborn baby.
16.______ The gradual lessening of a woman's ability to produce mature ova.
17.______ A surgical operation that makes it impossible for a woman to conceive.

Sexual Intercourse

A. Breasts
B. Chastity
C. Climax
D. Coitus
E. Condom
F. Continence
G. Contraceptive
H. Copulation
I. Ejaculation
J. Erection
K. Frigidity
L. Hymen
M. Impotence
N. Orgasm
O. Prophylactic
P. Semen

1.___, ___ Two other words used for sexual intercourse.
2.______ The enlarged and firm condition of the male sex organ during sexual stimulation.
3.______ The fluid that transports the sperm.
4.______ The discharge of semen at the height of sexual excitement.
5.___, ___ Two words for the highest point of sexual excitement in a man and a woman.
6.______ The general term for any device used to prevent conception.
7.___, ___ Two words for a rubber sheath placed over the penis to prevent conception and help prevent the transmission of venereal disease.
8.______ A membrane that usually partially covers a virgin woman's vaginal opening and that once broken, as during sexual intercourse, disappears.
9.______ A woman's organs that supply milk for a new baby and that are sensitive to touch during sexual excitement.
10.______ A woman's low degree of capacity to enter into sexual intimacy—physically or psychologically caused.
11.______ The inability to perform normal sexual intercourse. Usually the term refers to men.
12.______ The practice of abstinence from premarital intercourse (usually refers to women).
13.______ The practice of self-restraint in sexual intercourse, especially complete abstinence (usually refers to men).

General Terms

Part A

A. Adultery
B. Fornication
C. Heterosexuality
D. Homosexual
E. Incest
F. Masturbation
G. Mistress
H. Promiscuity
I. Prostitute
J. Rape
K. Seduce
L. Virgin

1.________ A woman who has not had sexual intercourse.
2.________ A woman who offers to have sexual intercourse for pay.
3.________ A person who derives his sexual excitement and satisfaction from other persons of the same sex.
4.________ A woman who usually limits her sex relations to one man to whom she is not married.
5.________ Normal interest in a person of the opposite sex.
6.________ Sexual intercourse of an unmarried man with an unmarried woman.
7.________ Indiscriminate sexual intercourse without limiting to one person.
8.________ Sexual intercourse of a married person with a person other than husband or wife.
9.________ Sexual intercourse with a close relative.
10.________ Forced sexual intercourse.
11.________ Fondling, caressing, or manipulating one's sexual organs, sometimes to climax.
12.________ To persuade a woman to give up chastity.

Part B

A. Douche
B. Genitals
C. Gonads
D. Hormones
E. Menstruation
F. Seminal emission
G. Venereal

1.________ The periodic discharge of endometrium from the uterus.
2.________ The flushing of the vagina with a liquid.
3.________ A man's or woman's external sex parts.
4.________ Reproductive organs, male or female (ovaries or testes).
5.________ The chemical substance in the body that causes male or female characteristics.
6.________ Term describing all diseases transmitted through sexual intercourse.
7.________ The discharge of semen from the penis during sleep, usually accompanied by a dream.

Document 10-3 ***What Is Moral and What Is Immoral?***

All our decisions need to be based upon the universal wish for acceptance and love and centered around the concern for the improvement of human interrelationships. The following moral code has been developed by Dr. Lester A. Kirkendall to serve as a basis for building a life-affirming moral code. The criteria are:

"Moral Behavior leads to:	Immoral Behavior leads to:
Integrity in relationships	Duplicity in relationships
Trust of others	Distrust of others
Broadening of human sympathies	Barriers between persons and between groups
Cooperative attitudes	Uncooperative hostile attitudes
Enhanced self-respect	Diminished self-respect
Consideration for others' rights and needs	Exploitation of others
Individual fulfillment and zest for living	Stunting of individual growth and disillusionment"[1]

An educator observed: "Schools sometimes try to create school unity and morale by building a rivalry with another school that may end in distrust, suspicion, and hard feelings." Is this school tactic moral or immoral using the above criteria? Defend your answer.

React to these statements: Cheating results essentially from a breakdown in communication or the inability of pupils and teachers to communicate with each other. Students do not cheat on something which they believe is important to them and their well-being. Is cheating moral or immoral using the above criteria? Defend your answer.

---

[1] Lester A. Kirkendall and Elizabeth Ogg, *Sex and Our Society* (New York, Public Affairs Committee, 1964), p. 19.

Document 10-4 Learning from a Mistake

"Everyone makes mistakes at times."[1] The area of sexual activity is no exception. The important thing is to learn from your mistakes. "To err is human," but not if the same error is made over and over again. "Wallowing in self-pity"—feelings of guilt—or pretending that you enjoy being "bad" is not helping you to learn from this experience. Consequently, you can become more compassionate toward the weaknesses of others.

The first step in erasing a mistake is to face up to the facts. Admit to yourself that you have done wrong, that you may have damaged your reputation and been foolish. It is hard not to make excuses for yourself and pretend that the mistake did not happen. But you must be able to recognize the error so that you will not repeat it.

"Blaming others for what you have done will not help. You must also accept the responsibility for your own behavior." If you do not like your behavior, you are the one to change it.

Self-condemnation does not help. You need to cultivate self-understanding. Set aside a period when you can sit down and list your strengths, your strong points. Think about how these can help you to be accepted again. Next list your weaknesses so that you can be prepared not to give in to them. "Know yourself" is an old truism that will help you find the way back to your former reputation.

Take time to sit down and think through what it was that made you do what you did. Usually difficulties with one's sex drive arise when other areas of his life are upset. Make a plan of action and list some adjustments that will help smooth out some of your problems.

It may be helpful for you to talk over your problems with an adult in whom you have confidence. Your own father and mother may be able to help you if you will only confide in them. It is also possible that your partner in your mistaken action can be a confidant. In this way your relationship will be strengthened as you face the problem together.

As you work toward resolving your problem you will find that you can forgive yourself, not by excusing your behavior, but by realizing that you can trust yourself again. There will be times when you do not measure up to your standards or expectations, but you must continue to work, developing your strengths in the areas where you fall short.

---

[1] Quotations in Document 10-4 are from Evelyn M. Duvall, *Why Wait Till Marriage?* (New York, Association Press, 1965), pp. 105–06.

"It is up to you to start afresh." One mistake, even in the area of sexual behavior, must not destroy you as an effective person. "Make a clean break with the conduct that got you into trouble." Join in school activities, become active in your church, volunteer for some service project in your community. "Make your life and your time count for something." As time passes and people become interested in other things, your behavior will be forgotten and you will have learned to forgive yourself. Your life will never be quite the same, but your experience will have helped you to further understand yourself and others.

Document 10-5 ***Growing Toward Marriage: In What Stage Are You?***

Getting into a good human relationship results from a period of growth just as becoming a tall person requires a period of physical growth. One person may become closely associated with another in a very short time, but it cannot be said that a strong relationship has been established. Progress toward a good marriage relationship is a growth process, and as they date and move toward marriage, people pass through three stages or periods. These can be distinguished broadly.

The first period might be called the *getting started* or *exploratory* period. During this period one is simply getting used to associating with members of the other sex. Dating relationships are usually brief, and in this period most persons prefer group associations. A boy or girl who has had little experience in play or work with members of the other sex is likely to find a certain amount of trial and error experience necessary before he feels at ease. Boys and girls in the early teen years ask many questions which indicate their dating perplexities. Boys will want to know "what girls expect in boys." The girls' question is reversed. Questions on how to ask for a date, to express appreciation, or say good-night, and whether to express affection are common. These questions indicate a strong feeling on the part of the boy or girl that he is dealing with a very strange creature —a member of the other sex. These are the questions of the *exploratory period.*

In the *trial and testing* period a person becomes interested in a person of the other sex on the basis of his personal qualities and character. An

---

Document 10-5, *Growing Toward Marriage: In What Stage Are You?* is adapted from materials by Lester A. Kirkendall printed in the Hayward Unified School District's *Teacher Guide for Family Life Instruction* (Hayward, California, 1963), p. 37. Reprinted with permission. The Hayward Unified School District and Lester A. Kirkendall grant teachers permission to make copies of this document for use in connection with their own family life and sex education classes. On each reproduction the following copyright notice must be given: © 1969 by Harcourt, Brace & World, Inc.

exploration of personal characteristics and values of dating partners occurs. Personality traits are valued more than a mere interest in a person of the other sex. If self-consciousness over friendships with members of the other sex has existed, it should have disappeared by now. Dating relationships are likely to be confined to one person at a time. Affection grows from an awareness that the two have similar values and goals in life. Clearly two dating partners may be in different periods so far as their maturity is concerned.

Once two people have come to think seriously of each other as marriage partners they have reached the *period of decision.* One may have reached this period while the other is still in one of the less advanced periods. This *period of decision* may be further divided into the pre-engagement and engagement periods. Some very important things need to be accomplished in this period. The couple should engage in even more intensive efforts to understand each other as personalities. They should try to understand each other's views and values on such matters as religion, divergent ideas resulting from differing family backgrounds, attitudes toward children, money, sex and feelings toward such matters as the man's choice of a vocation, and the woman's interest in a career. If, after thorough exploration, the couple feel they would like to marry, then there will be a definite agreement and an engagement. Many couples announce their engagement before they are really engaged. Public announcements of the engagement and definite commitment to marry should be withheld until the exploration of personalities and values is satisfactorily completed.

Looked at in this way, movement into marriage is a process of growth and maturity. A couple may marry before they have accomplished this process of growth—some hurry through the exploratory period—but if they do, they face a greater hazard of finding themselves mismated than if they had worked through these periods.

Document 10-6 ***Are You Ready for Marriage?***

The following questions should stimulate thought about readiness for marriage. There are no right or wrong answers. Answer by drawing a circle

---

Document 10-6, *Are You Ready for Marriage?* is taken from Lester A. Kirkendall, *A Reading and Study Guide for Students in Marriage and Family Relations,* 4th ed. (Dubuque, Iowa: William C. Brown, 1968), p. 10. Reprinted with permission. William C. Brown Company, Publishers, grants teachers permission to make copies of this questionnaire for use in connection with their own family life and sex education classes. On each reproduction the following copyright notice must be given: © 1968 by Lester A. Kirkendall.

around the "Yes," the "No," or the "?". Use the question mark only when you are uncertain. After you are through think about the meaning of your answers, and if possible discuss them with someone. The questionnaire assumes you are now considering some specific person as a possible marriage partner.

Yes No ? 1. Even though you may accept advice from your parents, do you make important decisions for yourself?
Yes No ? 2. Are you often homesick when you are away from home?
Yes No ? 3. Do you ever feel embarrassed or uneasy in giving or receiving affection?
Yes No ? 4. Are your feelings easily hurt by criticism?
Yes No ? 5. Do you enjoy playing or working with small children?
Yes No ? 6. Do you feel embarrassed or uneasy in conversations about sex with older persons or members of the other sex?
Yes No ? 7. Do you have a clear understanding of the physiology of sexual intercourse and reproduction?
Yes No ? 8. Do you understand the psychological factors determining good sexual adjustment?
Yes No ? 9. Have you had the experience of using some of your earnings to help meet the expenses of others?
Yes No ? 10. In an argument, do you lose your temper easily?
Yes No ? 11. Have you and your fiancé(e) ever worked through disagreements to a definite conclusion agreeable to both of you?
Yes No ? 12. Can you postpone something you want for the sake of later enjoyment?
Yes No ? 13. Are you normally free from jealousy?
Yes No ? 14. Have you thought carefully about the goals you will strive for in your marriage?
Yes No ? 15. Do you sometimes feel rebellious toward facing the responsibilities of marriage, occupational or family life?
Yes No ? 16. Have you been able to give up gracefully something you wanted very much?
Yes No ? 17. Do you think of sexual intercourse chiefly as a pleasure experience?
Yes No ? 18. Do you find it difficult to differ from others on matters of conduct or dress, even though you disagree with what they think?
Yes No ? 19. Do you often have to fight to get your way?

Yes No ? 20. Do you often find yourself making biting remarks, or using sarcasm toward others?

Yes No ? 21. Do you find yourself strongly emphasizing the glamor aspects of marriage, e.g., the announcement, congratulations, showers, the wedding?

Yes No ? 22. Have you and your fiancé(e) associated with each other in a variety of non-amusement situations, e.g., caring for children, in a work project, in time of stress?

Yes No ? 23. Have you and your fiancé(e) discussed matters which might cause marital conflict? For example: (Underline those you have discussed) religious differences; plans for having children; attitudes toward sex; differences in family background; financial arrangement in marriage; basic values in life.

Document 10-7 ***When an Engagement Should Be Re-evaluated***

CHECK YOURSELF Which of the following engagements should be re-evaluated with the possibility of a definite break?

______1. John, engaged to Eunice, was in service and has been missing in action for almost two years.

______2. Bob is Catholic, Jeanne is Protestant, and neither will change religion; they avoid the subject after three months of engagement.

______3. Jim has returned from two years in the interior of Brazil, broken in health, quite possibly a permanent invalid—wishes to break his engagement of five years' standing with Eloise, since he will be unable to support her and a family in his condition.

______4. Jack has broken three engagements and is on the verge of a breakup of the fourth with Georgene, of whom his doting mother disapproves.

______5. A week before the marriage Susan meets quite accidentally the former wife of Frank, her fiancé, and learns details of his life he has never told her. His family assure her everything will be all right—Frank was only seventeen and infatuated—this time it will be different.

______6. John swears he will commit suicide if Dorothy breaks their engagement; he waves a revolver to prove it.

★ KEY All should be re-evaluated.

Document 10-8 **Why Is Marriage Choice More Difficult Today?**

When Harry Allen married Susie Robinson, some eighty years ago, the problem of mate selection was far simpler than it now is. To begin with, the range of selection for most young people was about as far as Dobbin could travel and get back the same day—probably ten miles or less. Within this radius there were perhaps a dozen available girls from among whom Harry could choose. Most of these were from the same general background. Today his great-grandson lives in a big city. His radius is easily fifty miles, and within this area live many thousands of potentially eligible girls. Furthermore, with modern travel, this radius becomes indefinitely expanded. A girl from Portland, Oregon, meets a boy from Portland, Maine, while they are on vacation at Miami Beach, Florida. Outwardly these people look, behave, and generally act alike, yet they may represent entirely different and often conflicting backgrounds and points of view.

In the second place, both Harry Allen and Susie Robinson knew the families into which they were marrying. Harry knew, as everyone else did, that Susie's Aunt Jane had run off with a man not her husband, and was living somewhere in Boston with her twelve-year-old son, supported partly by Brother Joe who was Susie's father. People knew Harry's Aunt May, who was "not very bright" and that Harry's mother had not been the same since her youngest child had died. Yes, young people then could often know, not only the persons they married, but the character of their in-laws. Today it is not so easy for young people to get to know much about the families into which they marry.

Harry and Susie also understood what marriage meant for them, far better than most young people do now. When Susie said "yes" to Harry she knew what she was getting into and, more important, she had learned to handle it. She could bake a cherry pie, tend a garden, raise chickens, make clothing, and manage a household. She and Harry would never have dreamed of discussing sex, though both of them had been brought up on farms where animals were bred and, in practical ways, knew more about it than do many young people today.

Because Harry and Susie demanded less of their marriage, they had a good chance of finding what they expected. Life was hard and often grim. Marriage might have its moments of romance and emotional glow, but

---

Document 10-8, *Why Is Marriage Choice More Difficult Today?* is taken from Sylvanus M. Duvall, *Before You Marry* (New York, Association Press, 1959), pp. 17–19.

its main concern was working together to produce the physical necessities of life. Harry would no more think of expecting glamor of Susie than he would of his sorrel mare.

Young people today very often marry without the least notion of what to expect—of what it means to be tied down by babies, bedeviled by bills, or to be responsible for a household. What they expect of love and sex may be so unrealistic that marriage brings, not happiness and joy, but bitter disillusionment. Susie and Harry demanded of their marriage partners only that they might be reasonably decent and good workers. Today we expect that the other person will make us happy. Hollywood and TV films often set unrealistic standards of the love and romantic bliss to be expected in marriage.

We ought not to expect too little, however, Marriage can bring great satisfaction and fulfillment—far more than most couples achieve. Intelligence, understanding, and co-operation can make marriage the rich, rewarding experience it could be.

Document 10-9 ***Predicting Success in Marriage—"Premarital Factors"***

Clifford Kirkpatrick, an expert in marriage and family living, has listed the factors reported by several studies that are most highly associated with marital success.[1]

Happiness of parents' marriage
Adequate length of acquaintance, courtship and engagement
Adequate sex information in childhood
Personal happiness in childhood
Approval of the marriage by parents and others
Engagement adjustment and normal motivation toward marriage
Ethnic and religious similarity
Higher social and educational status
Mature and similar chronological age
Harmonious affection with parents during childhood

---

[1] See Clifford Kirkpatrick, *The Family as Process and Institution* (New York, Ronald Press, 1955), pp. 350–54.

Document 10-10 ***Discussion Guide: How To Assess Your Family Background***

Students should be reminded of the need for family loyalty before class discussion is begun. The discussion should be centered around the idea that:

1. Before a person is mature enough for marriage he needs to be able to view and understand his own family background, the contribution it has made to his personality, and the implications it may have for his marriage.
2. If the student finds in his family background marriage failure and unhappiness, he must attempt to think objectively and constructively about the situation and try to avoid a repetition in his own life.
3. Research has shown that a background of unhappiness is a handicap, but, like any other family history of chronic illness, positive action can overcome it.
4. The student should be encouraged to give his parents credit for his strengths and achievements rather than blame them for his weaknesses and failures.
5. The student whose family background has been happy should not take it for granted that he is sure to be happy also; rather, he should try to understand the techniques of living that have meant happiness in his family.
6. Each student whose family life is unhappy should examine the possibility that he has been partly at fault, and try to behave differently when he gets married.

The specific problems of a student's family should not be discussed in the classroom. The teacher should tactfully remind the student of the public setting and refer him to his counselor for individual attention.

Document 10-11 ***Outline for Self-Study: Maturity for Marriage***

Much of the success of any marriage depends upon the maturity of the two people involved. Study yourself on the following criteria. If you find it difficult to rate yourself, ask a friend or a member of your family to help you. Few people are mature on all points, so do not be discouraged if you find some immaturities in yourself.

I. Have you developed a measure of objectivity?
   1. Can you see yourself as you look to other people?
   2. Can you see others as most other people see them?
   3. Can you discriminate between facts and feelings about yourself, other people, and things?
   4. Do you act on the facts in a situation, in spite of your feelings?

II. Have you developed a measure of maturity in handling frustration?
   1. What was your pattern of behavior when your wishes were blocked at age five? Age ten? Age fifteen? Your present age? Can you see growth toward maturity in your changing pattern of behavior?
   2. As you think of mistakes you have made in the past, can you think of specific things you have learned from your mistakes?
   3. How many times during the past month have you blamed others for something that was really partly your fault?

III. Are you developing characteristics of a mature adult?
   1. Do you have a philosophy of life that enables you to meet unalterable situations with poise?
   2. Do you practice a reasonable measure of self-discipline in getting your work done or meeting responsibilities and obligations?
   3. Do you live in the present and plan for the future, leaving the past behind, except insofar as you can profit by having learned from experiences?
   4. Can you support yourself financially?
   5. Have you had the experience of earning your own money and living within a fixed budget?
   6. Have you developed a degree of other-centeredness? Do you find it easy to fit in with and to meet the ego needs of others?

---

7. How many strong prejudices do you have? (Prejudice relates to matters like being a good or poor student, or living in a certain region, or to social and financial standing, as well as to race, politics, religion, and many other matters.) Do you have fewer than, more than, or about the same number of strong prejudices as you had five years ago?

IV. Are you approaching a maturity adequate for marriage?

1. Can you look at your family background and assess its contribution to your attitudes, views, and feelings about marriage?
2. Have your experiences with love and affection enabled you to grow in your understanding of love?
3. Do you see sex in marriage as a desirable and wholesome relationship designed to bring satisfaction and security to both partners?
4. Have you become emotionally weaned from your parents so that your spouse will have little reason to feel that you are too dependent on them?
5. Have you grown to the place where you can think first of your responsibilities to others and sacrifice your personal needs when necessary?

chapter **11**

suggested content for the eleventh grade

Overview

This unit begins with a study of communication. The relationship between communication breakdowns and sexual conflicts is examined. A detailed problem-solving outline is introduced to re-emphasize the importance of this method of appraising problems and seeking solutions.

The material on "Marriage Day by Day" is designed to focus the student's attention on the economics of marriage. An intelligent appraisal of methods of handling a family's anticipated income is needed to help students appreciate the many factors involved in deciding whether that income will be adequate. "Money matters" are cited as one of the chief causes of marital difficulties.

The study of divorce is included to serve as a review of the previous units in the family life program. Marriage failure can generally be traced to an inadequate preparation for marriage or immaturity on the part of one or both partners. Studying why marriages go wrong is one of the best ways to see what factors are necessary to make them go right. The special adjustments that teenage brides and grooms must make should be reviewed when studying about divorce.

The unit concludes with a study of the family responsibilities of the married couple in American society. Emphasis should be placed on the development of a democratic family and on the roles of the husband and wife. It is important for the students to understand that the rapid changes that have taken place in our society and culture require potential marriage partners to discuss frankly what type of family they wish to establish and the role each expects the other to assume. Serious marital problems may arise between couples with widely divergent viewpoints concerning roles.

Students should continually be aware of the distinct characteristics of the masculine and feminine point of view in each area of this unit so that they will be better able to understand their future marriage partners.

The basal text can be either Landis and Landis' *Personal Adjustment, Marriage, and Family Living* or Duvall's *Before You Marry.*

Curriculum Outlines

Instructional Objectives

The student understands that:

1. Systems for intellectual and emotional communication need to be established early in marriage.
2. Beginning families need to establish ground rules for routine married life.
3. An intelligent study of divorce is a good way to develop the attitudes and understandings that help build an effective marriage.
4. Our society recognizes the need to protect the unity and strength of the family.
5. Applying democratic principles to family living gives strength and flexibility to the family.

Content

Communication

A. Maturity for marriage

B. Systems for intellectual and emotional communication

1. These systems need to be established early in marriage. One of the critical tests of the adequacy of communication within marriage is the way the couple meets a con-

Suggested Learning Opportunities

- Briefly review the material covered in the tenth-grade unit.
- Discuss the ideas contained in Document 11-1, "Establishing Systems of Intellectual and Emotional Communication." Also see "Rules for constructive quarreling" on page 221.
- Divide the class into small groups and have each group prepare a skit showing trifling incidents that may

flict situation. As long as they keep silent and pretend that they have no problems, little progress can be made in getting through to each other. When one person leaves the conflict situation in anger, tears, or patient martyrdom, communication is not adequate.

2. As the husband and wife make a real effort to share their true feelings and their anxiety or fear, even though their feelings and values do differ, they will be able to bridge their differences. The couple must have open systems of communication through which each gets across to the other the comfort, love, understanding, sympathy, loyalty, and sense of purpose that a man or woman needs in order to feel truly married.

cause quarrels between a newly married couple. Following the performance of the skits, ask the class to select the point at which the trouble began. Then have the groups perform the skits again, this time either avoiding or solving the problem that arose the first time.

- Have the class discuss the following idea: It has often been noted that six persons are involved in every marital relationship: the husband as the person he really is, the husband as he imagines himself to be, the husband as the wife pictures him, the wife as the person she really is, the wife as she imagines herself to be, and the wife as her husband pictures her.
- Invite a marriage counselor to speak to the class on the problems of communication in marriage.
- Have the class discuss and arrive at a definition of effective communication.
- View and discuss the film *David and Hazel.*
- Have the class list the various methods of communication in marriage.
- Have small groups discuss the ways that people inadvertently stop one another from communicating effectively. Following the discussion, have the group reporters compile a list of actions that limit effective communication between persons. The class may want to list the actions according to the types of individuals who are trying to communicate, for example, parents, dates, teachers, friends, or other adults.

C. Problems of communication
   1. How to communicate effectively?
   2. How to establish bonds of communication?

- Review the problem-solving method introduced in the eighth grade and design a chart for class use. See Document 11-2, "A Pattern for Problem Solving," for an example.

3. What is a workable pattern of problem solving?

- View and discuss the film *Love Is for the Byrds.*
- Have the class discuss the statement: "Speeches won't help when a couple disagrees; however, conversation and discussion should be encouraged, for from them may come ideas for new approaches needed to resolve the conflict."

D. The effects a breakdown of communications can have on sexual relations in marriage

- Discuss the ideas contained in Document 11-3, "The Effects of a Communications Breakdown on Sexual Relationships."
- Have the class discuss how the use of sexual relations can be an effective way to solve a communications breakdown.
- Have the class discuss what sexual relations can communicate.
- Discuss how a wife's boredom with sexual relations may be related to a problem of communications. How can a husband's problems with his job affect his sexual relations?
- Read and discuss the ideas presented in *Understanding the Other Sex.*
- Read and discuss "What To Do About Disagreements" in *The Man That You Marry.*

Resources

(S) Document 11-1, "Establishing Systems of Intellectual and Emotional Communication."

(S) Film: *David and Hazel,* McGraw-Hill, b/w, 28 min. Describes need for communication between marriage partners, especially about business problems. Shows how communication or lack of it affects the emotional climate in home.

(S) Document 11-2, "A Pattern for Problem Solving."

(S) Film: *Love Is for the Byrds,* Brigham Young University, color, 23 min. Shows some of the problems of communication and understanding that develop in marriage, and pinpoints some of the "myths" commonly held by young people regarding marriage.

(S) Document 11-3, "The Effects of a Communications Breakdown on Sexual Relationships."

(S) Kirkendall, Lester A., and Ruth Farnham Osborne, *Understanding the Other Sex.* Chicago: Science Research Associates, 1955.
(S) Boll, Eleanor Stoker, *The Man That You Marry.* Philadelphia: Macrae Smith, 1963, pp. 108–11.

Content

Marriage Day by Day

A. One of the first problems a couple must solve is where to establish a home.

1. Securing suitable housing may be a difficult problem for some couples.
2. The needs of a family vary from time to time regarding the size of the home they require.
3. The choice of location and the floor plan of the house or apartment require careful consideration.
4. Living with relatives may create more problems than it solves.

B. A couple must also decide how to handle its money. A mutually satisfactory system for earning and spending money must be agreed upon.

1. Money matters can have a profound effect on a marriage. Their effects depend upon the intelligence with which they are recognized and handled. The amount of income neces-

Suggested Learning Opportunities

- View and discuss the film *When Should I Marry?*
- Have the class discuss: "Should one spend a large sum on a permanent home and wait a few years to buy furniture?"
- Have the class discuss: "Buying a House vs. Renting a House or Apartment."
- Ask students to investigate and report on the cost of the interest on a home loan.
- Ask some students to report on some local housing developments. Where will you get your money's worth? Which houses and which neighborhoods seem to be the best places to rear a family?
- Have the class discuss what percentage of their income most families spend on housing.
- Have the class list the factors to be considered in evaluating the floor-plan of a house or apartment for space and convenience.
- Discuss American traditions and customs concerning the handling of money.
- Assign Chapter 19, "Learning To Manage the Family Income," in *Personal Adjustment, Marriage, and Family Living,* or Chapter 5, "Financing Your Marriage," in *Before You Marry.*
- Have the class discuss what they feel

sary will depend on what standard of living the couple expect and desire. This expectation depends on the income to which each partner has been accustomed, how important material things are to them, and individual responsibilities they have, such as the need to support a relative.

would be an appropriate standard of living for newly married couples in their community.

- Discuss how American education and advertisements seem to produce differences in the values held by men and women.
- View and discuss the filmstrip *Learning To Manage Your Money.*
- Poll the class on the following problem: "Suppose you marry and are able to live in a comfortably but simply furnished apartment and can save $100 a month. Would you prefer to:
    1. Use the $100 for recreation.
    2. Buy a car.
    3. Put the $100 in a savings account without a specific purpose.
    4. Invest the money in a business, in stocks, or in a mutual fund.
    5. Begin to have children.
    6. Buy furniture of your own.
    7. Buy a house or land.
    8. Travel.

  Tabulate the answers of the male and female students and compare the values of the two groups.

2. There are several methods of handling money within the family. More important than the system is that there is agreement between the couple on the system they select.
3. What is budgeting? Financial planning is as important in marital relationships as it is in business. Spending beyond one's income just for routine living can become a serious family problem. If properly used, budgeting can stretch the family income and also bring a greater degree of unity between husband and wife. Whether an informal type of budgeting is satisfactory or whether a more detailed type is required depends on the couple. All couples, however, need to plan their finances together.

- Refer to pages 91–92 in *Before You Marry* for some workable ideas of how families may handle their money.
- Have the class use the following steps in designing a budget. Have them consult their family for realistic figures on income, household expenses, etc.
    1. Keep a careful record of family expenses for a month.
    2. List fixed expenses and obligations.
    3. List household expenses.
    4. List personal expenses.
    5. Set aside an emergency fund.

6. Set aside a small amount to be saved.

- Have each student make a list of twenty items on which they, as a young married person, would like to spend money. Indicate which ones they consider luxuries and which are necessities. Compile according to sex, and discuss.
- Have the class compile a list of possible unexpected expenses.

4. What types of savings and insurance are needed? The amount to be saved depends upon the size of the couple's income and the margin left after taking care of necessities. A budget does not necessarily guarantee savings, but a program that is well planned in advance will help. An important factor is to decide upon a definite amount to be put aside and then to save it regularly. Savings are not gained by lowering one's standard of living but by an appraisal of relative values. Kinds of insurance, their cost, their value at maturity, etc., should be thoroughly investigated before the couple commit themselves to a plan.

- Have a lawyer discuss the kinds of insurance available for families. Ask him to discuss the reliability of insurance brokers, the insurance provided by unions and companies at no cost to the worker, and state programs like social security. What does it mean to be "insurance poor"?
- Have students discuss with their parents the kinds of insurance they have carried and are carrying.
- Organize a debate on the subject of purchasing insurance versus putting the same sum of money in a savings account or investment program.
- Have some students investigate the amount of interest paid on savings accounts by the various types of banks, savings and loan companies, and credit associations.

5. How can a couple spend its money wisely? An advertisement is no indication that an article is of high or low quality, since extravagant claims are made for all goods. A couple should compare brands and prices objectively and seek advice to counter the confusion created by advertising. If one buys quality goods wisely, it means that the fam-

- Have students prepare a report on household items using the following sources:
  1. Consumers' Research, Inc., and its magazine *Consumer Bulletin.*
  2. Consumers Union of the U.S., Inc., and its magazine *Consumer Reports.*
  3. Advertisements in the newspapers and magazines.
- Invite an expert to speak on how to

ily has more money for other expenditures.

judge the quality of at least one article commonly needed in new homes.

- Have students bring in cartoons illustrating problems consumers face.
- Analyze various types of advertising to discover the psychology behind them.
- Have the class read and discuss Chapter 20, "Consumer Economics and Family Security," in *Personal Adjustment, Marriage, and Family Living.*
- Select a student to give a report on *The Hidden Persuaders.*

Resources

(S) Film: *When Should I Marry?* McGraw-Hill, b/w, 19 min. An examination of a minister's advice to a young couple eager to get married. Summarizes some points to consider when deciding marriage readiness.

(S) Landis, Judson, and Mary Landis, *Personal Adjustment, Marriage, and Family Living.* Englewood Cliffs, N.J.: Prentice-Hall, 1966, chs. 19 and 20.

(S) Duvall, Sylvanus M., *Before You Marry.* New York: Association Press, 1959, ch. 5, pp. 91–92.

(S) Filmstrip and record: *Learning To Manage Your Money,* Society for Visual Education, color, 33⅓ r.p.m. record, 9 min. Suggests proper attitudes and gives concrete advice for correct money management. Several answers are presented to help the teenager arrive at his own best solution.

(S) *Consumer Bulletin.* Consumers' Research, Inc., Washington, N.J.

(S) *Consumer Reports.* Consumers Union of the U.S., Inc., 256 Washington St., Mt. Vernon, N.Y.

(S) Packard, Vance, *The Hidden Persuaders.* New York: Pocket Books, 1957.

Content

Divorce

A. General

Divorce is so widespread in our society that an intelligent study of divorce is necessary if one is to have the attitudes and understanding that are needed to

Suggested Learning Opportunities

- Have the class discuss the statement: "*People* fail, not *marriages.*"
- Discuss the ideas contained in Document 11-4, "Marriage Is a Way of Life."
- Have the class discuss the idea that

help him build a good marriage and avoid the eventuality of divorce.

B. Causes
   1. Lack of preparation for marriage
   2. Immaturity of one or both partners
   3. Conflicting marital expectations
   4. Separation caused by military service or occupation
   5. Conflicts over sex

Americans may be oversold on the value of a marriage relationship for everyone.

- Have the class discuss the various social changes believed to contribute to our current high divorce rate.
- Read and discuss Chapter 21, "Avoiding Divorce," in *Personal Adjustment, Marriage, and Family Living.*
- Present current local and national statistics on the rate of divorce for teenage marriages. Have the class list their ideas on why teenage marriages have such a high rate of failure. Compile the reasons, and discuss in small groups.
- Have the class discuss the statement: "The best way to solve marital problems is to change yourself, not your spouse."
- Discuss the ideas contained in Document 11-5, "Motivations for Marriage That Cause Conflicts."
- Have a committee survey the community resources available for helping families in a crisis situation and report to the class.

C. Possible effects
   1. Emotionally, psychologically, and socially traumatic experience for both partners
   2. Change in economic status
   3. Adverse effect on growth and development of the children
   4. Bitterness created by divorce laws in many states because one partner must be identified as the wrongdoer

D. Problems after divorce
   1. Readjustments to living alone
   2. Living with oneself
   3. Adjustment of social life
   4. Creation of a financial crisis
   5. Reaction to emotional stress

- Have the class list some of the effects of divorce on children; discuss how they could be minimized.
- Compile a list of the legal reasons for a divorce in your state.
- Have the class list the deeper, nonlegal reasons for divorce.
- Discuss the ideas contained in Document 11-6, "Divorce: Social Implications."
- Invite a clergyman or marriage counselor to talk about how divorces can be prevented and how adjustments can be made after a divorce has been granted.
- Have a committee report on the efforts being made by a Conciliation Court or efforts being made to establish one in your community.

Resources

(S) Document 11-4, "Marriage Is a Way of Life."
(S) Landis, Judson, and Mary Landis, *Personal Adjustment, Marriage, and Family Living*. Englewood Cliffs, N.J.: Prentice-Hall, 1966, ch. 21.
(S) Document 11-5, "Motivations for Marriage That Cause Conflicts."
(S) Document 11-6, "Divorce: Social Implications."

Content

Family Responsibilities

A. The protective function
   1. The family supplies food, clothing, and shelter for its members.
   2. It provides economic security.
   3. It protects by supplying moral support and encouragement.

B. Center for the formation of ideals and attitudes
   1. It is effective in the development of moral and spiritual values.
   2. The role a young person plays in society develops largely out of family experiences.

C. Family democracy
   1. What is a democratic family? What are the roles of the family members?
   2. What is a mutually acceptable pattern of who does what and who is accountable to whom?

Suggested Learning Opportunities

- Discuss the ideas contained in Document 11-7, "An Effective Family."
- Invite a lawyer to explain the protection the law gives the members of families from birth to death, and the state's concern for the family as a unit and for the welfare of each member of the family. Have him briefly review the laws governing family property and rights; the laws governing the protection of children; and the legal responsibilities of the husband and wife toward each other, toward their children, and toward their own parents. The lawyer might also wish to comment on other laws that reflect the state's support of marriage: tax laws; military draft and pay laws; rent, housing, mortgage, and loan laws and policies.
- Read and discuss Chapter 25, "The Successful Family," in *Personal Adjustment, Marriage, and Family Living*.
- Read and discuss the pamphlet *Democracy Begins in the Home.*
- Have the class devise and conduct a survey among men and women of various age groups asking: "In what areas are teenagers of today given too much freedom in making their own decisions? In what areas should teenagers today be given more freedom in making their own decisions?"

- Use the same survey anonymously with the class members. Compile, compare, and discuss. If there is a division between the opinions of the teenagers and the adults, have the class formulate plans to help resolve these differences.

3. Who will be head of the household?

- Conclude this unit with a final discussion on: Who will be head of your household?

Resources

(S) Document 11-7, "An Effective Family."
(S) Landis, Judson, and Mary Landis, *Personal Adjustment, Marriage, and Family Living*. Englewood Cliffs, N.J.: Prentice-Hall, 1966, ch. 25.
(S) Osborne, Ernest, *Democracy Begins in the Home*. New York: Public Affairs Pamphlets, 1953.

Background and Teaching Materials

Document 11-1 **Establishing Systems of Intellectual and Emotional Communication**

One of the biggest jobs facing the recently married couple is that of communicating with each other. Two people may live in the same house, they may share the same bed and board, but unless they establish effective systems of communication between them, they might as well be miles apart. She may live through the days in tight-lipped silence, he may pout and mope through the evenings, with no awareness of what "is eating" either of them, unless and until they have developed the signs and signals, the words and the gestures that keep the state of affairs open to them both.

Human beings do not live in emotional vacuums, but in a climate of feeling that changes quite as often as the weather. Each of us as men and as women at times feel loving and at times feel hateful; at times are high

Document 11-1, *Establishing Systems of Intellectual and Emotional Communication*, is taken from Evelyn M. Duvall, *Family Development*, 2nd ed. (Philadelphia, Lippincott, 1962), pp. 137–41. Reprinted with permission. May not be copied without the written permission of J. B. Lippincott Company, East Washington Square, Philadelphia, Pa. 19105.

and at other times low; are sometimes mad and sometimes sad. Mental hygiene findings have indicated without question that the healthful way to live is to recognize emotional states for what they are, as they arise, and to deal with them realistically and honestly. Pretending that all is well while one seethes inside is not only hypocrisy, it is corrosive even to the point of gastric ulcers if it becomes habitual.

If two people are to live intimately together in marriage, they must learn to express their real feelings in ways that are acceptable and healthful. They must develop ways of communicating for the mutual planning and for the furtherance of mutual services; and for the sheer necessity of sharing the meanings of a moment in the sense we mean by true companionship—two people understanding and being understood in a system of mutual identification that is deeply satisfying.

The young husband who has been brought up in a home where his father communicated with his wife by asking one of the children to "tell your mother" this or that, may have problems when he marries, in learning to be as open with his wife as she may desire. Such a wife tries to share her husband's day by little inquiries upon his return home: "How did your day go, dear?" or "Did you have a nice lunch?" only to have her efforts met with either a mumbled grunt or an annoyed, don't-bother-me-now response that does little to further the communication between the two.

Communication is a two-way task and a mutual achievement. Just as the husband may have difficulties in getting out of himself at times, so too the wife may find it hard to project herself into enough of her husband's interests to get much beyond the homey superficial levels of their life together. One young bride took lessons in photography in order to be able to share more intelligently her husband's interest in taking and showing his Kodachrome slides. Another wife found that her part-time job in her husband's plant one rush season added a great deal to the level of communication between them. This may be one reason why we find that women with some regular work experience make better adjustments after marriage than those who move from the protection of their father's home to that of their husband's with no opportunity to learn by experience how a man spends his day at work.[1]

Communication is an intricate complex of words, gestures, signs, and symbolic actions that have meanings to the communicating people. Some of these words and meanings are universal. Some are peculiar to the language and cultural group. More subtle systems are highly individual and must be built up within the new relationship. One of the joys of courtship, engagement, and the honeymoon is found in the development and the prac-

[1] Ernest W. Burgess and Leonard S. Cottrell, *Predicting Success or Failure in Marriage* (Englewood Cliffs, N.J., Prentice-Hall, 1939), pp. 136–58.

tice of intimate, personal gestures and symbols that have meaning only for the two persons. They identify "our song," they walk by "our house" through "our park," and they repeat little ceremonies that convey more than words could the special significance each has for the other. Special gestures of affection become their own language of love that channel love feelings and add immeasurably to the satisfaction they get in each other's company.

It may be relatively easy to get through to each other with love and affection. But learning how to handle the inevitable negative feelings that arise from time to time is a difficult assignment for many couples. No two people see eye to eye about all things. No two people feel the same way about everything they share in life together. So some conflict is to be expected in marriage, especially during the establishment phase when the two people are learning to mesh their former ways of living into a unity of habits, aspirations, and values.

The romantic illusion prevalent in America calls for two people in love living "happily ever after" in a state of perpetual bliss that offers no room for the disagreements and differences that two normal people inevitably find cropping up between them. So, when the first quarrels occur, one or both of the pair mistakenly may feel that the marriage is failing, their love is not lasting, or they were not "made for each other" after all. The couple that is able to see conflict as a part of the close, intimate marriage relationship, accepts its reality and assumes the responsibility for meeting constructively the differences that arise.

One of the critical tests of the adequacy of the communication established within a marriage is found in the way in which the two people meet a conflict situation. As long as they keep silent and pretend that they have no problems, little progress can be made in getting through to each other. When one person leaves the conflict situation in anger or in tears, or in patient martyrdom, communication between the partners is poor. As the husband and wife make a real effort to share their true feelings and to accept without anxiety or fear the fact that their feelings and values do differ, they are able to learn to bridge their differences. . . .

It takes time to learn to live constructively with differences in ways that increase the harmony of the marriage and the understanding of each other. It may not be fully accomplished during the first establishment phase of the marriage, but it should be begun well enough so that further tasks will not be rendered more complicated by failure to communicate effectively in moments of strain and tension. The husband and wife who establish good systems of communication for handling the hot spot areas of their relationship find real satisfaction in knowing "if we can handle this, we can weather anything that comes."

Unity as a couple is established by the network of bonds that weave the two into two-in-one. The bonds are not ties in the sense of fetters. There are open systems of communication through which each gets across to the other for the comfort, the love, the understanding, the sympathy, the loyalty and the sense of purpose a man or woman needs to feel truly married. Without such communication a person may ache with loneliness even while beside the mate. With a well-established communication system, the husband and wife feel united even though they may be separated by many months and miles.

Document 11-2 **A Pattern for Problem Solving**[1]

Steps	*Key Questions*	*Purposes*
1. Face the problem	What is the matter? Why do I/we think it is a problem?	To get problem into words. To uncover the fear involved.
2. Look at the causes	What has been happening? What has made it a problem now?	To get the build-up of the problem. To get a clear statement of what is bringing it to a head.
3. Set some goals	What do I want to accomplish for myself? For the other person? What do we/I want the situation to be?	To be sure of desires for self. To be sure that decisions will benefit others as well as self. To set a definite change to work toward.
4. Get more knowledge and understanding	What knowledge from the biological, psychological and social sciences are applicable? Have I found all the available material in technical and popular literature? What has been the experience of other people in similar situations?	To increase understanding. To gain insight.
5. Be the other person (Try to be each of the other persons or groups of persons involved in the problem)	Just how would I, as this other person, think about it? And as this other person what does he or she feel?	To get the other person's point of view and emotional slant. To allow thinking and feelings of others to be a framework for the next step.

6. Consider what to do	What could we/I do about it?	To get a list of possible actions.
	Will that bring me to my goals?	To be sure they lead to the goals.
	Will it fit the thoughts and feelings of the other person?	To be sure they will be acceptable to other person.
7. Make a plan of action	Just how can this be done?	To plan how to do it.
	Who will do each part? How will I do it?	To develop a 1, 2, 3, plan.
	Who will help me?	To select the person to help at each point if needed.
8. Check the plan with the goals	Will this plan lead you to your goals?	To be sure the plan is really directed at the desired solution.
	Does it provide for each goal?	To be sure it covers all the goals set.
9. Plan the follow-up	What shall I/we watch for to be sure the plan is working?	To encourage watchfulness in using the plan.
		To encourage abandonment if it seems to be failing.

[1] An adaption of "A Pattern for Counseling" by L. A. Lynde, Extension Specialist in Parent Education, January 30, 1947.

Document 11-2, *A Pattern for Problem Solving*, is by Mrs. Girdie Ware, Associate Professor Emeritus, Department of Family Relations and Child Development, College of Home Economics, Oklahoma State University, and Consultant, Child Welfare Division, State Department of Public Welfare, Austin, Texas. Mrs. Ware grants teachers permission to make copies of this chart for use in connection with their own family life and sex education classes.

Document 11-3 ***The Effects of a Communications Breakdown on Sexual Relationships***

When marital partners are unable to share their joys, angers, fears, and hopes, they no longer share a personal intimacy. When we have to hide our feelings, it is difficult to feel anything about people or things. A symptom of this loss of personal intimacy is usually sexual conflict.

Sexual intercourse is not only a physical act. It is not simply a matter of relieving certain physiological tensions. Every human act expresses feelings, attitudes, and concerns. We put an arm around a friend in trouble, or hold a child to comfort him, and these physical acts are important because of the concern and feeling that they convey. This is even more true of sexual intercourse. It is a means of deepening and strengthening intimacy. The breakdown of communications in marriage tends to empty the sexual act of its substantial meaning. Sexuality without mutual intimacy is hollow. It pretends to symbolize attitudes that no longer exist. This kind of counterfeit sexuality becomes more and more distasteful to the wife, since it does not meet her need for personal intimacy. But sexuality becomes a means of reassurance for the man under this threat to his adequacy as a man. Thus, the cause of marital problems appears to be sexual conflict rather than the true cause, the lack of effective communication between marriage partners.

Document 11-4 ***Marriage Is a Way of Life***

Marriage is a way of life rather than a goal or destination. We all believe in individuality; then why do 94% of the Americans join the institution of marriage? Read the following statements. Discuss them. How valid are they for you? Is everyone suited to marriage?

1. Marriage is a means of achieving together more than either person could have achieved alone.
2. Marriage requires unity of two individuals, yet allows for each to retain his uniqueness.
3. Marriage can give you a sense of importance and security.

---

4. Marriage channels the sexual feelings toward creative and constructive goals for the partners and society.
5. Marriage offers the best of all opportunities for the enrichment of our sex life.
6. Marriage has one of the best records for the satisfaction of human needs.
7. Marriage offers the best safeguard against loneliness.
8. Being married means you are wanted.

Document 11-5 ***Motivations for Marriage That Cause Conflicts***

1. Escape from an unhappy home. This type of person may have been unable to get along well with his family and is looking for a relationship that will remove him from the source of his unhappiness. His predominant motivation for marriage is escape.
2. Escape from feelings of loneliness. This type of person may have personality difficulties. He may believe that changing his environment by marrying will make life more pleasant and meaningful. However, he usually finds out that marriage is no solution for inner problems.
3. Marriage for the purpose of living through others. This type of person usually regards himself as less worthy or inferior and seeks to find meaning in life through the accomplishments of a marital partner.
4. Marriage for material possessions and wealth. This type of person may be ruthlessly ambitious with little interest in the needs of others; or he may have been unable to establish a stable love relationship and has given up and decided to marry for material possessions. People who deny that love is possible find it hard to develop a meaningful marital relationship.
5. Marriage on the rebound. This type of person has had an unsatisfactory love relationship and usually feels very unworthy; such a person hastens to resolve these feelings by finding another marital partner.

It is important to understand one's motives for marriage. If one seeks marriage only as a tool to help escape from an undesirable condition, a period of disillusionment is almost inevitable. The marriage partner is not regarded as an end in himself, but rather as a means to an end. Bitterness occurs when one discovers that neither marriage nor a marital partner can solve these difficulties; their resolution depends on one's coming to grips with them personally.

The five motivations listed are unsatisfactory if they are the *only* or *main* reason why a person wants to get married, but their mere presence is no proof that a person should not get married. Many people whose marriages are successful had traces of such feelings as *secondary* motivations.

Document 11-6 ***Divorce: Social Implications***

Some people believe that easy divorce, as it exists in our society, is a hazard to successful marriage, since a couple may sometimes think of it as a ready solution to the problems that arise in a marriage. The seemingly easier escape through divorce may prevent a couple from facing their marital problems in a mature manner. In former times, when divorce was not socially acceptable and was more difficult legally, many marital partners were forced to face their problems realistically and resolve them.

Many people still feel strongly that no divorces should be granted. This is the position of the Catholic Church. Some people accept divorce more tolerantly. From their viewpoint, while divorce is the termination of one relationship and in that sense painful, it may relieve an almost intolerable situation. It may open the door to happier, improved adjustments, and may even be the first step toward establishing a new, more satisfying relationship.

Unfortunately, divorce often involves exchanging one set of problems for another. The trauma involved, and the personality damage caused by the feeling of failure that divorce represents, is often worse than the difficulties people seek to escape. The decision to seek a divorce should only be made after all other sources of help have been exhausted. Until divorce is stabilized through marriage education, marriage counseling, conciliation courts, and the like, the increase in our divorce rate will reflect the instability of American families.

Document 11-7 ***An Effective Family***

An effective family illustrates the following characteristics:

1. The members are loyal to each other, show affection, and are cooperative.

2. The members enjoy living together and showing their happiness.
3. Members of the family contribute to the affairs of the community.
4. Family members help each other through times of stress and trouble and share spiritual values.
5. The family allows aggressive behavior at times and differences of opinions without getting upset.
6. Family members share tasks and activities and enjoy working and playing together.
7. The family encourages each member to develop to his fullest capacity at his own speed and in his own manner.

chapter **12**

suggested content for the twelfth grade

Overview

This final unit of the family life and sex education program is designed to reenforce the student's understanding of the importance of the family as an influence on each individual, as an influence on the larger community, and as the cornerstone of American democracy.

The maturity of the twelfth-grade students should enable the class to review effectively the "double standard" in our society, to understand the effects of an illegitimate pregnancy upon all family members, and to realize that premarital sexual experiences can increase the difficulties of building a permanent relationship.

The "Rules for constructive quarreling" (see page 221) should help students develop positive attitudes toward premarital and marital disagreements. Human reproduction is reviewed to clear up misconceptions. The need for prenatal care and the cost of child-bearing are examined. The crucial role of family planning in marriage and in our world today is stressed.

Major emphasis should be placed on the child care portion of this unit. Some students may lack interest in this subject, but they can be motivated by arranging appropriate observations of young children in nursery schools or nearby elementary schools. For a number of students this will be their only exposure in an academic setting to the basic principles of child care. The sharply increased number of emotionally disturbed children in schools today has made it mandatory for the high school to prepare both boys and girls to assume the role of effective parents.

The time available to the family life and sex education program in many schools will not be sufficient to permit child growth and development to be studied in great detail. The teacher should concentrate instead on helping the students to develop desirable attitudes and an awareness of their responsibilities as parents for the guidance of the children in their future families. The students should also learn where they can obtain reliable scientific information about children and the community resources available.

The family life and sex education program is completed with a discussion of "How Does a Parent Teach His Children About Sex?" and a final summation pointing out that the quality of our own family life depends on our own emotional resources.

The recommended basal text is Duvall and Hill's *When You Marry* (high school edition), or Allen Fromme's *Sex and Marriage* and Smart and Smart's *Living and Learning with Children.*

Curriculum Outlines

Instructional Objectives

The student understands that:

1. Marriage has one of the best records for the satisfaction of human needs.
2. A good marital sexual relationship is the product of mutual understanding and adjustment.
3. Establishing a workable philosophy of life as a couple gives unity to a marriage.
4. Bearing children is socially approved only if it occurs within the institution of the family.
5. Good parenthood demands an appreciation of children's needs.
6. The quality of our family life depends on our own emotional resourcefulness.

Content	Suggested Learning Opportunities
Functions of the Family A. The family is the medium for mutual love and companionship of husband and wife.	• Have a student report on *Cheaper by the Dozen,* discussing the advantages and disadvantages of a large family. • Ask students to read *What Makes a*

B. Every household has these four "managerial" functions:

1. The management of time
2. The management of money
3. The guidance of growth: physical, mental, emotional, social, and spiritual
4. The making and enforcement of decisions

C. Bearing children is socially approved only if it occurs within the institution of the family. No completely satisfactory alternative to the family setting has been found.

D. Sexual relationships are most meaningful in the family setting.[1]

1. A marriage certificate is a beginner's permit.
   a. Premarital sexual experiences may increase the difficulties of the unmarried person in adjusting to his sexual nature and may cause him other difficulties once he gets married.
   b. Pressuring a girl for intimacy is usually not based on mutual affection but is a form of exploitation.
   c. Our society still has a "double standard" that will ostracize the girl for the same behavior for which it will only criticize the boy.
2. Sexual experiences can build

Good Home?

- Assign Chapter 1, "Family Life Has Changed," in *A Guide for Family Living*. Discuss in small groups.
- Discuss the making and enforcement of decisions.
- Invite a speaker from an agency administering foster homes.
- Have students read studies on foundling homes and report to the class.
- Discuss how an effective family contributes not only to the individual couple and their children but to society as a whole.
- Discuss the ideas contained in Document 12-1, "The Functions of the Family."
- Discuss: "It is an important emotional experience for a woman to give up her virginity. The experience causes her to feel a very special attachment to the man, and is thus a sound beginning for a marriage." Discuss: "Is it better for a man to enter into marriage a virgin, so that the sexual relationship he establishes with his wife need not be compared with past experiences?"
- Discuss the concept that most premarital sexual relationships are in reality "pre-nothing," and so using the term "premarital" is a form of delusion.
- View and discuss the film *How Do I Love Thee?*
- Discuss the concept that a girl has to be more concerned about sexual relations because (1) she can't deny that

[1] The emphasis in this area should be: that the ability to communicate effectively is vital to a married couple; that they must be understanding, patient, and considerate with each other, rather than merely make critical judgments; that mutual sexual satisfaction usually takes a period of time to achieve. Sexual techniques are not suitable topics to be discussed in the classroom. Misconceptions that show up in questions in the Question Box or in comments in class should be cleared up in individual discussions, however. Your best source for personal preparation is Chapters 4 and 5 of Dr. Allan Fromme's *Sex and Marriage*.

constructive or destructive attitudes toward sexual relations in marriage.

3. Good personality adjustment is the best basis for good sexual adjustment.
   a. Sexual compatibility is important in marriage, but basic personality factors are more important. A good marital sex life is a product of mutual understanding and adjustment.
   b. However, a clear understanding of the biological aspects of sexuality and reproduction is also necessary.

a baby is hers; (2) she can't escape her normal feelings of dependence upon her lover; (3) she can't escape her desire for love and tenderness.

- Discuss: "The ability to wait is related to one's maturity."
- Have the class discuss the "double standard."
- Read and discuss Document 12-2, "If They Had Only Waited." Bring out these points:
  1. Paul and Nancy's breaking the moral code.
  2. The double standard: "Paul is under age and must have his parents' permission to marry."
  3. The effects on each family and each family member.
  4. The responsibilities Paul and Nancy will have as parents toward their own child.
- Discuss: "The fundamental principle of morality concerns the idea that one individual shall not take advantage of another or exploit another for his own satisfaction."
- Arrange a panel discussion with representatives of the clergy, the medical profession (psychiatrists), and the legal profession on problems involved in promiscuity.
- Discuss the various attitudes described in the book *Premarital Sexual Standards in America.*
- Assign pp. 160–65, "The Honeymoon," in *When You Marry.*

4. If problems do occur, where may reliable help be secured?

- Discuss the ideas contained in Document 12-3, "Marriage Counseling."
- Discuss sources of professional help to solve marital sex problems.
- Have each student write an outline or essay for his own personal use describing the development of his attitudes toward sex.
- Review local resources surveyed in the eleventh grade.

Resources

(S) Gilbreth, Frank, *Cheaper by the Dozen.* New York: Thomas Y. Crowell, 1963.
(S) Wolf, Anna W. M., and Margaret C. Dawson, *What Makes a Good Home?* New York: Child Study Association of America, 1965.
(S) Jenkins, Gladys Gardner, *A Guide for Family Living.* Chicago: Science Research Associates, 1956, ch. 1.
(S) Document 12-1, "The Functions of the Family."
(S) Document 12-2, "If They Had Only Waited."
(T) Reiss, Ira, *Premarital Sexual Standards in America.* New York: Macmillan, 1960.
(S) Duvall, Evelyn M., and Reuben Hill, *When You Marry* (high school edition). Boston: Heath, 1965.
(S) Document 12-3, "Marriage Counseling."
(S) Film: *How Do I Love Thee,* Brigham Young University, color, 30 min. Uses the stories of two couples as a basis for a discussion of the moral problems that confront young people who feel they are in love.
(T) Fromme, Allan, *Sex and Marriage.* New York: Barnes & Noble, 1950.

Content

Philosophy of Life

A. What pressures are exerted to force a young couple to take a stand on social issues?

A community is a group of families with some interest in common. A town, a county, a state, and a nation are examples of political communities. Neighborhoods are communities because the people who live in a neighborhood have many of the same interests. A town is a good community for family living when it has adequate provisions for health and safety, good schools and active churches, and a high degree of morale among the residents. Every town can be made better than it is by the active participation of its citizens in community affairs. Children learn citizenship practices through example and direct teaching. The neighborhood is a

Suggested Learning Opportunities

- Discuss decisions a couple must make regarding:
  1. what church to attend
  2. the general political situation and how to vote
  3. filing income tax returns
  4. what social groups to join
  5. what newspaper or magazines to subscribe to
  6. local city problems
- Assign the following topic as the subject for an essay or debate: "The role of the family as the primary source of citizenship education."
- Have a speaker from a service club or the school board discuss individual civic responsibility.
- Discuss the ideas contained in Document 12-4, "Your Marriage Will Be Different."
- Have students read and discuss pp.

practice ground. Learning opportunities widen as a child goes beyond his neighborhood and makes contacts on community, state, and national levels. Many parents are led into community service through the needs of their own children. A neighborhood is as good as the families who live in it.

B. Must a couple write a family creed? What is mutually important to the family unit must be decided upon: the blending of the two individual philosophies of life into a family philosophy.

C. How should a couple agree to disagree?
Productive quarrels are those which leave the marriage stronger by defining the situation causing the conflict.

Rules for constructive quarreling:

1. Spell out exactly what you don't like and how you want things changed.
2. Stick to the point and avoid side issues.
3. Stay with it until you thrash things out.
4. Go on to some simple next step for improvement.
5. Get it out; don't let it fester.
6. Attack the problem rather than each other.
7. Avoid dragging in your relatives.
8. Give each other clues as your tension lets up.

119–21, "Love Easily Disappears in an Atmosphere of Disrespect," in *Sex and Marriage.*

- Ask students to write a theme on the kind of family they would like to establish. Have them include statements on their philosophy of life and on the kind of person they would like to marry.
- Discuss the difference in a family creed or philosophy that is child-oriented, home-oriented, or parent-oriented.[2]

- Define and discuss the difference between quarrels, disagreements, discussions, and arguments.
- Discuss (or invite the school nurse to talk about) the effect a person's physical condition has upon the tendency to quarrel, specifically, the effect of:
    1. illness
    2. hunger
    3. fatigue
- Read and discuss pp. 121–24, "Honest self-expression is bound to create strong disagreements occasionally between husband and wife," in *Sex and Marriage.*
- Discuss: "Is marriage a means of self-expression or self-enslavement?"
- Debate: "Self-control and tact are not inconsistent with honesty."
- Discuss: "Self-expression within the family and mental illness."
- Assign the test on page 207 of *When You Marry* to clarify the difference

[2] See Evelyn M. Duvall, *Family Development* (Philadelphia, Lippincott, 1962), pp. 99–100.

between destructive and productive quarreling.
- Review the film *Handling Marital Conflicts.*
- Assign students to report on Chapters 4, 5, 6, and 7 in *Becoming Men and Women.*
- Ask students to report on the pamphlet *Building Your Philosophy of Life.*
- Have a student report on pp. 231–38, ("What About Quarreling?") in *Personal Adjustment, Marriage, and Family Living.*
- Assign Chapter 10, "Common Conflicts," in *When You Marry.*

Resources

(S) Document 12-4, "Your Marriage Will Be Different."
(S) Fromme, Allan, *Sex and Marriage.* New York: Barnes & Noble, 1950, pp. 119–21, 121–24.
(S) Duvall, Evelyn M., and Reuben Hill, *When You Marry* (high school edition). Boston: Heath, 1965, p. 207, ch. 10.
(S) Film: *Handling Marital Conflicts,* McGraw-Hill, color, 14 min. Portrays the development of an argument between each of two couples. Comparative points are made regarding the elements of constructive and destructive conflict.
(S) Neugarten, Bernice L., *Becoming Men and Women.* Chicago: Science Research Associates, 1955, ch. 4–7.
(S) Smith, T. V., *Building Your Philosophy of Life.* Chicago: Science Research Associates, 1953.
(S) Landis, Judson, and Mary Landis, *Personal Adjustment, Marriage, and Family Living.* Englewood Cliffs: N.J.: Prentice-Hall, 1966, pp. 231–38.
(T) Duvall, Evelyn M., *Family Development.* Philadelphia: Lippincott, 1962, pp. 99–100.

Content

Expanding the Family
A. Human reproduction (review)

Suggested Learning Opportunities

- Show the film *The Human Body: Reproductive System* if the class desires a review.
- Advise the students of the availability of the book *Love and Sex in Plain Language* in the library.

- View and discuss the film *From Generation to Generation.*
- Encourage students to submit any questions they may have about reproduction to the Question Box, and clear up in class any misconceptions that are revealed.
- Assign Chapter 13, "Where Babies Come From," in *When You Marry.*
- Invite the school nurse to discuss human reproduction. Have her discuss briefly heredity and genetic counseling.

B. Family planning

Since the earliest times recorded by history, women and men have recognized the need to control their reproductive power, to balance their capacity for producing children against their ability to provide for them. Egyptian hieroglyphics carved in stone tell of ancient powders and potions used to prevent pregnancy. Hindu physicians 2,000 years ago noted "periods of absolute sterility," certain days of the month when women were unable to conceive. The American Indians made crude edible extracts from wild plants to discourage fertility, and these plants, recently tested, were indeed found to inhibit fertility to some extent.

In addition to these ancient but scientific attempts to prevent conception, people through the ages have experimented with fanciful and traditional "home-remedies" to avoid conception —with varying success and with many problems.

This is the first age when pregnancy can be prevented with safety and almost complete certainty, yet without disturbing the intimate relationship between man and wife. However, the degree of certainty and safety depends on understanding.

1. Definition of family planning

- Discuss population dynamics and socio-economic reasons for controlling family size.
- Discuss current mass media materials on the problems of overpopulation in some of the newly developing countries.
- Discuss the work of Margaret Sanger (opened first birth control clinic).
- Read and discuss *A New Chapter in Family Planning.*
- Discuss the work of Anthony Comstock (responsible for the restrictive laws relating to birth control measures).
- Invite a doctor or teacher to discuss the legal aspects of conception control. Federal laws deal with importation, transportation, and interstate traffic of devices; state laws establish regulations within each state (some 39 states have laws).
- Discuss laws as a guide for personal conduct, and as an enforcement for it.
- View and discuss the film *Family Planning.*
- Discuss the statements listed in the content column.
- Discuss the legal and moral birthrights of children.
- Discuss how family planning can contribute to family stability.

a. The concern should be for the quality of life instead of the quantity.
b. A child's first birthright is to be wanted.
c. Parents have the right to freedom of choice as to the number of children in their family; they can choose either to deliberately limit the number of their children, or to leave the number up to chance. Freedom of choice is based on freedom of information.

2. Control of conception
   a. Birth control is any form of intentional limitation of the size of family.
   b. Contraception is the use of a procedure or a device to control reproduction.
3. Historical birth control methods
   Contraception was recognized as preferable to abortion in the first century. Medical literature has frequent references to contraceptive measures, usually teas and potions. One form of birth control, *Coitus interruptus,* is mentioned in the old testament story of Onan. Aristotle made reference to the use of an intra-uterine device when he spoke of the camel drivers putting pebbles in the camel's uterus to prevent pregnancy, for "pregnant camels are poor workers." Additional methods used for population control were male castration and female infanticide.
4. Modern birth control methods
   a. Temporary (mechanical and

- Discuss how family planning can contribute to the total interpersonal relationship of the marriage. Consider it from the point of view of:
  1. establishing effective communication
  2. making decisions together
  3. setting short- and long-term goals
  4. sharing responsibility
- Clarify for the class the terms "birth control" and "contraception."
- Discuss the history of birth methods.
- Discuss the role abortion plays in our society today in the United States, Japan, and Sweden.
- Read and discuss Document 12-5, "Understanding the Control of Conception."
- Discuss the various methods of birth control.
- Discuss the role of the United States Food and Drug Administration in approving drugs sold for fertility control.
- Discuss the concept that the most suitable method of contraception from a religious, medical, and psychological point of view will depend on the feelings and desires of the individual couple.
- Investigate the various agencies available to give family planning advice: private doctor, public health center, hospital clinic, and Planned Parenthood Clinic.
- Discuss the following three axioms of contraception:
  1. Any method is better than none.
  2. The most effective method is that one used most consistently.
  3. Acceptability of method is a critical factor in effectiveness.

chemical): diaphragm, cervical cap; intra-uterine devices; condoms; drugs, such as local spermicides, creams, and foams; systemic oral medication ("The Pill")

b. Natural: coitus interruptus; rhythm method

c. Permanent: surgical sterilization

5. Future methods under study
At present the area under study is physiological control.
   a. Immunological control: male (inhibits sperm production); female (inhibits placenta formation)
   b. Oral medication (inhibits sperm production in the male)
   c. Hormone therapy (increases safety of the rhythm method by more accurate determination of ovulation time)

C. Prenatal care

Though pregnancy is a normal state, not a disease, it is important that the mother place herself under medical care. Pregnancy does entail physical adjustments of the mother's system and should be supervised by someone who is medically trained. Her doctor will explain what is going on inside her body, how her body is reacting to these changes, and what to expect in the future.

While the mother acts as the incubator of this new human-in-the-making, the father's job is to give support—not financial so much as moral. The mother must make emotional adjustments as well as physical ones. Knowing that she is even more loved because of her role in this joint venture is important.

- Discuss the role of the obstetrician, general practitioner, and prenatal clinic.
- Read and discuss *A Baby Is Born.*
- Have the school nurse discuss prenatal care as a way to prevent birth defects. She should stress the importance of the current nutritional status of the girls in relation to their future role as mothers, and also emphasize the need of follow-up care of the mother after delivery.
- If the girls are interested in further discussion of nutrition, arrange with the school nurse or home economics teacher to meet with them after or before school.
- Check with the County Medical Society regarding the cost of prenatal care.

The mother will receive and should follow the instructions of her doctor. She will be advised about diet, exercise, rest and relaxation, and clothing. The father-to-be ought to know what these instructions are and should help his wife follow them. After all, this is not just Mary Jones who is pregnant; there is a pregnancy in the John Jones family.

D. The cost of a new baby
   1. Cost of physician
   2. Cost of hospitalization
   3. Insurance

E. Necessary adjustments
   1. Arranging for the physical care of the baby
   2. Developing new patterns for earning and spending income
   3. Evaluating and re-evaluating procedures for determining who does what and where the authority rests
   4. Adapting patterns of sexual relationships to pregnancy
   5. Expanding communications systems for present and anticipated emotional needs
   6. Reorienting relationships with relatives
   7. Adapting relationships with friends and associates and participation in community activities to the realities of pregnancy
   8. Acquiring knowledge about planning for the specifics of pregnancy, childbirth, and parenthood
   9. Maintaining morale and a workable philosophy of life

F. The time and attention a new baby must have

Becoming a parent is an awesome undertaking that requires the ability to sacrifice, to postpone personal wants

- Have students make inquiries of the local hospital regarding charges for mother and baby.
- Have a committee of girls plan a layette and necessary baby furniture and compile the cost.
- Ask a student to report on *Babies Are Human Beings.*
- Discuss the utter helplessness of children in the early years and the restrictions on a couple's freedom a baby makes necessary.
- Have the class list how a child can aggravate the personal differences between a husband and wife. Then list the rewards of parenthood.
- Ask a student to report on *These Are Your Children.*
- Discuss the concepts presented in *Sexual Relations During Pregnancy and the Post-Delivery Period.*
- Ask students to report on *Living and Learning with Children.*
- Read and discuss Chapter 9 in *Sex and Marriage.*
- Have students write a short answer to the question: "How much time will we need to spend with the baby?"
- Show and discuss the film *The New Baby.*
- Design and administer a questionnaire on attitudes toward children. See Document 12-6 ("Would I Make a Good Parent?") for an example.
- Arrange for the students to observe a young baby, either in the classroom or preferably in the baby's home.
- Compare observations in a class discussion.

for the welfare of others, to give of oneself because this is what one wants, and to accept another without qualifications. Children have a right to loving parents who want them—want them enough to direct all their efforts toward being adequate, responsible, mature adults.

Resources

(S) Film: *The Human Body: Reproductive System,* Coronet Films, color, 14 min. Presents a clear and objective description of the human reproductive system. Shows the similarities and differences between male and female reproductive organs, locates them in the body, and describes specific functions of each in the creation of new life.

(S) Johnson, Eric W., *Love and Sex in Plain Language.* Philadelphia: Lippincott, 1965.

(S) Film: *From Generation to Generation,* McGraw-Hill, color, 30 min. Tells the story of human reproduction as an integral part of the universal pattern of nature, explaining that childbearing is an emotional and spiritual experience as well as a physical one.

(S) Duvall, Evelyn M., and Reuben Hill, *When You Marry* (high school edition). Boston: Heath, 1965, ch. 13.

(S) Ogg, Elizabeth, *A New Chapter in Family Planning.* New York: Public Affairs Pamphlets, 1966.

(S) Film: *Family Planning,* Walt Disney Productions, color, 10 min. Explains what family planning means, why it is important, and how man can use it wisely.

(S) Document 12-5, "Understanding the Control of Conception."

(T) Aldrich, C. Anderson, and Mary M. Aldrich, *Babies Are Human Beings.* New York: Macmillan (Collier), 1962.

(S) Jenkins, William A., et al. *These Are Your Children.* Chicago: Scott, Foresman, 1949.

(S) Smart, Russell, and Mollie Smart, *Living and Learning with Children.* Boston: Houghton Mifflin, 1961.

(S) Film: *The New Baby,* Sterling Educational Films, color, 20 min. A family expects a third child. Emphasizes mother's prenatal medical supervision and daily care of the baby. Discusses a medical check-up for the mother and baby. Shows how parents prepare other children for the new arrival.

(S) Document 12-6, "Would I Make a Good Parent?"

(S) Maternity Center Association, *A Baby Is Born,* 2nd ed., New York: Grosset & Dunlap, 1965.

(S) Fromme, Allan, *Sex and Marriage.* New York: Barnes & Noble, 1950.

(T) Himes, Norman E., *Medical History of Contraception.* New York: Gamut Press, 1963.
(T) *Sexual Relations During Pregnancy and the Post-Delivery Period.* SIECUS Discussion Guide No. 6, 1855 Broadway, New York, N.Y.

Content

Child care

A. What are the basic principles of child care? Parents must have:

1. A desire to accept the responsibilities of parenthood.
2. An honest willingness to share their child's life everyday.
3. A willingness to make their children feel that they are secure, that they are wanted, that their values are respected, and that their attempts at self-expression and friendships have the complete support of the family.
4. A commitment to providing a happy home.

B. What are the patterns of child development?
The students should understand the broad general pattern of growth and development of youngsters, and they should be made familiar with reliable sources of information for future use. They must understand that some individual variations from basic growth and development patterns are natural, but they should also realize that deviations should be noted, questioned, and checked out with a doctor or clinic at the earliest possible time. When parents are in doubt about the normalcy of a particular pattern of behavior, their best policy is to ask for professional advice. The students need help in learning not to trust the old saying, "He'll grow out it."

Suggested Learning Opportunities

- Read and discuss pp. 171–73, "Self-understanding is an important requirement for good parenthood," in *Sex and Marriage.*
- Invite the school nurse, the home economics teacher, or a parent to discuss principles of child care.
- Discuss: "The child's feeling of status in the world is primarily determined by the emotional atmosphere of his home." "The soundest principle of child care is to be concerned with the quality of the total parent–child relationship, rather than with the innumerable problematic details and incidents in his daily behavior."
- Assign students to report on *Helping Children Develop Moral Values.*
- Read and discuss pp. 170–71, "Children benefit more from the forgiveness and patience of loving parents than they do from the knowledge of a psychologically well-informed parent," in *Sex and Marriage.*
- Assign students to report on *Emotional Problems of Growing Up.*
- Assign Chapter 14, "What It Means To Be a Parent," in *When You Marry.*
- Have students answer a questionnaire similar to Document 12-7, "Questionnaire on Parenthood."
- Have students read pp. 286–89 of *These Are Your Children.*
- Arrange for student observation in kindergarten or elementary grade. Ask students to read *Living and Learning with Children* before making these visits.
- Ask students to arrange a visit to a

nursery school or the home of a one- or two-year-old child.

- Have a committee visit a local hospital nursery and report to the class.

C. How can a parent share his children's lives?
Children give their parents the opportunity of recapturing the thrill and enthusiasm of youth. They change the atmosphere of a home. A husband and wife's opportunities for pleasure-seeking are extended beyond the boundaries of their own tastes to include those of their children. Children keep a home alive in response to the growth that is taking place within them. They make the future seem more significant for parents because parents see so many potentialities in them. The pattern of daily contact between a couple, however satisfying it may be for a while, tends to wear thin if it is not enriched by the development of a mutual concern for others. Children help parents develop this concern and interest better than anyone else in the world.

- Have students list ways that a typical student shares his life with his parents. Discuss how he might improve his relationship with them.
- Discuss: "What stops a student from sharing more with his parents?"
- Read and react to the statement on pp. 176–77 of *Sex and Marriage:* "Parents who impose their will on their children are primarily interested in themselves."

D. How does a parent teach his children values?

1. Parents teach their children best by first creating in them a desire to learn.
2. Children become what they are because of their parents rather than any obscure hereditary forces.
3. Children respond to parental attitudes even in infancy.

- Read and discuss pp. 168–69 in *Sex and Marriage:* "How do I teach my children values?"
- Discuss pp. 174–75 in *Sex and Marriage:* "Children rarely manifest greater self-control than we ourselves possess."
- Read and react to p. 173 in *Sex and Marriage:* "The problems of child care are enormously increased by parental disagreement."

E. How does parental disagreement influence children?
Parental disagreements do exist in every family. How to handle them constructively in relationship to the children in the family needs to be explored and understood.

- Read and discuss pp. 177–78 in *Sex and Marriage:* "Self-love undermines our ability to be effective parents."

F. How should a parent discipline his children?

- Discuss: "Does a parent rule by divine right?"

There are many ways to discipline children. The method of discipline should change as the children grow and develop. It is vital that the parents agree about the method of discipline to use and be consistent in using it in their family setting.

- Discuss: "Consistency is probably the most important ingredient in good discipline. The two parents should be consistent in how they treat their child; one should not undermine the other."
- Have each student write three rules that he would make for his children, and explain why each rule is important.
- View and discuss the film *The Bright Side*.
- Discuss: "The most difficult lesson in life is to take 'no' for an answer."
- Discuss: "The child's future happiness depends not on how *much* we teach him but rather on how *well* we teach him to control his own desires."

G. How can a parent know if he loves his children enough?

1. Extreme self-sacrifice among parents must be regarded with suspicion.
2. Loving one's children does not mean overindulging them.
3. The happier a husband and wife are together, the happier they will be with their children.

H. How does a parent teach his children about sex? Students who have completed the family life and sex education course should have the facts and information about sex to enable them to answer their children's specific questions of a biological nature. Their and their marriage partners' attitudes about human sexuality will determine their ability to help their children develop positive attitudes and feelings about sex. The key point the students must remember is to answer their children's questions when they are asked and not postpone them until "later."

- Discuss the statements listed in Content item G.
- Discuss: "How shall I tell *my* children about sex?"
- View and discuss the film *Parent to Child About Sex*.
- View and discuss the slides *How Babies Are Made*.
- Have student review the following books: *The Wonderful Story of How You Were Born. A Baby Is Born. The Story of a Baby. What To Tell Your Children About Sex*.
- Distribute Document 12-8, "Bibliography for Future Reference."

Resources

(S) Fromme, Allan, *Sex and Marriage*. New York: Barnes & Noble, 1950, pp. 168–78.
(S) Montague, Ashley, *Helping Children Develop Moral Values*. Chicago: Science Research Associates, 1953.
(S) English, O. Spurgeon, and Stuart M. Finch, *Emotional Problems of Growing Up*. Chicago: Science Research Associates, 1951.
(S) Duvall, Evelyn M., and Reuben Hill, *When You Marry* (high school edition). Boston: Heath, 1965, ch. 14.
(S) Document 12-7, "Questionnaire on Parenthood."
(S) Jenkins, William A., *These Are Your Children*. Glenview, Ill.: Scott, Foresman, 1966, pp. 286–89.
(S) Smart, Russell, and Mollie Smart, *Living and Learning with Children*. Boston: Houghton Mifflin, 1961.
(S) Film: *The Bright Side*, International Film Bureau, b/w, 23 min. Stresses that being a parent is not a problem but a source of pleasure, and indicates that the anxiety of parents can hurt the children. Points out how parental enjoyment of family living can provide a good emotional climate for children.
(S) Film: *Parent to Child About Sex*, Henk Newenhouse, color, 31 min. Presents when and how sex facts are taught, and more importantly, the way they are taught—the comfortable relationship and the free communication between parent and child that are essential in building a foundation for responsible, healthy, mature attitudes.
(S) Slides: *How Babies Are Made*, General Learning Corporation, color, 34 slides. These slides show the story of reproduction in plants, animals, and humans.
(S) Gruenberg, Sidonie M., *The Wonderful Story of How You Were Born*. Garden City, N.Y.: Doubleday, 1952.
(S) Levine, Milton, and Jean H. Seligmann, *A Baby Is Born*. New York: Golden, 1949.
(S) Ets, Marie Hall, *The Story of a Baby*. New York: Viking, 1939.
(S) Child Study Association of America, *What To Tell Your Children About Sex*. New York: Pocket Books, 1959.
(S) Document 12-8, "Bibliography for Future Reference."

Content

The Quality of Family Life

The quality of family life depends on the emotional resources of the parents. The more easily parents are upset in general, the more easily will they be

Suggested Learning Opportunities

- Discuss the ideas in Document 12-9, "Questions for Couples Considering Early Marriage."
- Conclude this unit with a brief review and an opportunity for students

upset in particular by their children. Often we fail to see the matter this simply; a child just "seems like a burden," and that's that. Family life consists of such a subtle and complex pattern of personality interaction that we easily confuse cause and effect. It doesn't take very much to recognize what demands a child makes of us, but how often do we see with equal clarity the elements of our own personality that cause us to feel that these natural demands are a burden? Few of us mind going out of our way for people we love. But first we must have the capacity to love. Offensive as it may sound, not all of us enjoy the same capacity to love even our own children. Without being especially aware of it, we frequently react to them with resentment, anger, and annoyance. Since, as parents, we are the most important influence in their early development, such behavior unwittingly sets the pattern for the difficulties our children soon enough present to us. In other words, our own emotional problems will undermine not only our marital relationship but also our relations with our children, thereby diluting our chances for the enjoyment of family life. But if we can face our own problems, resolve them, and maintain a vital relationship with our marriage partners, the quality of life in our families will be satisfying to us and beneficial to our children.

to ask questions that they may have been "putting off."

Resource

(S) Document 12-9, "Questions for Couples Considering Early Marriage."

Background and Teaching Materials

Document 12-1 ***The Functions of the Family***

The family is the most basic, most universal of the social groups to which man belongs. The biological influence of the family is very great, but its social influence is equally important, for it is from the family that man learns his social roles. Most sociologists speak of the family as the master social institution, the basic institution out of which other institutions have developed.

The functions of the family have varied greatly, from age to age and from family to family. Families in this country were large when the nation was new, but today they are smaller. One family may be strong in love and affection and yet be in financial trouble. Another family may do a good job of intellectual training but a poor job of moral and religious training. Some families perform all functions poorly, while still others may perform their affectional, economic, educational, and religious functions well.

An adequate income is a desirable goal for any family. Today's family is most likely to sell its labor for money. This money is then spent for the products the family requires. In cases where a family's income is cut off or greatly reduced because of prolonged illness, unemployment, or the desertion or death of the chief breadwinner, other provisions have to be made. Many wives work in order to maintain or supplement the family income. The number of women gainfully employed in the American labor force has increased greatly in recent decades. When a family is in great difficulty, the Public Assistance Program, operated as a joint endeavor by the national, state, and local units of government, may help out.

The economic significance of the family is not limited to the problems of getting and sharing income but extends to the obtaining of credit and the holding and transferring of property.

Husbands and wives expect a wide variety of roles of each other. These expectations differ from couple to couple and from family to family. In one home a woman may be expected to work outside the home, while in another her place is considered to be in the home. In one family a man may be expected to be a companion to his wife and children; in another his roles may be more traditionally defined. In general, the trend is for the husband and the wife to expect more of each other than they formerly did. Each now

---

tends to expect the other to be an understanding companion, a stimulating colleague, and a loving and sympathetic parent.

The family has declined as a center of family worship and formal religious education. However, it is still tremendously effective in the development of idealism, moral and spiritual traits, and values in its members. In cooperation with the church and other religious institutions, the family is also finding many new opportunities in religious education. When we think of what religion may do for the individual, we understand why a religious faith should contribute to success in marriage and family living. The inner security of a religious faith may help one to be more understanding and perceptive in meeting the needs of others.

The family is the key to the transmission of a society's cultural heritage from generation to generation. It is also the first important social world for training the young child in the ways of the group and his culture and the social roles that he will have to fill. The process of learning is called socialization. Children are not born with a language, they must learn it. They must learn moral values, customs, and manners as they gradually become more socialized. The family, of course, no longer attempts to train a child to be self-sufficient, to do all things well; the help of other institutions such as the school and church is taken for granted. However, the family still performs many informal training functions such as teaching the child about social groups, social relations, customs, and standards, as well as aiding the child in the development of an acceptable personality. Probably the family's most vital training function is to teach a child his native language. From his parents the child learns to pronounce words and becomes acquainted with some of the ideas that each word represents. Certain words bring laughter, and for saying others he gets reprimanded. As the child grows older and learns more words, he also picks up from his family more complicated attitudes or ideas about what words mean. For instance, a child may develop a favorable or unfavorable ideas of the word "work," depending on whether his family speaks of it only as drudgery and hardship or rather as opportunity and challenge.

Similarly, children can best learn the meaning of the word "democracy" in a democratic family where the individual members have both rights and responsibilities. In some homes the pro's and con's of an issue are discussed freely; decisions are made after everyone has expressed his opinion and the family's values have been considered. All family members, including the children, can express their ideas and know they will receive fair consideration. Through learning to make plans together, to accept responsibility for decisions, and to obey regulations, the children learn what democracy means. The relationship between family structure and the form of our government, in short, is quite close. If we wish our government to remain democratic, we should practice democracy in our homes.

The words a family uses may reflect certain prejudices, and so both words and attitudes are passed on to the child. Some families show their lack of tolerance by the way they talk about a family of different race, national origin, or economic level. Other families never by word or action associate ideas of superiority or inferiority with social, racial, or national groups. In either case the child will probably develop certain habits of thinking and behaving, according to what he sees and hears at home.

The child learns ideas of right and wrong through association with the words "bad," "naughty," "good," "fine," "nice," which he hears many times daily. His parents' standards of behavior are also communicated by example. He learns that it is naughty to lie, yet he may hear lies told over the telephone when social excuses are being made. Out of his first confusion he begins to wonder if there are shades of right and wrong. The two adults who keep him daily company thus pass along their own prejudices and principles.

Document 12-2 ***"If They Had Only Waited"*** (Anonymous)

I had to wait six months before I could write this article, even anonymously. The hurt was so deep that only time could partially heal the wounds. Then with time came the insistent belief that perhaps, by telling our story, we might help others avoid the senseless tragedy that has twisted the lives of two families. For no matter how we try to avoid admitting it to ourselves, tragedy is what has occurred—and we parents must share the blame.

It was a lovely moonlit Saturday evening in May. My husband and I were reading in our modest home in a typical Midwestern town. Our 18-year-old son, Paul, had left a couple of hours earlier to escort his steady girl friend, Nancy Crawford, to their high school prom.

When the door opened at ten o'clock and Paul walked in alone, both Nathan and I looked up in surprise. Even before Paul spoke, I knew that something dreadful had happened. His large hands clenched at his sides, he said slowly, "Nancy is going to have a baby. We're getting married. We just told her family."

For a moment, as if I hadn't heard, I gazed at Paul's strong, handsome

---

face. Then what he had said began to penetrate my consciousness. Stunned, I looked over at Nathan. He had raised his hands to cover his face.

I turned back to our son, the dependable Paul we had been so proud of, the senior voted Most Likely To Succeed, the basketball star. How delighted we had been when Paul settled down to going steady with Nancy—a beauty with brains and character, president of her class. We had attributed Paul's improved grades to Nancy's influence. Now he said huskily, "Mother—Dad—I'm sorry to hurt you. I'm so terribly sorry."

I heard my words tumbling out: "So this is how you proved you loved Nancy! Just how can you support a wife? And we trusted you! Oh, Paul, how could you do such a thing?"

Nathan, a high-school history teacher, has often acted as counselor for students in trouble. But this time the student was, with bitter irony, his own son. Paul responded forthrightly to his father's questioning. A few days before, he had taken Nancy to our family doctor. Earlier that evening, they had phoned for the results of the pregnancy test. Nancy was two months pregnant. The doctor had made them promise to inform their parents during the weekend.

Suddenly, I was thankful that our 12-year-old son, Tony, was away on a Boy Scout camping trip. "What did the Crawfords say?" Nathan was asking.

Paul ran his fingers through his crew cut. "Mrs. Crawford didn't say much. She just cried." Then he went on quickly, "Nancy's dad was awfully mad. But he said I didn't *have* to marry Nancy, and I—"

"Yes," I interrupted. "Nancy can go to a home and have the baby and give it to an adoption agency."

Paul shook his head. "Oh no!" he said, almost in a whisper. "I wouldn't let Nancy do that. At first, we were going to run away, but we knew that wouldn't solve anything." His face was so serious, so pitifully immature; the words were so sincere; "We want to get married and make it right."

Abruptly Nathan stopped pacing the floor. "Paul, you realize, of course, that if you marry, you can't go to the university? It was going to be a tight squeeze anyway." Nathan lifted his hands helplessly; he had counted so proudly on his son's college education. "You know that the Crawfords won't be able to help you. They can't even afford to send Nancy to the women's college right here in town."

Paul's chin quivered slightly. "I'll get a good job—and save money. And I've got money in the bank."

Nathan shook his head. "You can't possibly earn enough to be a husband and father and go to college, too."

Though white-faced and shaken, Paul insisted that no matter what the consequences, he loved Nancy and wanted to marry her. My heart ached for his naive faith in the power of young love.

How often I had heard Nathan speak publicly on the rise of teenage marriages. Studies revealed, he pointed out, that more girls now marry at 18 than at any other age; that one out of six brides is already pregnant; that the divorce rate for teenagers is higher than that of any other age group. Statistical odds were overwhelmingly against a lasting marriage for Paul and Nancy—under any circumstances.

Eventually that awful night passed, and it was Sunday. Nathan phoned the Crawfords and invited them to our house. Oscar Crawford is a bookkeeper in our town. His wife, Ethel, and I had become superficially acquainted through Paul's romance with her daughter, the oldest of four children. I dreaded facing the Crawfords. But when I saw them coming slowly up our front walk—Nancy, her head down, walking between her parents—momentarily I felt even sorrier for them than for ourselves.

All four adults exchanged embarrassed amenities. I had half-expected that I would want to speak out, to tell Nancy and Paul what their selfish act had done to our two families. But Nancy's brown eyes were as fearful and beseeching as a wounded fawn's. I held my tongue.

Nathan asked the young couple to leave us alone. Then Oscar Crawford began tonelessly, "We're not here to insist on a shotgun wedding."

Nathan's face colored. "You *can't* insist. Paul is underage, and must have our permission to marry."

Mrs. Crawford sniffed. "Well, your boy certainly fooled me. I thought Nancy was safe with him."

"It always takes two," I snapped.

Suddenly Mrs. Crawford's face softened. "I'm sorry. I didn't mean it that way. We're all in this together."

A look of perceptive understanding passed between us. We parents whose lives were being entangled groped and floundered to reach a rational level of communication. What exactly *were* we to do? Eventually, we decided to let our children marry, for it seemed unrealistic to expect, or force, Nancy to choose having an illegitimate baby over marrying Paul.

During the next three weeks before school ended, we tried to behave as though it were normal to arrange for a sudden wedding of 18-year-olds. But one day a perplexed Tony confronted me. "Some kids at school said that Paul *has* to marry Nancy. What does that mean?"

It was the most disturbing question I had ever had to answer. I hope I handled it without showing too much of the resentment I felt toward Paul.

There were so many questions I couldn't answer. Paul and Nancy had received sex education in school and instruction in a decent moral code from various sources, including their parents. Who or what was to blame for our two seemingly nice adolescents getting into trouble?

It was easy to point a finger at society, with the mass media emphasizing gratification of sexual drives as natural and glamorous. Or perhaps at the 20th century, in which so many people fear that there may be no tomorrow—only today. It was easy to blame the prevalence of attitudes that ridicule chastity as old-fashioned.

It was harder to blame myself. But when I honestly reviewed my life as Paul's mother, certain scenes emerged into focus.

Long ago, I had given up attending church, assuming that Paul could learn the difference between right and wrong at home, could select his own religion when he was older. Naturally, he had soon abandoned Sunday school. But what spiritual inspiration had I given him as a substitute for church?

And I had been ridiculously eager to have him date, to succeed on a social level. I had encouraged him to earn money to buy a jalopy. I had coerced him into growing up too fast. Now, inevitably, he must grow up faster than I had ever dreamed would be necessary.

A recurring argument between Nathan and me returned to haunt me. Nathan had worried that Paul and Nancy were together too much, had pointed out the well-known pitfalls of "going steady." When he questioned me about their studying together for hours in our basement playroom, I scoffed. Now, too late, I realized that our playroom was the place where the tragedy had started.

They were good youngsters. But, as parents, we should have talked to them directly, candidly about the tremendous power sex has to quiet conscience. We should have made clear to them how aware they must be of the dangers—*before* passion took over. We had given them no concrete wall to lean on when their emotions started running strong.

Gradually, I recognized myself as a guilty member of the lax society I condemned.

On graduation night, Nathan and I listened to the oratory extolling the glorious future for youth. Paul received his diploma, and as we clapped we tried not to think of how thrilled we would have been—if . . .

Two days later, Paul's '55 Ford roared into the driveway of our home and he burst into the kitchen. "I've got a swell full-time job at Blakely's garage." His eyes shone. "Of course, I'll be just a gas jockey at first. But I know I can work up to mechanic." Excitedly, he described how much money he could save.

As enthusiastically as I could, I said, "That's fine, Paul."

I watched him as he flipped through the pages of the morning paper. Only momentarily did his eyes scan the feature listing the colleges chosen by his classmates. "Where's that ad—a nifty one-room furnished apartment with kitchenette?"

He dialed a number and talked briefly. Crestfallen, he turned from the telephone. "The rent is $125—more than half my month's paycheck."

Paul sat down heavily at the kitchen table. He rested his chin on his hand. "Mom, we're sure to find something nice soon—don't you think?"

I watched Paul go slowly down the hall to his room and shut the door. I knew then that my son realized, for the first time, that life had closed in on him, that the door of the future had shut—hard.

The wedding day arrived—a day I had once dreamed of; now I dreaded it. Twenty-one people crowded into the Crawfords' narrow, spotless living room. Besides the immediate families, the only guests were schoolmates of Paul's and Nancy's. The room seemed hot and close as a girl sang in a thin soprano, "I Love You Truly."

My heart quickened when Paul, so straight and handsome, stepped up to stand in front of the minister. How proud I would have been—otherwise.

The out-of-tune piano faltered bravely through "Here Comes the Bride." And there was Nancy, coming slowly down the short hall on her father's arm. Her lovely face somehow sad. Then she and her stoic father were beside Paul.

The minister began, "Dearly beloved, we are gathered together—" I focused my mind on emptiness. Not even one tear would escape. Nathan nudged me. I rose for the final prayer.

When Paul had helped Nancy cut the wedding cake, we all had punch. Soon afterward the wedding party assembled on the front lawn. Finally, the new husband and wife emerged from the doorway amid a shower of rice. They hurried toward Paul's jalopy. He open its door with a flourish. "Come on, wife, we have a long way to go."

We all waved vigorously as they drove off on a five-day honeymoon. And that would be the end of Paul's hard-earned college fund.

The others went into the house. Nathan and I stood at the curb until the car had disappeared around the corner. "The Lord help them—and us, too," Nathan said fervently.

He put his arm around me. We walked forlornly back to the house. I knew that we were both thinking the same thought. If they had only waited!

Forever seared on my heart today are the words I have not been able to say to Paul. I say them now, not out of bitterness or anger, and not because they will help our Paul; but, rather, because some boy, some girl, sometime may remember them before it's too late. *Paul, no rationalizations, no tricky sophistry, no "modern" moral twists can change the fact that your life and the lives of those who love you most will never be the same, will never be as contented or happy or hopeful as they once were, because for one selfish moment you ignored your responsibility to Nancy, to your society—and to yourself.*

Document 12-3 **Marriage Counseling**

Marriage counseling is as old as marriage itself, but as a profession it is relatively new. Standards for licensing and practice are almost nonexistent. This lack of licensing requirements permits quacks to "hang out their marriage counseling shingle"; in addition, it has allowed many a well-intentioned but incompetent person to enter the field of marriage counseling. Such nonprofessional counselors have caused severe problems in the lives of many people. Even seeking the advice or counsel of one's neighbors, friends, or relatives can create more problems than it solves. Well-meaning friends can and do cause as much trouble as the charlatans; they just do not get paid for it.

Competent marriage counselors are very necessary to help persons experiencing marital difficulty. Basically, marriage counseling is a method of education, a method of reducing emotional tension, a method of helping the marriage partners solve a problem, and a way of establishing better problem-solving patterns. One distinction must be clearly understood: marriage counseling is not psychotherapy. True, some marital difficulties may be symptoms of more serious emotional problems, but most of the marital problems a counselor in our society must consider are brought to him by emotionally normal people. Therefore, persons who are experiencing difficulties in their marital relationship and who seek the help of a professional marriage counselor have a right to expect to have their marriage relationship examined but not necessarily their heads.

The most reliable source a person can turn to for help in selecting a marriage counselor is the American Association of Marriage Counselors, a professional organization that has set up standards all of its members must adhere to and that is actively working to implement legislation in the various states. Write to the American Association of Marriage Counselors, 3603 Lemmon Avenue, Dallas, Texas 75219, and ask them to refer you to a marriage counselor in your area.

The criteria for judging a good marriage counseling service are simple. They have been briefly summarized as follows:

"A Good Marriage Counseling Service

1 Doesn't promise quick results or make snap judgments.
2 Doesn't diagnose until after a careful study has been made.
3 Keeps all information confidential.
4 May charge nominal fees which are frankly discussed.
5 May call in other trained specialists to help.
6 Uses only trained professional workers from reputable colleges specializing in such fields as social work, human development, psychiatry, and related areas. (At least a master's degree in the specialized area is the usual professional standard.)
7 Is affiliated with such reliable bodies as local councils of social agencies, and nationally with such professional organizations as the National Conference of Social Work, and the National Council on Family Relations.
8 Does not advertise or try to drum up business, relying instead on slowly building up a clientele of satisfied users through referrals from other agencies and professional persons.
9 May have a membership and a board of directors of reliable citizens who take the responsibility for supporting and interpreting the program to the community."

Document 12-4 ***Your Marriage Will Be Different***

Back a few generations ago a man was really boss of his family. It was his *natural* right. His wife took orders and maybe even addressed him as "Mr. Brown." If any discipline were required for the children, he laid down the law and perhaps emphasized his recommendations with a trip to the woodshed. It sounds pretty kingly, doesn't it?

But when you stop to think about it, there are many advantages to modern marriages that never existed in earlier times. While an old-timer may have had a little woman who would rush about and do his smallest

---

Document 12-4, *Your Marriage Will Be Different,* is taken from *Becoming Men and Women* by Bernice L. Neugarten.

bidding, it's doubtful that his wife could give him the kind of companionship your future wife, with her better education and understanding of the world outside her home, will be able to give you.

And you'll be better able to understand your wife and her interests, too, because of your participation around the home. Actually men and women today can share more experiences, and, as a result, they can enjoy closer companionship in their marriages.

A man today is still the head of the house. Both by custom and by law, he is morally and financially responsible for the welfare of his wife and children, but modern marriage is a much more cooperative and sharing relationship than it once was. Husbands and wives consult each other about their problems, and together they reach satisfactory solutions. There is a give-and-take relationship, a sharing of ideas and desires and opinions that result in closer bonds of affection between man and wife.

A marriage today is a shared experience, to which two individuals bring their best traits and emerge with something better and wiser and richer than either of them could achieve alone. And marriage today is seen as a partnership between equals with full democratic rights for both partners.

Possibly because of this new emphasis on companionship and democracy, men and women are now marrying people with about the same amount of education as their own. In fact, marriage experts advise us that if the educational level is just about the same for a man and a woman, the marriage stands a better chance of success.

Nowadays, most married couples share the same hobbies and the same leisure-time activities. Men no longer expect to spend most of their evenings with male cronies with their wives going to "hen" parties. Couples go out together, and when their children are old enough, the family as a group spends more of its leisure time together.

Document 12-5 **Understanding the Control of Conception**

The use of fertility control methods can greatly reduce the risk of pregnancy, although no method or device is perfectly reliable. Probably more pregnancies result because of the faulty manner in which a device or method is used than from any defect inherent in it, however. The following birth control methods are widely used in the United States today.

Mechanical and Chemical Barrier Devices

Hormone pills (oral contraception) works by mimicking the action of the natural hormones that prevent the ovary from releasing an egg cell so that no pregnancy can occur. Must be taken only under a physician's direction.

Intra-uterine devices (I.U.D.) a small plastic or stainless steel ring or coil placed in the uterus. Exactly how the appliance prevents pregnancy is not yet understood. Must be placed by the physician, only after having had one pregnancy.

Diaphragm a flexible rubber device that covers the cervix or entrance to the uterus. Must be fitted by the physician.

Condom a rubber or latex sheath shaped to fit the erect penis. Must remain in place and intact during intercourse.

Spermicides aerosol foams, creams, jels, and vaginal tablets and suppositories that can be placed in the vagina to kill the sperm on contact. Directions must be followed explicitly.

Natural Methods

Rhythm method refraining from sexual intercourse during the wife's monthly fertile period. This is the only method of family limitation (short of total abstinence) approved at present for Roman Catholics by their church. Persons who decide to rely on this method should first seek the advice of a physician to correctly identify the eight days or so that the wife might be fertile.

Coitus interruptus, or *withdrawal* the man withdraws his penis from the woman's vagina just before he reaches his climax or ejaculation, but often a little semen is discharged before ejaculation begins or ejaculation begins before the man expects it. This method requires unusual self-control and sexual experience to prevent conception. It is risky and does not permit a joyous response in sexual intercourse. *Note:* If semen is ejaculated too close to the vaginal entrance, pregnancy can result.

Permanent Methods

Surgical sterilization Female: the Fallopian tubes, which carry the egg cell from the ovary to the uterus, are tied. Male: the vas deferens tube, which carries the sperm, is tied. Sterilization is not castration and does not impair sexual function in any way. There is no guarantee that surgical sterilization can be reversed in either men or women.

Document 12-6 ***Would I Make a Good Parent?***

The following list of questions has been prepared to help you understand the problems of parenthood. There are no right or wrong answers. Indicate your answer to each question by drawing a circle around the "yes," the "no," or the "?." Use the question mark only when you are certain that you cannot answer "yes" or "no."

Yes No ? 1. Do you like to work or play with small children?
Yes No ? 2. Do you like to read or tell stories to children?
Yes No ? 3. Do you ordinarily feel concerned when you see a child crying?
Yes No ? 4. Do you sometimes answer a small child's questions in a teasing way?
Yes No ? 5. If you had children would you have a strong preference for a boy or girl?
Yes No ? 6. If you had a child, do you know what vocation you would want him to follow when he grew up?
Yes No ? 7. Can you mention any particular skills or abilities which will be helpful to you in working with children?
Yes No ? 8. Do you ever have the feeling that children will interfere with your plans or happiness in marriage?
Yes No ? 9. As a result of your childhood, have you some things you are resolved to do, or not do, as a parent?
Yes No ? 10. Do you believe quite strongly in the maxim, "Spare the rod and spoil the child"?
Yes No ? 11. Do you think the mother has a greater responsibility than the father in the rearing of children?
Yes No ? 12. Would you feel humiliated and embarrassed if your 7-year-old offspring had been found to have taken some money?
Yes No ? 13. Would you feel embarrassed to have it known among your friends that you had been acting as a baby sitter?
Yes No ? 14. Do children get on your nerves?
Yes No ? 15. Do you expect a small child to learn to obey immediately?

Document 12-6, *Would I Make a Good Parent?* is taken from Lester A. Kirkendall, *A Reading and Study Guide for Students in Marriage and Family Relations,* 4th ed. (Dubuque, Iowa, William C. Brown, 1968), p. 99. Reprinted with permission.

Document 12-7 ***Questionnaire on Parenthood***

Male_______ Female_______

Directions

I. If you agree, encircle A. If you disagree, encircle D.

A D 1. The average parent underestimates his child's capacity for understanding and insight.

A D 2. The average parent underestimates his child's capacity to be neat, orderly, and coordinated.

A D 3. There is little chance that the things which happen to a child in his first year of life will affect his later adjustment.

A D 4. The parents should reprimand or punish the child for expressions of hostility ("I hate you") toward them.

A D 5. We should strive to have the sex education for the son given by the father; for the daughter by the mother.

A D 6. The average woman has more preparation than the average man.

A D 7. The average man is better prepared to be a good father to his sons than to his daughters.

A D 8. The average man is better prepared to be a good father to older children (10–15 years) than to an infant or a very small child.

A D 9. It would be harder to love an adopted child than one of your own.

II. Encircle the correct answers. ND means "no difference," or "no feeling either way."

1. As I was growing up, when I needed comfort or advice I was most likely go to:	Mother	Father	ND
2. In our family the sterner, harsher discipline was likely to come from:	Mother	Father	ND

Document 12-7, *Questionnaire on Parenthood,* is taken from Lester A. Kirkendall, *A Reading and Study Guide for Students in Marriage and Family Relations,* 4th ed. (Dubuque, Iowa, William C. Brown, 1968), p. 85. Reprinted with permission. William C. Brown Company, Publishers, grants teachers permission to make copies of this questionnaire for use in connection with their own family life and sex education classes. On each reproduction the following copyright notice must be given: © 1968 by Lester A. Kirkendall.

3. When there was some silly little thing I liked to play or do, the parent most likely to understand was:	Mother	Father	ND
4. In our family, the parent who was most likely to give me my allowance or the money I needed was:	Mother	Father	ND
5. If you could have only one child, which sex would you prefer:	Boy	Girl	ND
6. Which seems in general easier to rear:	Boy	Girl	ND
7. How would you feel if your 4-year-old son wished:			
a. to play with dolls	Pleased	Displeased	ND
b. to play with a football	Pleased	Displeased	ND
8. How would you feel if your 4-year-old daughter wished:			
a. to play with dolls	Pleased	Displeased	ND
b. to play with a football	Pleased	Displeased	ND
9. How would you feel about kissing your 8-year-old son to show your affection?	Glad to	Wouldn't like to	ND
10. How would you feel about kissing your 8-year-old daughter to show your affection?	Glad to	Wouldn't like to	ND

Document 12-8 **Bibliography for Future Reference**

Butterfield, Oliver M., *Sexual Harmony in Marriage.* New York: Emerson, 1964. (A book about sex techniques)

Fromme, Allan, *Sex and Marriage.* New York: Barnes & Noble, 1950. (A book about marriage)

Offen, Allan J., *Adventure to Motherhood.* New York: Taplinger, 1966. (A picture-story of pregnancy and childbirth)

Schaefer, George, and Milton Zisowitz, *The Expectant Father.* New York: Pocket Books. (The role of the father during the wife's pregnancy)

Spock, Benjamin, *The Pocketbook of Baby and Child Care.* New York: Pocket Books. (A guide for child rearing)

Gruenberg, Sidonie M., *The Wonderful Story of How You Were Born.* Garden City, N.Y.: Doubleday, 1952. (To read aloud to young children)

Ets, Marie Hall, *The Story of a Baby*. New York: Viking, 1939. (To read aloud to young children)

A Healthy Personality for Your Child. Breast Feeding. Foods Your Children Need. Infant Care. Your Well Baby. Your Child from One to Six. The Adolescent. Superintendent of Documents, Government Printing Office, Washington, D.C. (Pamphlets on child growth and development)

Child Study Association of America, *What To Tell Your Children About Sex*. New York: Pocket Books, 1959 (Suggested answers for young children's questions about human reproduction)

Document 12-9 ***Questions for Couples Considering Early Marriage***

These points are intended to bring out issues which will help a couple contemplating early marriage. Persumably the answer "Yes" indicates marriage readiness.

1. Have either or both had success in holding a responsible job? Yes No
2. Have either or both had experience in caring for children? Yes No
3. Can you talk freely on such matters as money, religion, sex, relationships with your families, and expectations in marriage? Yes No
4. Have you been engaged for at least six months? Yes No
5. Do you know where you will live after marriage? Yes No
6. Do you know how you will earn your living after marriage? Yes No
7. If there is strong parental opposition, can you "take it"? Yes No
8. Have you talked over all the reasons for wanting to marry now? Yes No
9. Have either or both had the responsibility of managing a household? Yes No
10. Do you get along well with each other's parents? Yes No
11. Have you weighed advantages and disadvantages of marrying now? Yes No

---

Document 12-9, *Questions for Couples Considering Early Marriage,* is taken from Lester A. Kirkendall, *A Reading and Study Guide for Students in Marriage and Family Relations,* 4th ed. (Dubuque, Iowa, William C. Brown, 1968), p. 48. Reprinted with permission. William C. Brown Company, Publishers, grants teachers permission to make copies of this questionnaire for use in connection with their own family life and sex education classes. On each reproduction the following copyright notice must be given:

12. Have you seen each other react to trouble and disappointment? Yes No
13. Is the sexual side of your relationship such that you are fully at ease and free from anxiety about it? Yes No
14. If your educations are not completed, can you see the way clear to completing them? Yes No
15. Projecting your plans for six months to a year, can you meet the probable financial needs? Yes No
16. Are you clear on whether you want to postpone the coming of children or have an early pregnancy? Yes No
17. Are you fully ready for the sexual family planning side of marriage? Yes No

part V

teaching methods and program evaluation

chapter 13

effective teaching aids and techniques

Experienced classroom teachers know that some instructional methods and devices are more effective than others for presenting specific types of subject matter to students. This chapter is concerned with the teaching aids and techniques that lend themselves most readily to the presentation of family life and sex education. The attempt here is not to include all possible teaching techniques, but rather to describe those which have been found to be most successful in coursework pertaining to family life and sex education.

This chapter is divided into three parts. The first part provides specific observations about some of the basic categories of teaching aids, such as books and tape recordings; the second examines role playing; and the third comments on such teaching techniques as the small group discussion and use of the question box. Whatever aids and techniques are used, certain basic purposes underlie the presentation of any subject matter, and they should never be lost sight of as a result of an excessive concern with instructional apparatus. In family life and sex education courses we are concerned with helping the student establish positive attitudes about his role in life. The basic goals of the program are to increase the student's self-understanding; to increase his understanding of others; to provide him with practice in social interaction; to increase his readiness to recognize, accept, and promote beneficial social changes; and to sharpen his ability to recognize, appreciate, and help preserve what is genuinely beneficial in the culture and society that have come down to him from the past.

Teaching Aids

The teaching aids that serve most effectively in helping the teacher to achieve the goals of the family life and sex education program fall into four categories:

1. Case studies
2. Literature
3. Sound tapes
4. Films and filmstrips

The first two categories appeal to the learner's visual process. The third appeals to his auditory process, and the fourth involves both the visual and the auditory. All of the above teaching aids can be used to illustrate examples of family interaction, which serves as the basis for concept and attitude formation. Determining which aids will be most useful for a given class depends largely on the ease with which the teacher handles the subject and the device. Instructors should not attempt to use any aids that they do not understand well or cannot handle in a comfortable and effective manner. This is particularly true with role playing, which will be discussed in detail later.

The Case Study

The situational case study is an effective means of helping students to develop self-confidence in interpersonal relations and to gain insight into the behavior of others. The cases usually focus on the prejudices, attitudes, and sentiments of people caught in a problem situation. The various situations chosen for class study can be geared to the grade level of the individual class and thus depict problems that might arise in the student's own life.

Children identify quickly and naturally with the problems of others. When the hero of a children's book is in danger or is unfairly treated, the young reader feels threatened. Students often relate in much the same way to the case study. When they analyze a situational problem that could be their own, they are in essence analyzing themselves. Should they be faced with the need for decision making in a similar situation, they will have had valuable "trial run" experience to help them to make the right decision.

Another value of the case study method lies in the fact that students become aware of problem situations that might have been prevented had there been better understanding between the principals concerned. If a case study features an eleven-year-old boy who rebels against his parents because he has misunderstood what they expect of him, the sixth-grader studying the case not only gains an understanding of causative factors, he has also learned a valuable lesson in interpersonal relations.

One example of a case study that was found to be very useful by a sixth-grade teacher gave the life history of a twelve-year-old boy who was the only male member of the family. He had six sisters, and his father had abandoned the family. The case was discussed from the standpoint of sibling relationships and the problems encountered with no male member of the family to help the boy learn what ordinarily are considered male activities or roles.

Another case study used at senior high level and in adult education classes was the life story of a twenty-year-old girl who was dating a boy four years her junior. The girl had money and did not work. The boy came from a broken home and had spent much of his life in foster homes. The girl's father, who was twenty years older than the mother, had exercised very strict control over the family until his death. The girl's mother had used the daughter as a buffer to engage in extramarital social life. The guidance counselor (to whom the girl had turned when the personnel of a social agency objected to her pressuring the boy for marriage) was trying to help the girl evaluate her life.

The age level of the boys in the two cases offered an opportunity for empathy by male students in both school classes. The second case provided the adult education group a broad basis for discussion of the pro's and con's of a significant age span between marriage partners. The second case also elicited considerable discussion on the exploitation of children by parents. Although questions had been prepared by the teacher in both cases, there was no need to use them. The two school classes and the adult group were able to recognize the major areas of concern.

Case studies suitable for use in family life and sex education classes may be obtained through school social service files or school guidance counselor's files, or from book compilations of case studies.[1] Popular magazines are another fruitful source. When a case study is selected from the counselor's files for classroom use, the teacher must be certain that it is not a report on a member of the class or his siblings. Serious harm could result from an oversight of this sort.

Case studies may be used to help individual students or as a basis for group discussions. Good leadership is naturally a marked asset in any discussion stimulated by a case study. The teacher can add more meaning to

[1] See also Phyllis B. Heller, *Look to This Day: A Case History of Family Life in the Form of a Novel* (New York, typewritten report [Ed.D.], Teachers College of Columbia University, 1953).

the procedure if he prepares a series of questions for the group leader to start the group talking. However, if only a teacher, and no other specially trained leader, is available to lead the group discussion, well-thought-out questions distributed to the students still can serve to guide the discussion into profitable channels. Whether the case study is used on an individual basis or by the group, the questions prepared to direct the study are of the utmost importance.

When cases are made the basis for a group discussion rather than assigned for outside reading by individuals, more meaningful solutions to the problems posed often result because of the variety of experiences students bring to the discussion. Awareness of thought that may not have occurred to an individual student is introduced. This in turn often stimulates debate, and even the more retiring students can find themselves deeply involved. Two other positive results of the group method may be noted. The first is that the group members feel a greater sense of achievement when a solution has been attempted through group consensus. The second is the group solidarity that results when members tackle a problem together.

Case studies may also serve as the basis for role playing. In role playing, individuals within the student group assume the roles of the principals described in the problem situation. Students sometimes alternate in assuming roles, since one student may feel that he can contribute more insight into a character being portrayed by another member of the group.

In addition to their uses with students, case studies are helpful for teacher training in family life and sex education, and also for helping the local community understand the value of the program. In workshops, where small discussion groups are used to help teachers prepare for the classroom situation, the case study is a valuable tool. If a school is considering including parents and community representatives in some aspects of the course, the case study group discussion may be the proper place to start.

The following study is an example of the cases that can be used in building appreciation for the family life and sex education course in the local community. The case involves a seventeen-year-old girl enrolled in a family life course. The girl had married when she was fifteen. Her husband was three years older, a high school senior at the time of their marriage, and an outstanding athlete. Theirs was not a forced marriage—that is, out-of-wedlock pregnancy was not the motivating factor. The two young people came from middle-class homes where siblings and both parents were present. In neither instance did they appear to have had any unusual problems during their growing years. The decision to marry was made after a few dates. Although both sets of parents suggested that they were rather young to marry, no strong objection was made.

The girl remained in school and was in her senior year when this case study was written. Her friends were excluding her with increasing frequency from their social activities. Her husband had no problems in his male peer group or in heterosexual groups. Friction was developing between the husband and wife because of their inability to find the mutual social activity they had enjoyed prior to and early in their marriage. The wife was confused and asking for help.

After her experience with the twelfth-grade unit in family life and sex education, the girl began to understand many things about herself and her husband that she felt she should have known sooner. She more fully understood her sexual obligations as a marriage partner. Her teacher reported that the girl felt strongly that courses in family life and sex education should have been offered at a much earlier grade level. With the sources of help that she had found in the coursework even at so late a date, the girl believed she would be able to salvage her marriage.

In summary, the case study method would seem to have four chief values. First, the cases afford the class an opportunity for dealing with problems of human relations or interpersonal relations. Second, the cases stimulate analytical thought. Third, the cases provide the student group with the basis for a venture in cooperative thinking and action. Fourth, the cases give individual students an opportunity to look at situations with which they can identify strongly, and also help the students to understand the causative factors in these situations and so to avoid certain problems in their own lives.

Literature

Many kinds of literature are included in family life and sex education courses. Books, both fiction and nonfiction, newspaper and magazine articles, and short stories are all important resources. The imaginative short story is a particularly effective teaching aid. Because short stories can often be read and discussed in one class period, students can study many of them during the year and thus gain insight into a variety of situations and behavior responses. The "literary" short story or sketch is often a pure study in character and offers older students a revealing picture of the dynamics of intrapersonal change and interpersonal relationships.

Popular magazines are an excellent source of short stories, since the theme often centers on current boy–girl relationships or on family situations that are pertinent to incidents in the student's own life. From the earliest grades popular magazines of a suitable interest level are available. Such magazines as *Children's Digest* and *Jack and Jill* are examples of resources for the elementary grades. For the secondary level, movie and television magazines that the students enjoy reading may be employed in coursework. Women's magazines also have many fine stories dealing with problems of maturity and understanding.

The short story or novel portrays life situations that the student would rarely have the opportunity to experience first hand. By identifying with a fictional character he can grasp and visualize important family life and sex education concepts. If the story is subsequently discussed in class, the student can be assisted in determining why he identifies with or rejects certain fictional characters. This can result in a clarification of his values and of his concept of individual roles within the family constellation and within his peer group, and he will gain an increased awareness of his own strengths and weaknesses. Self-understanding gained in this way may increase the student's self-respect—that is, his acceptance of himself and his place in society. Self-respect is a key element in an individual's ability to be comfortable in situations where his personal beliefs and feelings are concerned, and particularly in sexual, family, and interpersonal relationships, in his ability to motivate other people, and in his competency as a member of a family.

Imaginative literature can also be helpful in reducing negative feelings toward persons from different ethnic or socio-economic backgrounds. Careful selection of stories is necessary if the students' prejudices are to be reduced. For example, stories that have their setting in slum areas may, if not handled skillfully in discussion, intensify a middle-class student's contempt for those of lower socio-economic background, rather than heighten his understanding and acceptance.

The imaginative story can also be used as a basis for role playing. This activity gives the student practice in social interaction and the teacher an unparalleled opportunity to gain an insight into the student and his beliefs and prejudices.

Imaginative literature can also reduce a student's fears about growing up. Many young people, though eager to experience the pleasures and privileges of adulthood, tend to back away from assuming adult responsibilities. When they can experience through the vicissitudes of a fictional character the demands and stresses of growing up, they will be better equipped to deal with similar problems, to form judgments, and thus to cope with the duties that the expectations of society impose upon them.

The values of imaginative literature in a family life and sex education course can be summarized as follows: (1) Through identification with fictional characters the student can learn about his own emotional needs and attitudes and can better understand the motivations and behavior of others; (2) through exposure to a variety of characters and plot settings he is given an opportunity to assess interpersonal behavior as it is conditioned by cultural influences, family structures, and individual choice.[2]

Sound Tapes

Sound-recorded tapes used in the area of family life and sex education fall into two categories: those made by high school students or teachers to record interviews or group discussions; and commercial recordings that dramatize particular concepts or episodes.

In recordings of dramatic episodes, voices carry the burden of establishing character and communicating emotion. Volume, pitch, timbre, and rhythm are all important attributes in depicting character and mood. A loud, blustery voice will indicate a person with these unpleasant characteristics; a staccato rhythm or a marked change of pitch will indicate a shift in emotion. For example, an actor portraying the role of a boy who has been admonished by his father may reply in a matter-of-fact manner. The words he speaks may indicate unconcern, but a change of pitch or rhythm in his voice will reveal the agitation or anger that he feels.

In many respects dramatic recordings function like films in stimulating the audience to identify with the actors. Although the recorded tape lacks the film's visual stimulus, it has the advantage of allowing the student to create a mental picture of the characters to suit his particular needs. The student will draw heavily on his past experience in visualizing the characters. He will usually choose one character in particular with which he can identify closely and will unconsciously ascribe to that character many of his own feelings and behavior responses.

There is a natural tendency on the part of most people to shy away from self-analysis and discussion of intimate personal feelings. When a student can identify closely with a given character in a taped drama—a character he has helped to create by giving the voice a physical identity—he will be able to examine and discuss some of his own feelings by attributing them to his alter-ego, the fictional character. The protective cloak provided by the fictional character helps to increase his self-assurance. The student begins to relax, to feel that he is in control of the situation. He begins to view social interaction more objectively and with a greater sense of confidence. As his self-assurance grows, he may acknowledge many of the

[2] See also Rose Marie Somerville, *Family Insights Through the Short Story: A Guide for Teachers and Workshop Leaders* (New York, Bureau of Publications, Teachers College of Columbia University, 1964).

feelings and responses he has described as being his own and proceed to direct self-analysis.

Tapes produced by school personnel often record real-life experiences of local students. A teacher, guidance counselor, or school nurse may interview young people who have had premarital relations, out-of-wedlock pregnancies, or similar experiences known to the youth of our time. While the best of these tapes offer a high degree of student identification, a number of risks are inherent in their use. Extreme caution must be taken to insure that voices are not identifiable. In addition, since most students are minors, legal clearance to use the tapes must be obtained from the parents of the children interviewed. Many willing parents and students can easily be found.

Perhaps the most common weakness of amateur recordings lies in the quality of the interview precedure. Frequently the interviewer is inexperienced and may slant the questions to the point where the tape sounds like a prepared script with nonprofessional actors woodenly enacting the parts. The immediacy and dramatic impact are thus considerably diminished, if not lost entirely. Only an experienced interviewer, skilled at establishing rapport with teenagers and capable of eliciting straightforward, pertinent responses, should attempt to use this demanding medium.

Commercial or professionally produced dramatic recordings can help students understand themselves and others in a more immediate way than educational films, which are also used to teach principles of behavior. Such films are usually written to demonstrate a psychological principle or concept. They are often heavy with some moral message and are rejected by the students. Recordings of plays made by professional actors are believable and moving; the characters become real people with real problems, and the student's emotions are touched. The tape recording has another advantage over films in that tapes can more easily be played and replayed to reinforce lessons learned or to introduce fresh insights.

Examples of commercially available dramatic recordings that might be used at the senior high school level are Ibsen's *A Doll's House,* Arthur Miller's *Death of a Salesman,* or Eugene O'Neill's *Beyond the Horizon.* These dramas are relevant to the content of the family life and sex education course, and they can be very helpful when used by a skillful teacher. The success of the recordings depends on the skill and understanding of the teacher. The value of audio tapes lies in the opportunity they give students to recognize and identify the interactions between characters and to be able to internalize these as their own. If the class discussion that follows the playing of a recording is dominated by the teacher's presentation of his own conclusions, the value is lost to the student. For teachers who have not used this technique before, handbooks and discussion guides are usually available where the recordings are obtained.[3]

Films and Filmstrips

Of all audio-visual aids, films enjoy the widest use. Since films and filmstrips are routinely accompanied by explicit directions, little explanation is needed; moreover, the majority of teachers have had some training in their use in preparatory coursework. The most important consideration is using films, that is, selecting the right ones to accomplish the objective in view, has been covered in earlier chapters.

Role Playing

The need to bring real-life situations and theoretical knowledge together is of great concern to educators. In the family life and sex education course, role playing serves as one of the major means by which the gap may be diminished. Role playing has been described as an unrehearsed involvement, or spontaneous acting out, of social situations arising from problems in the area of human relations. The technique seeks to effect better interpersonal understanding by permitting individuals to experiment with different roles, to test new behavior patterns, and to establish new concepts.

Role playing serves three major objectives: (1) It helps the role players to gain insight and empathy into the behavior of others; (2) it provides an opportunity for exploration and practice in a variety of problem solutions; (3) it both interprets and imparts information about a particular issue or problem.

One of the chief advantages of role playing is its versatility. The method can be used with any age level and in connection with virtually any controversial issue, although it serves its greatest purpose in the field of human relations. Role playing is an exceptionally effective means of aiding young children to develop the concept of socialization. It has been said that a child's later personality development is greatly determined by his opportunity to enact new roles in the play situation. The give-and-take and

[3] See also Earl Owen Goodman, *Procedure for the Use of Sound-Recorded Dramatics Episodes in Cultivating the Ability To Understand Social Interaction* (Ann Arbor, Michigan University Microfilm, 1962. A microfilm copy of an original typewritten report [Ed.D.], New York, Teachers College of Columbia University, 1962).

imaginative demands of social play help children to acquire an understanding of others, which in turn sets the pattern for appropriate behavior in social interaction.

Some authorities are so convinced of the value of early experience in trying out a variety of social roles that they feel that maladjustment and interpersonal problems in adulthood can be traced directly to insufficient childhood opportunities in this area. This theory might lead one to question the value of using role playing with adults if the patterns are so firmly established in childhood. However, role playing as a means of aiding adolescents and young adults to acquire an understanding of social interaction is widely employed, and its value has not been disproved. Older youths have little opportunity to experiment with new behavior experiences because they are expected to conform to the conventions of the segment of society to which they belong. The hippies and flower children of today, in revolt against these conventions, are experimenting in areas of behavior widely different from those of their parents and their community; unfortunately, theirs is a real-life adventure, instead of role playing.

The first step in role playing is the selection of the problem for study. The topic must be well defined and have specific meaning to the group as a whole in order to generate the interest and spontaneity so necessary to this activity. For example, students in early secondary grades are interested in dating patterns. The subject of study might be how boys can learn to hold a comfortable conversation with the parents of his date when he arrives at their home. The role playing might take the form of a family discussion of the hour the girl is to be brought home. For a junior high class the subject might be whether young teenagers should be encouraged to participate in dances and other boy–girl social relationships. For younger children the discussion might center around which household chores are appropriate for boys and which for girls.

Problems to be used in role playing may be suggested by the students in "buzz sessions," or lists of problems may be turned in by individual students. Case studies, short stories, or recorded dramas can also be used as the basis for role playing.

After a decision has been made regarding the type of problem to be used as the basis for role playing, the group must decide on the number of persons to be involved. Role playing may be enacted by small groups or large, though many teachers favor the small group. The physical setting in which role playing is to take place, the length of time to be allotted to the role playing, and the decision as to whether or not a suggested outcome is to be decided upon need not be predetermined in every case. Some matters may be left up to the group. Too precise structuring of the procedure inhibits the interest of the group. The alert teacher will constantly be evaluating the effectiveness of the activity and will determine the time when it ceases to be productive.

Whether or not role playing should be used to find an answer to a question or simply to aid in further clarification without reaching any conclusions depends on the type of fictional situation or problem that is chosen as a basis for the activity. Again, the awareness of the teacher to the type of problem or situation being role-played must determine the pattern that follows. For example, if a situation has to do with the understanding of a parent's reaction to a student's driving his car after having been arrested for some infraction of the law, then a suggested outcome of the discussion will be fairly important. If the problem is concerned with the aspects of dating patterns, however, probably no conclusion will need to be reached. One part of the role playing that must *not* be predetermined is the dialogue, for if it is not left entirely to the role players, the real benefit of the procedure is lost.

A specific story or situation proposed by a student gives the group members a real-life situation that can be role-played. Assume that in a sixth-grade class a student named Mary tells of her experience in her aunt's home when her cousin John, a seventeen-year-old junior in high school, was refused permission to go out and forbidden to use the telephone for a month because he had lied to his parents about his whereabouts the night before. His father had heard from friends that John had been seen in a local tavern with a girl several years his senior and whom they did not consider socially acceptable. Mary does not understand the importance of this situation. She does not see what the problem is since John, in her frame of reference, is old enough to decide what he does or does not do. Mary has no older brothers or sisters. Development of this situation permits the group members to contribute individual ideas and feelings to the solution of the problem and to have some sense of personal involvement in the life situation.

After the roles or characters to be played have been decided upon, the students should be given an opportunity to volunteer for parts. Students not wishing to participate should not be coerced; instead, they should be asked to participate as observers to interpret the behavior of the students enacting the roles. Once the dialogue has started, a reticent student will often decide that he can portray the role better than the original volunteer and will ask to take over the part. Role playing, like any other classroom activity, probably will not elicit 100% involvement. The teacher who is unable to get the whole group to participate should not be discouraged.

A brief warmup period is sometimes helpful in making the students feel more comfortable and thus more willing to participate. Students who have had the most experience in role playing or who are at ease in addressing the class might demonstrate the activity. Props may help some students get the "feel" of a character, thereby enabling them to concentrate on the problem rather than on characterization. For example, if a girl is portraying her father, wearing a man's hat may help her create the impression she wants. A particular arrangement of chairs or other furniture may also contribute to the general atmosphere. If the situation is a family conclave, chairs and a table can easily be arranged to simulate a dining room.

Nonparticipating students in the group are still involved in the learning situation in their function as observers. It is important that they be made to feel that their contribution is an active one; if they do not feel this, they may view the role-playing performance as merely another classroom exercise of little pertinence to them, and the ensuing learning will be negligible.

The students who are to act as observers must decide what and how they are going to observe. One observer may wish to look for certain behavior characteristics or physical mannerisms among the role players. Another may wish to concentrate on what the role players say to each other and how what they say affects the other players. Still a third observer may wish to envision himself in a particular role and watch that player's sensitivity to the feeling and behavior of the other players.

In a procedure known as *split-group identification,* the observers divide themselves into units and attempt to identify as groups with one or two role players. Assume, for example, that the role playing is to be based on a situation in which a ninth-grade girl is being pressured by three boys in the eleventh grade to ignore parental restrictions on riding in the boys' car. Using the split-group identification plan, the boys in the class might observe the performance of the girl, while the girls could divide into three groups to observe how each of the boys performs. A group of observers will generally give a broader and more valid assessment of character and portrayal than an individual observer working alone. The laggards in the class will be stimulated to participate more actively in order to keep up with their peers.

Just as there are different types of observation, there are different types of role playing. One practice is *role reversal,* in which any two group members may change their roles during the play situation. In a second type, sometimes called the *alter-ego technique,* a group member other than the role player verbalizes what he believes are the latter's unspoken thoughts and feelings. A third type is *multiple role playing,* in which the same problem is played by different groups at the same time, with the various outcomes subsequently reported back to the entire group. In still another procedure, members of the audience spontaneously take over roles that they feel are not being adequately portrayed.

The ultimate goal—indeed, the very essence—of role playing is total group involvement in the problem and the behavioral patterns under study. The road to this involvement is the spontaneous discussion that follows the completion of the role-play activity. The students who were performers tell the observers how they felt about the characters they portrayed, why they responded as they did to specific situations, and what insights they believe their portrayals contributed to the study. Following this, it is the observers' turn to speak. They may decide to question the performers about various aspects of the role enactment, or they may simply have a general discussion among themselves, questioning each other on their views and reactions to the performance.

Whatever form the discussion takes, it must be clearly understood by players and observers alike that the behavior manifestations of a character in the drama are not necessarily the student actor's own, but rather what he perceives the play character's would be. The participants must first have the opportunity to explain and, if they wish, to defend their role enactment before being questioned by the observers. Their objective assessment of character motivation clears the way for the observers to question—critically, if need be—details of the portrayal without fear of offending the performers.

Teachers may sometimes find it difficult to interest certain students in taking an active part in role playing. This reluctance is found most often among younger children, who may be shy or even a little afraid to project themselves into a role, or with the very young child who, though receptive to play acting, finds it difficult to grasp the whole concept of role playing. For these students, a variation of role playing known as *indirect introduction* may be the answer. In this method a teacher or group member will say, "Why don't you show me how . . ." or "Pretend that I am someone else and tell me what would happen if . . . ." No mention is made of playing a role, but the child is nonetheless led into doing just that.

Some teachers experienced in role playing have stated that students who participate as performers are more prone to change their attitudes and show a greater understanding of behavior motivation than those who are instructed merely to identify with the performers or to act as observers. This may well be true. However, role playing cannot be forced upon students who for one reason or another do not wish to portray a character in the problem situation. These students must be allowed to find their own level of participation if they are to grow in the area of personal introspection.

Role playing must be used judiciously if it is to retain its value for students. Children may become bored if too much reliance is placed on this or on any other teaching device. By alternating the various teaching aids and techniques in this chapter, and by using different presentation approaches within a technique, the teacher will be able to sustain the interest of the class, and more students will profit from the family life and sex education program.

For the teacher who is concerned about his ability to use role playing as a teaching aid, books, pamphlets, and films are available to help him.[4] In role playing, as in all instructional methods, the teacher must understand and feel comfortable with the procedure if he is to put it to effective classroom use.

Other Teaching Techniques

The major goal of family life and sex education is to develop sound student attitudes. Dialogue between students is one of the best means of accomplishing this. In fact, the key to teaching the course successfully is to keep it "dialogue centered" and to place the main emphasis on pupil-to-pupil interaction as opposed to teacher-to-pupil interaction.

It is widely accepted in the field of education that lectures by the teacher do little more than impart facts. To develop attitudes the student must actively participate and become deeply involved in the ideas presented. He can best find this involvement in the forum of open discussion. On the whole, students are grateful to the school that recognizes this need and provides an understanding teacher to help them in the classroom setting. Some family life authorities believe that such dialogue-centered courses can contribute to a lower incidence of divorce by giving students an opportunity to learn how to communicate freely and honestly with the opposite sex and to learn to say what they really mean—not what they think the opposite sex wants to hear.

Five techniques bearing on the quality of classroom dialogue will be discussed in turn:

1. Class discussion
2. Small group discussion
3. Guest speakers
4. Lectures by the teacher
5. The question box

Class Discussion

A teacher who makes appropriate arrangements for classroom discussion is likely to be gratified by seeing a truly worthwhile discussion develop

[4] Mark Chesler and Robert Fox, *Role-playing Methods in the Classroom* (Chicago, Science Research Associates, 1966); and Mathilda J. Jansen and Lawrence M. Strolurow, *An Experimental Study of Role Playing* (Washington, D.C., American Psychological Association, 1962, 1963).

when the students go into action. Several factors must be arranged or controlled, however. To begin with, the class size should be kept to twenty-five or less. This size not only permits the total class to become better acquainted and thus more spontaneous in expressing their views, but it also enables the teacher to keep the discussion on course. The teacher must have sufficient control of the class to prevent students from discussing each other rather than the problem under study. If he notes any such tendency, he should remind the students that the study is problem-centered, *not* person-centered. At the same time the teacher must carry the reins of his authority lightly, lest the discussion become a student–teacher–student exchange. He must keep tossing the conversational ball to the students, intervening only when necessary.

To assure the most effective results of class discussion, classes should be planned to include students from all levels of academic achievement and ability. The slow readers can become active participants by engaging in panel discussions or debates. The better readers can assume the responsibility for reading the supplementary books (each student using a different source) and presenting a position based on that source. Thus, the academically slower students are informed of additional points of view without being asked to cover materials above their level of ability or speed of reading. The potential dropout, who often is also the slow reader, can benefit from this arrangement, for such students have been identified as keen observers and generally demonstrate good oral communications skills.

The mere fact that students are talking is no assurance that learning is taking place. A poorly planned classroom discussion may be as ineffective as a poorly planned lecture. The topic chosen for a discussion must be one about which the students are sufficiently well informed or about which they can become well informed as they prepare for the discussion. One means of giving the class the information it needs about a topic is to lead off the discussion with reports on outside reading done by a few students. Frequently this will set off a spirited class debate, particularly if one published authority disagrees with another. The stage is thus set for a meaningful exchange of views. Reports on two books about marriage, for example, might well lead to an animated period of discussion in an upper-level family life and sex education course.

Small Group Discussion

The small group discussion permits freer and wider student participation in a given number of minutes than the classroom discussion. Another advantage is that the student who is reticent about expressing himself before the whole class may feel less reserved in a small group.

The views of the whole class on a subject may be ascertained within the small group format by using the multiple discussion method, in which several small groups simultaneously discuss the same topic and report their separate conclusions to the reassembled class. This reporting procedure can lead to difficulties unless it is carefully managed. Detailed reports from each group would be lengthy and time-consuming to read; they would also tend to be repetitious. One way to avoid this problem is to provide each group with a sheet of paper listing the topic to be discussed and the names of the student leader, recorder, and observer or resource person assigned to the group. Space is provided for the recorder to write down the major points covered and conclusions reached by his group. These record sheets are then turned in to the teacher.

Prior to the next class meeting, the teacher reviews and summarizes the various group reports, noting areas of agreement and dissent and, if necessary, aspects of the problem that the class failed to consider. For example, assume that the topic for discussion was "Homosexual Behavior as a Legal Problem" and that all the discussion groups reached the same conclusion: men demonstrating affectionate behavior toward each other in private are not harming anyone and therefore should not be prosecuted. If none of the group discussions made mention of female homosexuals, the teacher would call this omission to the attention of the class.

As the students in small group discussions begin to exchange views on problems that concern them, they soon discover that there are many ways to approach a problem. Evidence that one person accepts as valid may not be recognized as relevant by another person, even though they are discussing the same issue. By listening to and evaluating conflicting viewpoints, the student adds a new dimension to his understanding of the problem. This is particularly true of topics such as the influence of religious beliefs on family planning and contraception control. Various faiths will normally be represented in a public or non-church-affiliated school. Even in schools sponsored by particular religions a variety of viewpoints on such topics may be expressed.

In addition to his gain in understanding of the topic, a student's knowledge of himself and of the world is broadened by exposure to the variety of personal experiences that other group members bring to a discussion. One student may be the child of divorced parents, for example; another may have lived in foster homes or have lost a parent or sibling. As a student listens to the experiences of these other children he may achieve a sudden insight into a problem that he had previously been unable to understand or to bring into focus because of a lack of knowledge or experience.

As an individual changes group affiliations he tends to adjust his attitudes to the norms and expectations of the new group. This group can be either a membership or reference group or both. A membership group is one in which the individual has personal contact with the other members, while a reference group is one with which he identifies. In school the student may well feel very much a part of the class group to which he is assigned. If this group is discussing the topic "Why Wait Until Marriage for Sex Relations?" the student may experience a positive reaction to concepts he had never heard or thought of in family discussions. This would be particularly true if his family held strong views in favor of premarital chastity. The student's affiliations to both membership and reference groups are undergoing changes. This provides an opportunity for attitude change. It may also lead to attitude reinforcement.

The new reference group will be of primary importance, particularly at the secondary school level. The change from family-centered life to high school sets in motion an imbalance of attitude systems. If this break in what has been an essentially monolithic structure as to family attitude domination is used properly, it can be of immeasurable value. For example, the student whose family code insists on premarital chastity may be in rebellion against this code: he may espouse instead the sexual freedom he has seen on television, in films and magazines, and in other mass-media outlets. When the subject of chastity is discussed by his class group, the student may find that the majority of his classmates agree with his family. Because he identifies with his reference group, he is forced to re-examine his attitude on the subject itself and, in the process, to question any mass-media concepts to which he may have subscribed.

Students often experience an increase in self-confidence within the small group. As each participant presents his ideas, interpretations, and beliefs, a student may gain a different vision of his own worth. He may find that other members of the group listen attentively to him and respect what he says. Consequently, he places a new prestige value on his own experiences and his ability to assess them. He may, in fact, discover that he has leadership qualities that had not been brought out in the larger classroom setting. This is particularly true where a student has excessively dominating parents who have never given him an opportunity to express views or make decisions about his own behavior. Leadership skill, whether it be exercised within the family or in society at large, is a necessary and sought-after trait. It is one of the traits that students must be helped to gain in school, and they should be helped to gain it in the family life course in particular. Small group discussions give the students opportunities to acquire experience in leadership roles.

The leader of a group discussion has two important functions. One is to establish a climate that will be conducive to group participation. The other is to utilize whatever tools are necessary to help each individual within the group to achieve his maximum power of expression. The climate of a discussion may be one of positive feeling, such as curiosity or interest; or it may be one of negative attitudes, such as suspicion, fear, or hostility. A negative climate must be dispelled if the group is to function well in open discussion. If, for example, abortion is the topic for study, the discussion might become overly concerned with physical danger. Fear might be created on the part of girls in the group. The leader would need to guide the discussion into the broader aspects of the question, including social and legal considerations, and away from the threatening concepts of death, permanent sterility, and the like.

The well-prepared leader, rather than taking a place of special distinction, tries to make himself a part of the group through the seating arrangement that he plans. It is preferable that the group be seated in a circle so that everyone has a face-to-face view of his neighbors. If this is not possible, the leader takes a seat somewhere in the middle of the group. However, physical arrangement alone will not create the desired atmosphere. It is the leader's attitude that is of utmost importance. There must be no doubt in the minds of the group that the leader accepts all participants in the group as individuals with an equal right to be heard. This acceptance must be reflected in his demeanor, his actions, and, most important, his words. The leader must be careful to appear to give equal weight to all statements made. He will alienate members of the group if, in his desire to demonstrate acceptance, he tells one member of the group, "You are right," or "I agree." His is the difficult task of charting a course of strict impartiality.

There are times when the leader must keep the group discussion within the limits established by outside authorities, such as the school administration or the P.T.A. It is essential in such cases that the leader tell the students the source of the limitations and spell them out. For example, the topic of contraception may have been banned. At other times restrictions will have been set prior to the discussion by the teacher, the leader, or the group itself. The topic for discussion may be the legal aspects of homosexuality. The teacher may feel that he wants the group to have some depth of understanding of the legal implications of the subject before they study the broader aspects at a later date. It is the job of the group leader to confine the discussion to the assigned area. In so doing he must be careful not to appear to be throttling members who tend to stray from this area.

The student leader is the agent of the group. He is given his position to aid group members in understanding the topic, to stimulate and synthesize the discussion, and to assist the group in reaching a collective decision.

He reports to the group prediscussion plans and assists the group in setting whatever limitations they desire. The leader must make sure at the outset that all members of the group know each other. If they do not, name-cards and brief introductions can be used. The extent to which these procedures are necessary varies according to the size of the school body and the amount of contact students have with each other.

The student recorder is another important member of the discussion group. He notes and summarizes the problems, issues, and facts discussed. He provides periodic summaries whenever required during the course of the discussion and prepares a final report to be given to the class group after a consensus has been reached.

A third special member of many small discussion groups is the observer, or resource person. He assists in keeping the discussion flowing with clarity and ease and keeps a tally of the time given to various members of the group. In this way a degree of equality in the opportunity to speak is given to all group participants.

Group thinking and discussion constitute a cooperative enterprise. The small group discussion should not be an exercise in the use of argumentative skills simply for the fun of arguing. The contributions of each member must be meaningful or the discussion becomes frustrating and a waste of time. Some teachers believe that the small group discussion is the only effective way to cover material in the classroom—and particularly family life and sex education material. In support of this view they cite the great gains in attitude development that the small group process is said to contribute. However, some follow-up studies comparing small group and large group discussions have suggested that very little difference in attitude formation took place in one process as opposed to the other. Teachers who use the small group discussion exclusively should look again to see whether a combination of discussion procedures is not in fact a better way to attain the desired goals of the course.

Guest Speakers

A number of family life and sex education teachers rely heavily on guest speakers. While it is certainly true that a well-informed person can contribute much to a discussion of family life and sex education, this method does not give students much exercise in first-hand learning and self-understanding that is the goal of the course. The student's ability to develop his own attitudes and make independent judgments can even be lessened, especially if the guest speaker is prone to moralize (and, regrettably, such is often the case).

A built-in problem with guest speakers is that they must be arranged for in advance. If the class is in the midst of studying a particular topic of interest, the interjection of a guest speaker lecturing on a different topic may offer a jarring note. Many professional people also have heavy commitments that necessitate last-minute cancellations, thus leaving the teacher without a plan for class activities. However, one use of guest speakers has been reported that avoids some of these difficulties and can be quite stimulating. This is the so-called "hot seat" approach. It eliminates the lecture and places the burden on the students. For example, a local obstetrician may be invited to help the class study family planning. Prior to his visit the students are asked to read about the subject and to be ready to ask questions. The physician makes a brief statement of definition and states any limitations he wishes to place on the discussion. The remainder of the session is devoted to questions and discussion by the class members.

Lecture Method

Most teachers have listened to or taken part in discussions about the relative merits of the lecture method as opposed to the discussion method—or to a combination of the two. In fact, many have heard lecturers condemn the lecture method as the worst possible way of teaching. Those who espouse the discussion method usually feel that they are the liberals—the avant-garde in the field. As is usual in cases of this sort, there is no black or white to be found. There are times when a properly formulated lecture can be the most efficient way of changing attitudes and other times when a discussion can be the most effective means; each technique has its logical time and place. The determination of this time and place is essential to the success of all teaching.

If a teacher finds that the majority of his students are unreceptive to a particular point he is attempting to make, it would be wise to postpone a discussion. His class is not ready for discussion; the lecture is the appropriate form of instruction. For example, one teacher sensed a very limited class interest in discussing the legal aspects of sterilization due to ignorance of vital statistics and medical rationale. She discontinued the discussion and began a lecture giving facts and figures. With more substantive material for background, the discussion format was resumed successfully. Role playing and other instructional activities can be used just like the lecture to get a straying discussion back on the track. Studies have shown that a dissident minority will be brought to the majority point of view when discussion makes them aware of the majority position. Some students will yield their opinions to ridiculous points if they feel that the majority of the group is against them. When the teacher observes this happening he should turn to the lecture or some other activity so that discussion can later resume on a more meaningful basis.

The Question Box

One device that is widely used in many courses, and particularly in family life and sex education courses, is the question box. Each student is asked to put a slip of paper in the box, whether or not he has written a question on it. This reduces the possibility that students who submit controversial questions will be identified and therefore encourages the students to ask about the problems that really are worrying them. By skillful use of this technique, the teacher can pass over questions that are outside the area to be discussed or that are too inadequately worded to be meaningful. He may group several questions together, explaining to the class that he has done so to save time. He may also suggest that persons whose questions were too personal or too controversial to be included in the class discussion seek a personal interview with the teacher or guidance counselor or some other person equipped to work with that student.

The best time for use of the question box is near the middle or end of the course, for when it is used early, most of the questions the students ask concern matters that the class will take up at a later date, and so answers must be postponed. If, however, the teacher wishes a preliminary indication of student interests to help him shape the content of the course, then there is some value in using the question box during the first session or two.

This chapter has commented on some of the teaching aids and techniques that have been tried in family life and sex education courses and found to be successful. The teacher who has reservations about any of these techniques should acquaint himself further with their use through reading and individual investigation. Teachers and other educational leaders who are willing to make use of a variety of techniques derive a sense of satisfaction that they would otherwise miss. By trying various methods of presenting the course material, the teacher has a better opportunity to establish meaningful relationships with his students and to establish a climate for positive attitude change, formation, or reinforcement. Learning new teaching methods or changing some aspects of one's teaching approach may sometimes appear burdensome, but change is inherent in the whole philosophy of the family life and sex education program. Hopefully, teachers will accept the challenge of change and will do whatever they can to foster that change to give the student the opportunity to lead the fullest possible life as a member of his peer group and later as an adult with the right and responsibility of family life.

chapter **14**

program evaluation

Evaluation is an important component of any educational endeavor. In evaluating the effectiveness of educational procedures, we are interested not only in measuring the changes that education helps bring about in children and youth, but also in judging the desirability and adequacy of these changes.

The primary objective of a program of family life and sex education is to "develop attitudes and conduct so that the individual's sexual nature will contribute to his self-development and happiness and at the same time conserve and advance the welfare of society."[1] Typically, however, the community views the program in a different light, and parents soon begin to ask: "Has the number of illegitimate pregnancies decreased? How many divorces have you prevented?"

All these questions may be posed within a few months of the inception of the family life program. Naturally, such questions have no simple answers, partly because statistical data are rarely as easy to interpret as untrained persons often assume. If the family life and sex education program is truly effective, for example, the rate of venereal disease will show an immediate *increase* as students are motivated to seek medical diagnosis after discussions of the problems created by premarital relations. The community should be made aware of the fact that the local statistical rate of venereal disease might increase and that there are many problems inherent in

[1] Anaheim Union High School District, *Family Life and Sex Education Course Outline: Grades Seven Through Twelve* (Anaheim, Calif., 1965), p. 10.

collecting accurate statistics; and they should also be alerted to the chain of infection, demonstrated in the study of "The Infectious Syphilis Outbreak, Primarily Among Teenagers."[2]

The only valid answers that can be given to queries regarding the number of divorces that have been prevented are subjective answers. Divorce statistics, like statistics on venereal disease, are usually far from self-explanatory.[3] Reports volunteered by students often provide a far clearer picture of the influence the family life and sex education course is having in preventing divorce and illegitimate pregnancies. The following comments were volunteered by students who had taken the family life and sex education course in Anaheim, Calif.:

> Bill and I have been going together for almost a year and a half. We had decided on getting married next year after I graduate. Since we realized that we wouldn't have much money and that Bill would be in the service shortly after we were married, we decided that it would be better if we waited until after he got out of the service. This would give me a chance to go to a business school, to find a job and save some money.
>
> I had never before realized the harm a long engagement could bring. I knew that an engagement meant that marriage would follow, but now I can see that teen-agers are definitely not ready for engagement unless they are extremely mature. I have also changed my attitude towards marriage—not as an institution itself, but concerning the responsibility of it. I understand now that the foundation of marriage has to be more than just love and affection; it has to have a good financial basis, a strong mutual companionship and an extreme amount of maturity. I'll think of these and a lot more that I've learned, before I accept that engagement ring my boyfriend was talking about. I've still got my college education to think about. He's finished his hitch in the service (or will in February), but I know he's not ready yet, either. He says he loves me and if it's true, it'll last. But I know that I have to help too. That's because I love him.
>
> I used to think that being engaged was *only* for the purpose of getting financially ready for a wedding. Now, I realize that's the most important step before marriage. Its purpose is to find out whether or not you can live with a person for the rest of your life. You get a chance to talk about marriage and both express your ideas about marital problems. It should be a time of finding out whether you are willing to sacrifice for this person—finding out if

[2] *Today's VD Control Problem* (New York, American Social Health Association, 1963), pp. 36–37.

[3] In California, for example, divorce statistics do not separate the number of people getting second and third divorces from the number seeking a first divorce. Legislation is now being prepared to correct this defect in the reporting system, however.

> you care for this person more than you care for yourself. Finding out whether you *really* love this person.
>
> I've found myself not mature enough for either engagement or marriage. I now have a realistic understanding of the problems. I had always realized there would be problems, but I didn't know exactly what problems or what solutions. I find marriage more than a happy life. I find it to be a challenging one, too. In marriage there are almost as many thorns as there are roses.
>
> Now I realize some of the pressures of being married that I hadn't realized before. I will consider marriage more seriously now.
>
> I feel differently about going steady now. If a boy asks me to go steady, this time I might be able to say "no" since I recognize the immaturity of going steady just because it's the thing to do and because some poor fool asks you to!
>
> I probably won't go around tryen knock up any girl I can find cause I know it could cause trouble, but I think sex is beautiful its the most pleasing thing God gave us and I intend to make use of it but I'll be more careful.

Analyzing comments such as the following is also very helpful in evaluating whether attitudes are being developed that will contribute to more stable marriages:

> I now realize that sex is not the dirty thing I thought it was. It is a wonderful thing if used properly.
>
> I feel differently towards sex. I used to think you found sex in dirty alleys and scum places like skid row, and that sex was as dirty as those places, but now I know that sex is clean and wonderful, but only after marriage.
>
> I feel more enlightened now about women and sexual intimacy. Usually outside of family life people seem sort of hush-hush about sex questions, but in family life class you can learn things no one seems to want to mention.

Another subjective way that teachers can evaluate the impact of the family life and sex education course is simply to observe what happens in their classrooms. The expression on the face of a seventh-grade boy when he first realizes that his body probably contains live sperm and has the ability to create a new life can convince a teacher that he will always respect this function. Girls who have already made a mistake and are pregnant without the benefit of marriage often request to be assigned to a family life and sex education class before they are placed on home teaching status. This too in an informal way says a great deal to the teacher about the value of the program. The rest of the school staff will be able to make similar observations of their own. Restroom wall markings, pornographic pictures, and the telling of lewd jokes may diminish sharply or disappear. Increased respect for and cooperation between the sexes and the greater understanding of each person's responsibility to himself and others may be noticed by teachers in other subject areas.

What specific evaluation procedures can a teacher use to obtain some measure of the effectiveness of the family life and sex education program? First, the classroom teacher must have an instrument to measure his ability to communicate with his class. It has been found helpful to ask the students to evaluate the family life and sex education unit on the last day (see Document 14-1). Student replies to questions like these help the teacher evaluate the progress of the class and assess his own ability to meet the needs of the students. The students are usually very frank in their comments on the effectiveness of a teacher's presentations, the value of the class discussions, and the areas of the program that need improvement. The student also has an opportunity to give his reaction to the appropriateness of the curriculum and to make suggestions for revision. This provides the feedback so essential in meeting the needs of any group.

A second form of teacher evaluation is the use of a carefully designed question posed by the teacher, to which the students respond by writing a paragraph without using their names. One question designed by Duane F. Cain, a family life and sex education teacher at Loara High School, Anaheim, Calif., asked whether the student's feelings about any of the subjects covered in the family life course had changed as a result of the course. The question stimulated a variety of responses and gave Cain a basis upon which to form an opinion as to the effectiveness of the class.

A third form of teacher evaluation is based on an analysis of student behavior during classroom discussions. Conversations with parents form another source of relevant data, while discussions with teachers of other subject areas regarding changes in the behavior of the students after they had the family life class are still another source.

The use of personality tests is not recommended, for two reasons. The tests now available have received no general endorsement; they are still in a pioneering stage. Also, just as we do not expect clinical psychologists to be able to teach a chemistry lesson, we should not expect a classroom teacher to be able to administer and to interpret a clinician's test of emotional adjustment.

A partial evaluation of the effectiveness of the total family life and sex education program could be obtained by developing and standardizing an instrument to be used to pre-test and post-test students participating in the family life and sex education program and also a control group of students not in the program. Unfortunately, most of the tests developed thus far have been designed for college students or are primarily concerned with sex information. According to James Peterson,[4] two high schools in a large midwestern city did a comparison study of the number of illegitimate pregnancies occurring within their student population. One high school participated in a family life and sex education program and reported a 90% decrease in the number of illegitimate pregnancies when compared to the control school without a program.

The method most readily available to schools today for evaluating the family life program is to use a questionnaire to collect students' subjective reactions at the close of each unit and at the end of the total program. These subjective evaluations will reflect the professional and personal competency of the teachers, the suitability of the texts and other materials used, the adequacy of teaching methods, and the suitability of the curriculum in terms of the needs of the students. The evaluation that emerges from the student responses will be honest even though it is subjective.

To make a realistic evaluation of a comprehensive family life and sex education program, a great deal of specialized training and knowledge is required that is fully possessed only by behavioral scientists who have kept up with research developments in their particular disciplines. Typical school personnel are not trained to design the instruments needed to collect from students the information required to make an objective evaluation. This type of study involves many other difficulties as well; to better understand them, the reader is referred to the books[5] *Adolescent Character and Personality,* by Havighurst and Taba, *The Psychology of Character Development,* by Peck and Havighurst, and *Human Behavior: An Inventory of Scientific Findings,* by Berelson and Steiner. Hopefully, even in spite of all the difficulties involved, an instrument will eventually be designed that can yield objective evidence to check on the value of the program of family life and sex education for grades kindergarten through high school that educators have established on the basis of the best subjective evidence currently available. Until that time educators will have to do the most effective teaching possible and trust that their assumptions are correct. Just as it is difficult for some of the students to understand that science does not

[4] Professor of sociology and marriage counselor at the University of Southern California, Los Angeles.

[5] Havighurst, Robert J., and Hilda Taba, *Adolescent Character and Personality* (New York, Wiley [Science Editions], 1963); Peck, Robert F., and Robert J. Havighurst, *The Psychology of Character Development* (New York, Wiley, 1960); and Berelson, Bernard, and Gary A. Steiner, *Human Behavior: An Inventory of Scientific Findings* (New York, Harcourt, Brace & World, 1964).

have all the answers to questions in the area of human reproduction, it will be difficult for the community to understand that we do not have the means to do a wholly realistic evaluation of the program at this time.

The lack of objective evaluations should not stop us, as educators, from designing and implementing what we think is the most effective education to increase the stability of the American family. According to Evelyn Millis Duvall, "Marriage courses have proven to be remarkably effective in all measures used to evaluate them to date."[6] It is a well-known truth that not all of our students will become space scientists or engineers, but nine out of ten will marry and establish families.

[6] Evelyn M. Duvall, "How Effective Are Marriage Courses?" *J. Marriage and the Family,* vol. 27, no. 2, May 1965, p. 183.

Document 14-1 ***Student Evaluation of the Family Life and Sex Education Class***

Grade ———— **Sex** ————

Note: The worth of this evaluation depends on the student responding **fully** and **honestly** to each part.

Have you previously completed a Family Life and Sex Education class? **Yes No**

1. strongly agree
2. agree
3. undecided
4. disagree
5. strongly disagree

(*Note:* Select the one that best states your opinion. Then place the appropriate number in the corresponding box.)

☐ 1. *The family life and sex education class was worthwhile.*
Why:

☐ 2. *The whole presentation has been too frank.*
Why:

☐ 3. *My questions have been avoided.*
Why:

☐ 4. *The information was presented in such a way that it was easy to understand.*
Why:

☐ 5. *The class has helped me to gain new insights in human relationship.*
Why:

Answer the following with a sentence or paragraph (please be frank and specific):

1. What comments do you have to help the instructor improve? Why?

2. What areas did you find most interesting? Why?

3. What areas did you find least interesting? Why?

4. What class activities were most helpful to you? Why?

5. What other suggestions do you have for improving the class? Why?

addresses of film distributors

Association Films
600 Grand Avenue
Ridgefield, New Jersey 07657

Bailey Film Service
6509 DeLongpre
Hollywood, California 90028

Brigham Young University
Dept. of Educational Media Services
Provo, Utah 84601

E. C. Brown Trust
3170 S.W. 87th Avenue
Portland, Oregon 97225

Charles Cahill and Associates
P. O. Box 3220
Hollywood, California 90028

Calvin Productions
Calvin Building
1105 Truman Road
Kansas City, Missouri 64106

Carousel Films
1501 Broadway
Suite 1503
New York, New York 10036

Churchill Films
662 North Robertson Blvd.
Los Angeles, California 90069

Coronet Films
65 E.S. Water Street
Chicago, Illinois 60601

Sid Davis Productions
1418 N. Highland Avenue
Hollywood, California 90028

Walt Disney Productions
Doubleday and Company, Inc.
501 Franklin Avenue
Garden City, New York 11530

Du Art Film Labs
245 W. 55th Street
New York, New York 10019

Educational Films
250 W. 57th Street
New York, New York 10019

Encyclopaedia Britannica Films
425 N. Michigan Avenue
Chicago, Illinois 60611

Film Associates of California
11559 Santa Monica Blvd.
Los Angeles, California 90025

Rex Fleming Productions
Santa Barbara, California 93100

Guidance Associates
23 Washington Avenue
Pleasantville, New York 10570

Henk Newenhouse
1825 Willow Road
Northfield, Illinois 60093

International Film Bureau
332 S. Michigan Avenue
Chicago, Illinois 60604

McGraw-Hill
Text-Film Division
330 W. 42nd Street
New York, New York 10036

Society of Visual Education
1345 Diversey Parkway
Chicago, Illinois 60614

Sterling Educational Films
241 E. 34th Street
New York, New York 10016

General Learning Corporation
(slides)
3 E. 54th Street
New York, New York 10022

B 9
C 0
D 1
E 2
F 3
G 4
H 5
I 6
J 7